ADVANCE P

FOR

SOUL OF A PEOPLE

"A wonderful and engaging book ... David Taylor's *Soul of a People* will make you secretly wish that you could have been one of the thousands of writers who, during the height of the Depression, set out to paint an intimate portrait of a nation and its people. Taylor illuminates this history of the Federal Writers' Project with impressive research and deft storytelling."

—**Robert Whitaker, author of *On the Laps of Gods: The Red Summer of 1919 and the Struggle for Justice That Remade a Nation***

"During the Great Depression, the federal government paid out-of-work writers to capture American voices on paper. But *Soul of a People* is the first book to tell the stories of the Federal Writers themselves. In David Taylor's engaging narrative, this spunky, colorful, and entertaining crew comes back to life."

—**Ann Banks, editor of *First Person America*, an anthology of oral histories collected by the Federal Writers' Project**

"This intimate portrait of the Writers' Project, a gem of FDR's New Deal, is a nostalgic journey through America in the Depression Era. Familiar faces dot every corner, young writers from Studs Terkel to Richard Wright, John Cheever to Ralph Ellison. It's a journey well worth taking, a key formative moment in our literary common culture, well written and nicely researched."

—**Kenneth D. Ackerman, author of *Young J. Edgar: Hoover, the Red Scare, and the Assault on Civil Liberties***

"Long before Oprah and blogs, the WPA during the Great Depression of the 1930s gave America its first mass exercise in reading and writing—the Federal Writers' Project. Now David Taylor goes inside the project to give us intimate snapshots of the writers and what they saw and felt during that hard time. *Soul of a People* is a revealing and valuable resource."

—**Nick Taylor, author of *American-Made: The Enduring Legacy of the WPA***

"David Taylor has added a perfect chapter to the amazing saga of the Federal Writers' Project, with vivid portraits of some of the men and women who produced the American Guide series, an unmatched collective portrait of a people battered but not beaten by the Great Depression. *Soul of a People* should be mandatory reading as the storm clouds of hard times hover over us again."

—**Bernard Weisberger, editor of *The WPA Guide to America***

SOUL OF A PEOPLE

THE WPA WRITERS' PROJECT UNCOVERS DEPRESSION AMERICA

DAVID A. TAYLOR

WILEY

John Wiley & Sons, Inc.

This book is printed on acid-free paper. ∞

Copyright © 2009 by David A. Taylor. All rights reserved

Published by John Wiley & Sons, Inc., Hoboken, New Jersey
An Imprint of Turner Publishing Company, Nashville, Tennessee

For general information about our other products and services, please contact our Customer Care Department within the United States at (800) 762–2974, outside the United States at (317) 57-3993 or fax (317) 572-4002.

Wiley also publishes its books in a variety of electronic formats. Some content that appears in print may not be available in electronic books. For more information about Wiley products, visit our web site at www.wiley.com.

Library of Congress Cataloging-in-Publication Data:

Taylor, David A., date.
  Soul of a people: the WPA writer's project uncovers depression America / David Taylor.
    p. cm.
  Includes bibliographical references and index.
  ISBN 978-0-470-40380-8 (cloth)
  ISBN 978-1-68442-520-4 (paperback)
    1. Federal Writers' Project—History. 2. United States—Guidebooks—History—20th century. 3. United States—Social conditions—1933–1945. 4. United States—Intellectual   life—20th   century. 5. United   States—Civilization—1918–1945. 6. Federal Writers' Project—Influence.   I. Title.
  E175.4.W9T39   2009
  973.917—dc22
                                                          2008047041

Printed in the United States of America

10 9 8 7 6 5 4 3 2 1

CONTENTS

Foreword by Douglas Brinkley   v

Acknowledgments   ix

Prologue   1

Introduction: At a Crossroads   5

1   The Writers' Project   9

2   Point of Departure: New York   23

3   Chicago and the Midwest   39

4   Gathering Folklore, from Oklahoma to Harlem   75

5   Rising Up in the West: Idaho   97

6   Nailing a Freight on the Fly: Nebraska   111

7   Poetic Land, Pugnacious People: California   125

8   Raising the Dead in New Orleans   141

9   Cigars and Turpentine in Florida   161

10   American and Un-American: Back Around
the Boroughs   189

11   Converging on Washington   207

12   Traveling Beyond   227

Appendix: Resources for Readers and Travelers   231

Sources   235

Credits   251

Index   254

FOREWORD

By Douglas Brinkley

In the late 1970s, when I was in junior high school, my mother gave me a copy of John Steinbeck's *Travels with Charley*, a memoir about his journey across America by camper with only his French poodle as companion. The book resonated with me. Every summer our family left Perrysburg, Ohio, in a station wagon pulling a twenty-four-foot Coachman trailer in Steinbeck-like fashion. For six weeks, we visited national parks and literary landmarks while traveling down interstates and blue highways alike. These road trips galvanized my interest in America more than any textbook possibly could have. So my mother quite naturally thought that I would enjoy *Travels with Charley*, and I did.

An unintended consequence of my first reading of Steinbeck's 1962 book was that I started to collect WPA guidebooks as a hobby. Early in *Travels with Charley*, Steinbeck raved about the aesthetic excellence of the WPA guides compiled during the Great Depression. He called them the "most comprehensive account of the United States" ever written. Steinbeck had jammed his suitcase with the American Guides (as they were first known), and he insisted that they were worth their weight in gold. Intrigued by his promotion of these bygone relics, I soon asked my local librarian in Perrysburg to let me study the guidebooks up close. Before long, I was reading about the Oklahoma hills and the Florida flats, Chicago's Miracle Mile and Pittsburgh's great steel mills, the Great Smokies and Crater Lake. And the sections of photographs were simply tremendous.

From that moment, I was hooked. As a college student at Ohio State University, I used to scan the shelves of used bookstores and collected the WPA guidebooks as if they were stamps or coins. To date, I own 197 of the volumes, most of them with dust jackets (albeit torn). Everyone who becomes enamored with these volumes has his or her own favorite; mine is the *WPA Guide to Illinois*. William Least Heat-Moon said he couldn't have written *PrairyErth (a deep map)* (1991) without the Nebraska guide. When John Gunther hit the road for his memoir *Inside U.S.A.* (1947), his suitcase bulged with WPA guides, too. Anybody who takes the time to *read* a WPA guide (and not merely flip through one) comes away with an understanding that its regional, social, and economic histories were written, in many cases, by stellar prose craftspeople. With no disrespect to the transcendentalists, it's fair to say that the WPA guides were composed by the most dazzling group of writers America has ever produced.

Now, at long last in *Soul of a People*, David A. Taylor tells the behind-the-scenes stories of the WPA guides and much more. After rummaging through private and public archives and interviewing WPA veterans, Taylor has written a lively, informative, and often uplifting story of the Federal Writers' Project. Created in 1935 in the heart of the Great Depression era, the Writers' Project (part of the Works Progress Administration) at its peak supported more than seventy-five hundred writers, editors, and researchers and received four years of federal financing. When the government funds expired, Congress let the program continue under state sponsorship until 1943. Although people were grateful for even subsistence wages in a time of economic despair, few participants deemed it a badge of honor to earn $20 to $25 a week from the government. But their embarrassment at being on emergency relief work has been our great gain. Many of these young writers went on to create enduring works of American fiction, nonfiction, and oral history.

Taylor takes a different view from most New Deal scholars. For the first time ever, the multiculturalism of the Federal Writers' Project is explored. As you'll find in these pages, the Project's directors believed that the United States could (and should) build a national culture based on diversity. Facing a huge challenge from reactionaries like Martin Dies of Texas, the Ku Klux Klan in several states, and anti-immigration laws that were regularly passed in Washington, D.C., the WPA writers nevertheless forged ahead. They celebrated an astonishing range of often marginalized Americans: Florida turpentine workers, California grape pickers, Nebraska hoboes, and Louisiana folk artists. A roll call of the writers who worked on the WPA guides is a veritable Who's Who of our finest talent: Conrad Aiken, Nelson Algren, Saul Bellow, Arna Bontemps, Edward Dahlberg, Ralph Ellison, Zora Neale Hurston, Claude McKay, Kenneth Patchen, Philip Rahv, Kenneth Rexroth, Harold Rosenburg, Studs Terkel, Margaret Walker, Richard Wright, and Frank Yerby.

Reading *Soul of a People* made me want to hit the used bookstores for some of the volumes I'm missing. The Nevada and Maine state guides, in particular, I desperately covet. As for the city guides, I crave *Lexington and the Bluegrass Country* and *Atlanta: The Capital of the South*. They'll both soon be mine. Put another way, I'm ready for a road trip, and instead of Charley serving as copilot I'll bring along this wonderful new history by David A. Taylor.

Let the travels begin!

ACKNOWLEDGMENTS

Soul of a People has been a great collaborative effort. I would particularly like to thank Studs Terkel and Stetson Kennedy for their wisdom and generosity. Ann Banks, Christine Bold, Peggy Bulger, Jerrold Hirsch, and Bernard Weisberger showed the way as researchers and historians and provided the documentary team with important insights and guidance. The book and the documentary also owe a debt to the work of Jerre Mangione, Dennis McDaniel, Pamela Bordelon, and William Leuchtenburg.

My thanks to Douglas Brinkley for his enthusiasm for this topic. Louie Attebery, David Bradley, Michael Chabon, Jack Dies, Dena Polacheck Epstein, Dagoberto Gilb, Maryemma Graham, Herb Lewis, Sharon Maust, Gordon McLester, Mindy Morgan, Leo Seltzer, Ruthe Sheffey, and Susan Swetnam answered rounds of questions with good humor. Many more named in the text gave generously of their time and expertise, including the wonderful Grace Paley.

Andrea Kalin has been a supreme partner in making *Soul of a People*, with her ability to see the path, sharpen the storytelling, and inspire others. Olive Emma Bucklin's work on the documentary script uncovered valuable new insights. James Mirabello has been an irreplaceable stalwart on this effort for as long as the Writers' Project itself lasted and has earned special thanks for his patience and his dedicated research, professionalism, and production support. He also took a leading role in the photographic research, along with Bonnie Rowan, Lewanne Jones, Alicia Melton, Oliver Lukacs, Eitan Charnoff, and Zachary Ment. Other members on the Spark Media team who contributed their time and talents include David Grossbach, Nancy Camp, Dennis Boni, Lenny Schmitz, Luis Portillo, Wanakhavi Wahisi, Debra Jackson, Maribel Quezada, Danielle Metz, and Joseph Vitarelli.

Valuable support for the documentary came from Steve Rabin, John Y. Cole at the Center for the Book in the Library of Congress, Sandra Parks, Al Stein, and the Smithsonian Institution, particularly David Royle, Chris Hoelzl, and Addie Moray.

I am grateful for support from the National Endowment for the Humanities, particularly Tom Phelps, NEH director of Public Programs; David Weinstein, our program officer; and Sonia Feigenbaum, vice president for the Office of Public Programs. The NEH provided grants for the research, scriptwriting, and production of the documentary. Additional funding came from the Illinois Humanities Council; the Nebraska Humanities Council; the Maryland Humanities Council; the Wisconsin Humanities Council; Humanities Texas; and the Idaho Humanities Council. We also have enjoyed warm support from the American Library Association and the Library of Congress.

William Clark, my agent, believed in this book from the start and went to great lengths for it. Thanks also to Hana Lane, my editor at John Wiley & Sons, for perceptive guidance, Jennifer LaBracio for marketing strategy, and Kimberly Monroe-Hill, senior production editor. Rachel Cohen contributed insights and the example of her wonderful book *A Chance Meeting* and pointed out valuable connections. Tim Dickinson and Stephanie Joyce provided helpful suggestions on early drafts.

Librarians were a tremendous help in the research, particularly Mary Ellen Ducey with the Benjamin A. Botkin Collection of Applied American Folklore at the University of Nebraska–Lincoln Libraries, Archives and Special Collections; Michael Flug, senior archivist at the Vivian G. Harsh Research Collection of Afro-American History and Literature, Chicago Public Library; J. C. Johnson, archivist at the

Howard Gotlieb Archival Research Center of Boston University; Elva Griffith, formerly with the Ohio State University Libraries' Rare Books and Manuscripts Division; Dr. Alice Birney, curator at the Library of Congress Manuscripts Division; Susan Halpert, at Harvard University's Houghton Library; Bruce Tabb, Special Collections librarian at the University of Oregon; Darlene Mott, archivist at the Sam Houston Regional Library and Research Center in Liberty, Texas; and Genie Guerard, head of the Manuscripts Division at the UCLA Library's Department of Special Collections. Thomas Mann, reference librarian at the Library of Congress, is a master at finding hidden sources of information.

I'm grateful to my family for their constant support and, above all, to my wife, Lisa Smith, who has nourished me on this journey since we first borrowed a copy of the *WPA Guide to New Orleans*. She has enriched this project with her priceless enthusiasm, keen eye, encouragement, insight, and love.

PROLOGUE

ONE SUMMER DAY IN 1939, A GRAY, WEATHER-BEATEN MID-1920S Chevrolet coupe rolled down a dirt road on Florida's Gulf Coast, stirring up dust amid the pine trees of a turpentine camp. When it pulled to a stop, from the driver's seat stepped a poised woman named Zora Neale Hurston.

Hurston was working with the Federal Writers' Project and had come hoping to find kernels of Florida's black folk culture—the stories and songs that people share with one another—to record for posterity. What she found instead was a story of modern-day slavery.

Hurston was a nimble survivor. From an unsettled girlhood, she had launched a promising writing career in the Harlem Renaissance during the 1920s, gathering the stories of real people, especially in her native Florida. Then the Depression destroyed her funding sources. For her, the Writers' Project was a life raft that helped her weather hard times. Although Hurston bristled at bureaucratic management, with the government's support she had managed to gather songs that had not been previously documented and to reach deeply into stories that were being lost. What she really needed was the means to pursue her folklore research, to advance her career as a literary artist, and to create a new African American theater.

As a professional, she was accustomed to traveling through the South in her coupe, which she christened Sassy Susie, and gathering folklore that was both disturbing and vital. She knew that stories of conflict and hardship were essential to how people understood their lives. "Folklore," she wrote, "is the boiled-down juice of human living."

Still, entering the Aycock and Lindsay Company's turpentine camp near Cross City was like visiting a foreign country. Hurston was stunned by the conditions of the workers and their families and the stories they told of beatings and worse.

"Nobody allowed to leave," she scribbled in her notes. "Klan paraded last Saturday night." Workers had to buy their provisions from the employer at inflated prices, so that each day they dug themselves deeper into a future of debt and servitude. The company man was the unques-tioned authority for miles around.

Hurston's visit was part of the largest cultural experiment ever. The Federal Writers' Project was a small corner of the much larger Works Progress Administration, launched by Franklin D. Roosevelt in 1935. Like the rest of the WPA, the Writers' Project aimed to help people who were desperate for jobs when nearly a third of American families were hit by unemployment. Recruited from the millions of jobless, WPA writers drove along back roads collecting information about American history, interviewing Americans about how they lived, and gathering details about battles and landmarks, local histories and festivals, and lore. They were foot soldiers in an army against the Depression. From the start, Hurston and the rest of this army stirred up strong reactions.

In Washington, D.C., some months earlier, a very different interview had taken place. The congressional hearing room on Capitol Hill had the air of public theater. A congressman asked the witness whether it was her agency's "uniform policy to array class against class? And to encourage class hatred?"

"Yes," replied Louise Lazell, a former administrator for the Writers' Project.

"From your experience and contacts and observations, do you feel that the Federal Writers' Project is being converted into an agency to spread communism throughout the United States?" asked Congressman Martin Dies.

"I think so," answered Miss Lazell.

As chairman of the Committee Investigating Un-American Activities, Martin Dies aimed to intensify a debate that Roosevelt had started with the New Deal. Dies suspected that some New Deal projects were pawns of foreign propaganda and that the Writers' Project seemed to be stirring up unwelcome ideas about American values. He was well aware of the tinder keg of discontent that the Depression had created. His home district in East Texas was a potentially dangerous mix of dirt-poor farms and the booming oil ports of Beaumont, Orange, and Port Arthur. One historian called the ports "hellishly prosperous," with fierce competition for wages and jobs. In 1934, striking longshoremen in Houston had clashed violently with strikebreaker guards and nonunion workers. The conflict lasted for months and left three men dead. The idea of labor union complaints about downtrodden workers spelled trouble to Dies.

Dies had broken with FDR and the New Deal, and he was not alone in his suspicions about its values. By August 1939, he was one of the best-known men in the United States, and a Gallup poll taken that fall found that three out of four Americans approved of his investigation.

The people working on the Writers' Project were addressing the question of American values from a different vantage point. Each side held a different view of what exactly "American" meant. Leaders on each side branded the other's tactics "un-American." What did that mean? And how had a country that had rallied together for a war against the Depression a few years earlier come to such a turn?

INTRODUCTION

AT A CROSSROADS

[O]nly one expert ... is qualified to examine the souls and the life of a people and make a valuable report—the native novelist.... In time he and his brethren will report to you the life and the people of the whole nation—the life of a group in a New England village; in a New York village; in a Texan village; in an Oregon village; in villages in fifty States and Territories.... And the Indians will be attended to; and the cowboys; and the gold and silver miners; and the Negroes; and the Idiots and Congressmen; and the Irish, the Germans, the Italians, the Swedes, the French, the Chinamen, the Greasers; and the Catholics, the Methodists, the Presbyterians, the Congregationalists, the Baptists, the Spiritualists, the Mormons, the Shakers, the Quakers, the Jews, the Campbellites, the infidels, the Christian Scientists, the Mind-Curists, the Faith-Curists, the train-robbers, the White Caps, the Moonshiners. And when a thousand able novels have been written, there you have the soul of the people, the life of the people, the speech of the people. And the shadings of character, manners, feelings, ambitions, will be infinite.

—MARK TWAIN, "WHAT PAUL BOURGET THINKS OF US" (1895)

THIS BOOK AIMS TO PUT YOU IN THE SKINS OF PEOPLE WHO, IN the 1930s, set out on the kind of experiment that Twain had articulated four decades earlier: the unemployed people who signed up for the Federal Writers' Project to, according to its mandate from Congress, "hold up a mirror to America." This book attempts to place you in the passenger's seat with them for their drive and to reveal America through their eyes.

It was a bumpy ride. Few were, in fact, novelists—many didn't even call themselves writers—but they all wrote about "the life and the people of the whole nation." (At its height, in 1936, the Project employed about seventy-five hundred people nationwide.) The WPA writers' work is often presented in terms of politics, but the writers deserve a look as individuals. Through them, stories emerge of intense personal struggle. At their core, these experiences raise questions about what it means to be American, how we respond to crises, and the tension between the American ideal and American reality.

This book began from a chance discovery on the road. When my wife and I returned from living overseas and launched a driving trip across America, a friend lent me a copy of the 1938 *WPA Guide to New Orleans* from her father's attic. At first, I thought the book was a dead relic, but when we reached the Big Easy I was struck by how the text lured the reader from standard tourist sites to consider, for instance, voodoo rituals in the vaulted cemeteries. The guide mined local history, revealed surprising connections (for example, between Creole mourning practices and modern lawn furniture), and didn't sugarcoat anything. It made even an 1850s yellow fever epidemic intensely human with firsthand accounts. The WPA guide brought to life a city barely glimpsed in newer guides: black and white, sometimes distressed, authentic. It lingered to quote headstones and relish people's use of language. It was compelling.

Today's guidebooks do a fine job of digesting mountains of facts into sleek packaging and pointing us to what we should see. The WPA guide, by contrast, was messy with original accounts, tangents, and wry commentary. The book got inside the place and made it fascinating.

"It makes a big difference whether you see the world from inside or outside," said WPA writer Meridel Le Sueur. "It affects how you see history, how you see time . . . how you see people."

A book collector later told me of his amazement at discovering the *WPA Guide to Washington, D.C.,* in a used bookstore. A native Washingtonian, he found that the 1,140-page guide was a revelation, an anatomy of his city. Through its stories and block-by-block history, it showed the place as if it were a great body, down to its bones. The book inspired him to collect a complete set of the WPA guides, or, as they were called in the 1930s, the American Guides.

Historians, filmmakers, novelists, and other travelers have had their own transformational experiences with the American Guides. The New York City guide has been a perennial best seller, giving readers a way into the city that remains, along with a glimpse, as novelist Michael Chabon said, of "the city that in some ways is no longer there." In researching his Pulitzer prize–winning *Amazing Adventures of Kavalier and Clay*, Chabon found the New York guide invaluable. Recalling the guide from when he worked in bookstores, he bought a copy and pored through it.

"The thing that struck me most about the overall tone of that guide," said Chabon, "is that, coming out of this absolutely devastating period, there's this amazing tone of optimism and faith in the common people, the sense that there's a prevailing, quirky orderliness to life in New York City. . . . You have this great city going about its normal business of being an insane pressure cooker/volcano/petri dish of commerce and life."

The New Orleans guide led me to ask questions about the people who created the series, and I found their variety fascinating. Increasingly, what intrigued me were the dramas of the people *behind* the WPA books. What did life feel like for them? How did going from joblessness to reporting on their own communities (for a national bureaucracy, no less) affect artists with visions as varied as those of Jim Thompson and Zora Neale Hurston? What feelings—humiliation, anger, excitement, nostalgia, adventure—did that passage involve?

Pieced together, a new story emerged that was different from the images of breadlines and despair we typically associate with the Depression. WPA writers anticipated, and perhaps paved the way for, changes that came in the following decades. Meridel Le Sueur said that the Project marked a reaching forward in sensibility: a reach forward to the civil rights movement, to the women's movement of the 1970s. In that sense, the work of the WPA guides, created by many unknown, unemployed Americans, resonated throughout the twentieth century. Historian Michael Denning suggested that the Project's mandate to record people's lives echoed the call of the radical John Reed Clubs of the time, which urged writers to study trades and create novels that blended field research, autobiography, and fictional invention.

Given the Project's national scope, the stories of the handful of individuals recounted here, along with selections from the WPA oral history interviews, are obviously not comprehensive. But the accounts chosen do give a fair sense of the whole and explore the idea voiced by many people involved in it: that individuals "caught in the wreckage" of a national disaster (in the words of Mabel Ulrich, the state editor in Minnesota) uncovered something valuable and lasting. As we grapple with the critical events of our own time, we can draw strength and perspective from their energy and hopes.

The Project went beyond words, gathering music, flavors, and more. Suggestions for further explorations appear in the appendix. I hope that *Soul of a People* opens new paths for your experience of your home state and of America.

THE WRITERS' PROJECT

Had it not been for the Project, the suicide rate would have been much higher. It gave new life to people who had thought their lives were over.

—NELSON ALGREN

IN 1999, IN THE BASEMENT OF A UNIVERSITY building in Madison, Wisconsin, a professor discovered boxes containing 167 steno notebooks, a time capsule from the 1930s. Many were written in an unfamiliar language; others included sketches of ox yokes and lacrosse sticks. The authors were members of the Oneida, a branch of the Iroquois, who had worked for the WPA. The notebooks included interviews with Oneida elders and life stories of people now long dead.

Yet these stories from the past have importance for the Oneida community today. Copies of the WPA notebooks are now available in the small reading room of the Oneida cultural center. "Readers get so excited," said Carol Cornelius, an Oneida historian. "You're pulled right into the time period. It's engrossing."

"It's a vital connection to our early days," she added, noting that without the notebooks, there would be major gaps in the tribe's history. The notebooks also helped revitalize interest in the Oneida language, which was on the verge of dying out.

The 1930s writers who worked on the Oneida program and other parts of the Writers' Project had a sense of mission. Oscar Archiquette, the youngest of the Oneida writers, had floundered in his youth, as he himself admitted, but on the Project he had purpose. Others agreed. "For two years I have been working on Oneida Language Project," Guy Elm wrote. "I am very much interested in my work. . . . I hope to see it published in books so that the people can read it and find out for themselves, what Oneida people are really, bad or good."

Gordon McLester, an Oneida historian who now films oral histories, echoes that view. McLester learned his approach to education and history from Archiquette, and his efforts to record Oneida lives today grew from the WPA project. "The cycle comes around," he said. "They did it in the 1930s; we're doing it again in the twenty-first century. The main point is to get images of *real* Oneida life out there."

How controversial could that be? Today oral history is the province of preservationists and stewards of the past. But during the Depression, the effort spurred huge protests. "There still continues to be . . . a lot of useless, worthless WPA projects," one Wisconsin farmer complained to his congressman. He singled out the Oneida language project as full of "fat, lazy Indians" and marveled at their useless make-work at taxpayer expense. "Can you tell me who wants to learn the Indian language?"

The core of his complaint was economics: as long as members of the WPA staff could get $70 a month "writing the Indian language," they would never take farm jobs that paid less. "That is one project that should be halted immediately," he urged.

Welfare-to-work stirred debate in the 1990s, but it provoked much more intense feelings in the 1930s. A 1939 Gallup poll found that as the country headed toward a presidential election, more voters ranked WPA relief as the worst part of FDR's government—nearly one in four, more than for any other issue, well ahead of spending, farm programs, foreign policy, or even "packing" the Supreme Court. Yet the same poll found that more respondents ranked WPA relief as the administration's *greatest* accomplishment (28 percent). Clearly, WPA work relief was a lightning-rod issue.

The WPA guides to the states, U.S. territories, and selected cities remain the most visible legacy of the Writers' Project. The books—part travel guide, part local encyclopedia—together made up America's first self-portrait: a multifaceted look at America by Americans, assembled during one of the greatest crises in the country's history. The Project, as it was known, churned out more than three hundred publications in five years, including a hundred full-size books on topics ranging from zoology to ethnic history. The Project also left an archive of oral histories and interviews with people in many walks of life, including the most comprehensive firsthand accounts of slavery ever collected, from thousands of former slaves across the South. Plans to publish interviews went into limbo when the Project closed down in 1939. In recent years, the Library of Congress has posted thousands of these life-history interviews on its *American Memory* Web site.

At the time, the guides received the most public attention. "This is not the well selected, carefully sculptured mosaic of formal history or geographical description" of a typical guidebook, wrote Frederick Gutheim in the *Saturday Review of Literature*. "It is the profuse disorder of nature and life, the dadaist jumble of the daily newspaper. It gets in your blood and sends you crowing from oddity to anecdote, from curiosity to dazzling illumination of single fact." The guides formed an often irreverent portrait that revealed the eccentricity, humor, brutality, and ingenuity of the American people. Anything was fair game, as Jerre Mangione noted in *The Dream and the Deal*, from a colorful sketch of millionaire John D. Rockefeller with dimes in his pocket and doggerel he typed and gave his visitors to the exploits of a jovial but homicidal Delaware innkeeper. Illustrated with thousands of black-and-white images, the WPA guides provide a glimpse into America's window.

Now you can connect a WPA guide with relevant interviews in a few mouse clicks at the Library of Congress Web site (see the appendix for a full list of Web sites). Pull up a map of the country and browse interviews collected in each state, or search for a town name or an individual.

In Nebraska, you can read the recollections of a farm wife in Dakota City, the songs of a hobo in Lincoln, and a cattleman's memory of driving stock to Omaha. You can view photos of life back then taken by field photographers such as Dorothea Lange, Jack Delano, and Gordon Parks, who worked with the Farm Security Administration. It may be that nothing gets you closer to the life story of a place than this combination of guides, interviews, and photos.

The Writers' Project, like the rest of the WPA, had its roots in poverty relief, not in a patriotic desire to celebrate America. The Depression's bleakest days had passed, but families still slept on park benches and in stairwells. Across the countryside, thousands of families lost their farms in a foreclosure epidemic that sparked desperate protests. The economic hurricane didn't spare writers: by 1935, a quarter of the U.S. publishing industry was out of work. Women and minorities were especially hard hit. ("There is something about poverty that smells like death," wrote Zora Neale Hurston in *Dust Tracks on a Road.* "Dead dreams dropping off the heart like leaves in a dry season.") Roosevelt's efforts to jump-start the economy included the 1935 Emergency Relief Act, which authorized the Works Progress Administration, the most ambitious of all relief efforts during the Great Depression.

The whole WPA faced heavy skepticism from both ends of the political spectrum. Many saw it a haven for people who were too lazy to work. The gag was that WPA stood for "We Poke Along" (local variations included "Whistle, Piss and Argue"), suggesting that those involved had no work ethic and would accept any handout. One editorial warned that with the Writers' Project, pencil leaners would be added to the ranks of WPA "shovel leaners." In Chicago, the *Tribune's* front-page cartoons lampooned the WPA workers as goggle-eyed professors. "The word was 'boondoggling,'" said Studs Terkel in a 2004 interview. "They were loafing on the job at taxpayers' expense." (The word's origins are murky. It seems to have sprung to life in 1935 as part of a movement to fight government waste, but some sources trace it back to the cowboy era, when it referred to braiding together odds and ends of leather to make saddle trappings. Boondoggling was done when there was no other work on the ranch, so it was the equivalent of twiddling your thumbs.) On the left, radicals decried the Project as hush money designed to preempt the publications of pamphlets about the broken capitalist system. People questioned why any kind of writing deserved public support. In many places, introducing oneself as a "WPA writer" could raise hackles and end an interview on the spot. In the Southwest, the WPA writer became known as *el Diablo a pie*: "the devil on foot."

Initially, WPA relief was mainly intended to create jobs for blue-collar workers, for the building of bridges, roads, and other public works. But unemployed white-collar families demanded help, too. Unlike bridges, however, writing was not something the public thought it needed, so the program took some pushing. The Writers Union and the Unemployed Writers Association called on the government to create a policy for the broad category of writers "in the present economic emergency," or else "the writer must organize and conduct a fight to better his condition." In February 1935, the two groups picketed the New York Port Authority with placards that read "Children Need Books. Writers Need Bread. We Demand Projects."

In 1935, strikes in New York pressured the WPA to create relief jobs for white-collar workers.

Six months later, the WPA announced that it would sponsor projects to employ people on relief who were qualified in the fields of writing, art, music, and drama (a fifth was devoted to historical surveys). The Writers' Project established offices in every state.

A WPA poster on the meaning of work relief: Work Promotes Confidence.

It was intended to last six months. Not surprisingly for an emergency effort, things were thrown together. Henry Alsberg, the Project's director, had worked with WPA director Harry Hopkins on a larger relief program and was drawn to the new effort for writers. A fifty-seven-year-old bachelor, Alsberg had been a foreign correspondent, a playwright, and a director of the Provincetown Theatre and had organized humanitarian relief to Russia in the 1920s.

Few questioned Alsberg's qualifications, but, privately, friends marveled at the idea of him as a national manager. He looked the part of the distracted intellectual: poorly dressed, constantly fumbling for cigarettes, his clothes streaked with ashes and stains. One staffer described him as having "a cumbersome body and a voice that sounded like something from the Old Testament." Colleagues said that he was a completely impractical planner. How could someone who was barely able to administer himself lead a nationwide effort?

Alsberg had big ideas for the project. He wanted the WPA writers to document aspects of America that were already fading. His plan highlighted regionalism, the concept that America's unique cultures grew out of its varied landscapes and its natural and man-made vistas. In 1935, as historian Bernard Weisberger has noted, most Americans cared little about the rest of the world. In the South, Civil War memories still dominated politics and race relations, and there were still many Civil War veterans alive to parade on Memorial Day. In the West, pioneer days tinted the public's views about

Franklin D. Roosevelt (left) and Harry Hopkins, WPA director.

Native Americans. But by that year, signs pointed to factors that were changing the character of every region of the country. The influence of radio spread further every day, and the pace of news was quickening.

Alsberg imagined that the task would also provide a sort of training for young writers. "These writers will get an education in the American scene," he told the *New York Times* that fall. "A great deal of *real* American writing comes out of seeing what is really happening to the American people."

A time of national disaster may not seem like the best moment to raise such issues. With America's economic system flat on its back, people—especially young people—were searching for new solutions, for change.

It took time for officials to settle on an objective that resembled an economic engine that involved a pen: travel guides. But Alsberg was less interested in economics than in sociology and the arts. He wanted

Henry Alsberg, director of the Writers' Project, and Eleanor Roosevelt.

guidebooks that were also history books and that captured the gamut of America and its experience. He didn't seem fazed about making guidebooks too big for people to carry on a walking tour. Can you sightsee with a thousand-page book in your hand? It's not surprising that few people believed anyone would actually read these books.

Working with Alsberg, however, was someone who had a more practical view of guidebooks. Katharine Kellock, like Alsberg, had helped with humanitarian relief in Russia in the 1920s. That was when she saw how useful tour guides like the Baedeker series could be. Originally from Pittsburgh, Kellock had recently worked as a writer and a researcher for the Scripps Howard news service. When she joined the Writers' Project,

Katharine Kellock, national tours editor for the Writers' Project,
meets with George Cronyn, assistant director (right).

she proposed that part of each state guide consist of driving tours that
showed a traveler on the ground what to expect at each stop on the road.

In supervising the progress of the guides, the editors at headquarters
traveled tirelessly and were sometimes overwhelmed and appalled at
what they discovered. In late 1935, George Cronyn, an assistant director, found a nest of corruption in the California office. "Incompetence,
grave irregularities, political maneuvering, and sabotage of the American
Guide," he warned Alsberg in a memo. "This business is so messy I am
in despair," Kellock wrote to Alsberg, as she traveled through South
Carolina in January 1936. "Weird how much this state reminds me of
Russia—down here the rotten plumbing and scaly walls and curious
meal hours are reminiscent of Odessa."

After creating the guidebooks, a second goal of the Project was to
gather American folklore. The Project's first director of folklore was
John Lomax, the legendary ballad collector who had amassed cowboy
songs since his boyhood. Even before 1910, he had received Harvard
fellowships to haul around a massive recording machine, making disks

of "Home on the Range" and "Git Along Little Dogies." Lomax found himself widowed and out of work in 1932 when the bond market—his day job—collapsed. By 1935, he was making recordings for the Library of Congress, mostly in the South. Lomax spoke of field recording as capturing songs in their "native habitat." An unreconstructed Texan, he and his son Alan had met Huddie Ledbetter (aka Lead Belly) in a Louisiana prison in 1933, secured his release, and helped him settle in Manhattan. They published *Negro Folk Songs as Sung by Lead Belly* in 1936.

Lomax was nearly seventy when he took the WPA job. As the Project's folklore adviser, he brought to it his interests in folk songs, regional character, and black culture. He left after a year and a half, feeling that the spread of better roads and the rise of radio already spelled doom to folk music and regional cultures. But his influence on the Project remained, especially in the interviews with former slaves.

In May 1938, the folklore job passed to Benjamin Botkin, who was in some ways Lomax's opposite in personality—where Lomax was brash and full of Texas bluster, Botkin was shy and bookish. An intellectual who combined a knowledge of writing with a deep love for American culture, Botkin was the son of Lithuanian Jewish immigrants who had

Benjamin Botkin, national director for the folklore division.

settled in Boston. He was a cousin of George and Ira Gershwin's and loved low and high culture equally: jazz as well as opera, pulp fiction as well as classic literature, movies and Mark Twain. He had traveled widely and was fascinated by the entire country. Botkin had a Harvard degree and a PhD from the University of Nebraska and had been a professor in Oklahoma for nearly twenty years. He was deeply interested in how regular Americans talked about their lives and work, and he believed that writers had the job of "helping us respect one another." Even if writers weren't journalists who should show what was happening to America's traditions and point out spots of hope.

"As a nation, we have a genius for overstatement and understatement," Botkin told the *New York Post* in May 1944. "Both extremes are typically American." In time, he became the Project's spokesman for creating what he described in "WPA and Folklore Research: Bread and Song" as "a comprehensive picture of how America lives and works and plays."

This effort would show perhaps most clearly where many of America's various cultures came up against one another, sometimes deflecting, often cross-pollinating. From Chicago, where white musicians learned the vocabulary of jazz expression from black musicians (defying a 1920s racial ban on blacks and whites playing together), to Florida recordings of Spanish songs and Bahamian versions of old English folk tunes, these dynamics came through. Hurston described what was happening as a "revolution in national expression in music" equal to Chaucer's shift from Latin to vernacular English. In Harlem, Ralph Ellison found in the black community men who argued passionately the merits of their favorite sopranos, having themselves been extras at the Metropolitan Opera for years whenever there was a need for Egyptians or "natives." Ellison laughed at this unexpected crossing of race and culture. He called it an "outrageous American joke" and felt that his "appreciation of American cultural possibility was vastly extended."

To show America through people's lives, Botkin urged every WPA interviewer "to discover the real feeling of the person consulted and . . . record this feeling regardless of his own attitude toward it." For him, the Project's importance lay in showing "a living culture and understanding its meaning . . . in democratic society as a whole."

As a result, Peggy Bulger notes in *American Folklore: An Encyclopedia*, folklore became a way to improve people's lives, as well as to create understanding. It was a way to look at culture, and Botkin's method was to interview lots of people to find out what they valued. In other words, folklore was more than old folktales—it was a tool for national recovery.

The Project's designers believed that celebrating American diversity could prevent a wave of fascism like the one Europe was experiencing. The hard times had fueled a rise of anti-immigrant and fascist groups in the United States, like the group that Humphrey Bogart's embittered autoworker joins in the 1937 film *Black Legion*. ("No matter what it is or who commenced it, I'm against it," Bogart growled. "Especially if they're after my job and have an unpronounceable last name.") Eleanor Roosevelt crystallized this idea when she said that America's diversity was its strong point. This was in response to Hitler, who championed a monolithic, homogeneous population and viewed America as a great country weakened by fissures and subcultures. The Roosevelts essentially said, "No, that variety is our greatest strength." The WPA guides and interviews attempted to show that variety.

People realized that a program on such a vast scale would probably have an effect beyond whatever books were published, but nobody knew what that would be. At the time, the Writers' Project was called a charity for mediocre talents, and there is overwhelming evidence for this. There are many instances of plodding and awkward writing, and quite a few of the guides are rife with stereotypes of their time that can make today's readers cringe. Yet many of the guides show lively writing, and in the decades that followed, people who had never considered themselves writers would publish biographies and histories. In the case of Juanita Brooks, her 1950 book *Mountain Meadows Massacre* offers a nuanced investigation into the hidden story of a slaughter in Utah that would transform a community's view of itself.

A handful from the Project's roster would become some of the century's most important literary artists. Four of the first ten winners of the National Book Award in fiction and one in poetry came from this emergency relief project. Its effects have been cited in works as varied as John Cheever's *Falconer*, Ralph Ellison's *Invisible Man*, Saul Bellow's

Chicago novels, Zora Neale Hurston's later novels and plays, and Studs Terkel's interviews and books. The Project also influenced the poetry of Margaret Walker, May Swenson, and Kenneth Rexroth and the eyeballs-at-the-curb viewpoint of Jim Thompson's noir classics *The Grifters* and *The Killer inside Me.*

When Nelson Algren said that the Project gave hope to people who had lost it, he was not being melodramatic. The Writers' Project set a trampoline under many thousands, writers and nonwriters, who would otherwise have hit the pavement. The poet W. H. Auden called the Project "one of the noblest and most absurd undertakings ever attempted by any state." It put people in contact with one another, restored voices to many who had fallen silent, and gave us the closest thing to Twain's vision that America has ever seen.

2

POINT OF DEPARTURE:
NEW YORK

Till recently no one dared to say out loud that things were on the decline. It was merely a sort of public secret for years that everything was not as it should be. The unemployed—thousands of them—walked around like ghosts (they still do, you'll see them) or were hiding away in their shacks

—CONNECTICUT TRAVELING SALESMAN, IN "NEW
ENGLAND'S TRAGIC TOWNS" (1937)

THE GREAT CRASH OVERTURNED THE LIVES of all Americans like a surging wave. Not all at once, but dramatically and irreversibly. Many did not feel the effects immediately in October 1929. In Chicago, post office workers still had jobs. In New York, publishers kept releasing books. In the South, textile companies continued to operate. But within months, people would be staring around them, dumbfounded. For three years after the crash, companies fired an average of twenty thousand employees every working day, week in and week out. In some cities, half of the adults were out of work.

"With the leveling force of an earthquake, the stock crash had hit us all," wrote Anzia Yezierska in *Red Ribbon on a White Horse*, her novelistic autobiography. "Bankers, industrialists, ditch diggers, and authors were tossed together into the same abyss."

Yezierska was a brash woman who had always had a kinetic confidence. In the 1930s, she was in her fifties, and as her auburn hair turned gray, she remained attractive. Even as her financial straits worsened, she dressed in tailored navy serge or gray tweed suits.

As a young girl, Anzia had come to New York from Russia with her family, fleeing the anti-Semitic pogroms of the late 1800s. She grew up in a tenement on the Lower East Side, the youngest of many children and thus the most American of them in her habits. For years, the family lived in a dark, cramped flat that looked out at the blank wall of a neighboring building.

Soon, Anzia's older sisters were working as seamstresses in a sweatshop, while Anzia went to school and learned English. She helped the family by selling paper bags to the pushcart vendors on the street. As a teenager she joined her sisters, sewing buttons. In that era before child-labor laws, she often put in twelve-hour days. Anzia bridled against

A Lower East Side scene during the Depression.

her mother's traditional role and her father's paternalism, and she struggled for a way to carve out her own identity. When everyone else in the family was asleep, she would crawl up to the roof of the tenement "and talk out my heart," she recalled later, "to the stars and the sky. Who am I? What am I? What do I want with my life?"

Anzia went to night school every evening after work and set aside money to study at the New York City Normal College. She struggled to save money—against her father's wish that she share all of her wages with the family. Yezierska, as her daughter, Louise, wrote in her biography, *Anzia Yezierska: A Writer's Life*, "was seventeen or eighteen, fighting with her family even more because of the differences she now discovered between her own situation and that of the young Americans in her classes."

Anzia Yezierska in 1920.

Yezierska married, but she found that marriage didn't suit her and soon divorced. With a young child to care for, she taught elementary school for several years. She had an ear for the language of the street and began to write fiction. Coming from a talkative family and a convivial neighborhood would have honed Yezierska's ear, according to author Grace Paley, who grew up a generation later in a more Americanized Jewish neighborhood of the Bronx and who discovered Yezierska's stories as an adult. "Another marvelous thing is the English language," said Paley. "It is so receptive, it allows you to do so much. My generation of Ashkenazic Jews, we were just welcomed into English—we may not have been welcomed into the culture altogether, but our language was welcomed into literature. The English language says, 'Come in! Come in!'"

Yezierska got her first short story published in 1915. Five years later, she came out with a book of short stories, *Hungry Hearts*. It caught the eye of Hollywood studio owner Samuel Goldwyn, and she suddenly went from working as a house-cleaner and a button-sewer to instant fame. Hollywood packaged her as "the sweatshop Cinderella."

That label masked something much more complex: Yezierska's desire to capture human nature's contradictions. She first felt the impulse to write after an episode at the market, where a woman grew hysterical when her small son got lost in the crowd. "Find me my child! My Benny! My best child from all my children!" the woman cried. When a policeman came over, leading a pale-faced little boy by the hand, the mother slapped and cursed her Benny for giving her such a scare. Ironies and dramatic turn-arounds ("Her best child of all her children!") enthralled Yezierska.

Throughout the 1920s, she lived the American dream. She became a best-selling author and a Hollywood screenwriter for adaptations of her books. In the America of that decade, heady with a new generation of immigrant success, her stories combined fresh thinking and exotic old-world customs that captivated readers and moviegoers.

With the economy in shambles, however, the public was no longer interested in plucky immigrant stories. Nobody wanted to see immigrants in movies, either; now they were viewed as competitors for scarce jobs. The Cinderella of the tenements was back to sweeping ashes. Yezierska moved from a big apartment on Fifth Avenue to a small flat on the lower West Side. Then to a darker, smaller flat in a shabbier house, followed in quick succession by cheaper, dingier rooms and more crowded eating places. By 1934, she was sharing an apartment on Twelfth Street with her grown daughter and learned again the art of making do with a single room.

More than most Americans, Yezierska grasped how her own fall mirrored that of many thousands around her. She had seen the whole country on the rise, and now her world was shrinking to what it had been when she was a teenager on a rooftop, wondering what she could become. The Depression felt bound up with personal defeat and silence.

Yezierska visited a fellow writer she had known some time earlier to see about finding work and was rebuffed. "You? You want a job?" the other woman asked. Yezierska couldn't find words to explain what she was going through.

"Friends retreated before my failing fortunes just as I had once run away from my own poor people," she wrote in *Red Ribbon on a White*

Horse. "Occasionally I ran into some of the celebrities with whom I used to dine at the Algonquin. At first I was naïve enough to greet them with the warmth I felt at sight of a familiar face. Only after I saw their embarrassment did I learn to avoid noticing them at all."

Like many others, Yezierska felt ashamed of her fall from prosperity, as if it were her own fault. In time, she would embrace the idea that this anti-Cinderella story—her return to poverty—was a more universal story of the time, her true story.

Americans prize self-sufficiency above all—rugged individualism, we call it. To be unable to provide for your family in this new urban world produced a profound shame. Often, it was so humiliating that people didn't talk about it. Families moved away, leaving town without a word, under the shadow of eviction.

Activists protested the injustice of the broken economic system. For many young people of that generation, communism offered change and an alternative to a market system that had failed. What's more, the Hoover administration's repressive reaction to dissent had caused a backlash. "If you were against starving, you were a Communist," recalled Leo Seltzer, who in the early 1930s was a young engineering student-turned-filmmaker in New York. "If you were against unemployment, you were a Communist. If you were against what the government was doing in terms of making the rich richer, you were a Communist. . . . Everything 'anti' was Communist. So you end up being against the government, because the government is against you."

Most Americans, though, were simply stunned. People felt abandoned. People *were* abandoned, sometimes by those close to them, as Yezierska found. In 1935, she wrote to a close friend:

Dear Celia,

Thank you for knifing me in the back and betraying what I said to you in strictest confidence when I called on you for help. It's human nature to kick the ladder on which you once climbed. Maybe you need the sadistic satisfaction of belittling those relatives and friends whom you can no longer use to get on.

Anzia

People saw their worlds sliding away, and they were speechless.

One morning in the spring of 1936, while making breakfast, Anzia Yezierska's attention was caught by something she heard on the radio. "I was in the kitchen," she wrote in *Red Ribbon*, when "the radio broadcast a special news item about WPA: a headquarters had just been set up for the new Writers' Project. I hurried to the address, eager to work. . . . All I needed . . . was the security of a WPA wage to get my typewriter out of the pawnshop."

The address mentioned on the radio turned out to be a dingy, cavernous building with new, hastily made signs that read WPA. A huge crowd had gathered, and a guard was telling people to take the freight elevator. Yezierska was jostled into the elevator and dumped on the twelfth floor.

Clearly, she and many others were desperate for change. With the social meltdown of the Depression came an opening, like the clearing in a forest when a large tree falls. People scrambled for new ways to make life work again. Things *had* to change. So people were open to an experiment like the Writers' Project when in other times they might have said, "This is a waste of time. It can't work." In the Depression, new ideas were absolutely necessary.

On the other hand, the public saw the WPA as lamentable, a necessary evil at best. Politicians either supported the programs with noises of concern and pity or opposed them as misguided. One of those who railed against them was Congressman Martin Dies of Texas. In a June 1935 newsreel, he said, "If we had refused admission to the sixteen million five hundred thousand foreign-born in our midst, there would be no serious unemployment problem to harass us."

Dies, a big blond Texan, had concerns about un-American ideologies and foreign influences, a heightened version of the concerns that many citizens felt. Two events in early 1938 triggered the founding of his committee to investigate un-American activities. First came reports of a Nazi spy ring working inside the United States. Then in April, in the German Yorkville neighborhood on Manhattan's Upper East Side, the German American Bund, a pro-Nazi group established in 1936, threw a party for Hitler's birthday. During the celebration, participants got into a brawl with Jewish veterans of the American Legion after one of the legionnaires demanded to know whether the group was German or

American. In Congress, Dies argued that an investigative committee led by him would not be "inclined to look under every bed for a communist," but he claimed to have "information showing the establishment and operation of some thirty-two Nazi camps in the U.S.," with nearly half a million members "marching and saluting the swastika."

The national mood was fearful, with gangsters and international intrigue rampant. Newsstands brimmed with books that had titles like *Secret Armies* and *Secret Agents against America.*

In the immense building where Anzia went to sign up for the Writers' Project, she hoped that her credentials—her list of best sellers and Hollywood credits—would pave her way toward getting a job. "I've come to work on the Writers' Project," she told the guard at the desk when she got off the elevator. Asked for her relief number, she insisted, "I don't want relief. I want work as a writer."

The prerequisite for a WPA position was certifying that you were eligible for welfare. It was called "the pauper's oath," and it required you to prove that you had no money, no property, no job, and no prospect of getting any of those. For the Writers' Project within the WPA, you also had to show evidence that you were a writer. It can be hard to fathom the mix of competing feelings involved in certifying for emergency relief and qualifying for the Writers' Project. It was like studying hard for a test and, if you passed, earning a dunce cap. "Are you poor enough? Okay. Now, are you skilled enough?" It was a Kafkaesque situation.

Many of the WPA writers resented that stipulation; many were dispirited. Ultimately, the Project was a cross section of society, Yezierska later wrote in *Red Ribbon*:

> We were as ill-assorted as a crowd on a subway express—spinster poetesses, pulp specialists, youngsters . . . , veteran newspapermen, art-for-art's-sake literati, clerks and typists . . . people of all ages, all nationalities, all degrees of education, tossed together in a strange fellowship of necessity.

That variety made the Project more representative of the general population than most publishing ventures are.

On the Lower East Side, where Yezierska grew up, for example, Project writers would in time describe the neighborhood in the WPA guide with the authority of people who knew the life there. It was a two-square-mile slice of the city packed with tenements, shops, and noise from which a startling range of public figures emerged: "politicians, artists, gangsters, composers, prize fighters, labor leaders." Their guide shows tenement conditions in specific, visceral terms: "[T]he smothering heat of summer still drives East Siders to the windows and fire escapes of their ill-ventilated dwellings, to the docks along the river or to the crowded smelly streets, where . . . children cool themselves in streams from fire hydrants." And the writers got inside those families on the fire escapes to show that teenage rebellion like Anzia's was still simmering across the Lower East Side.

"Through appalling sacrifice, some Jewish families realized their fondest aspiration: a son became a doctor, teacher, or lawyer," notes the guide. "An East Side family was often divided against itself by the conflict of the old and the new." The WPA writers would even find an apt quotation from the Lower East Side novelist Samuel Ornitz: "Many of us were transient, impatient aliens in our parents' home."

From the tenements, the guide takes readers to work in the sweatshops of the garment district, as seen from the employees' viewpoint: the bare floors and whitewashed walls, the long cutting tables with motorized blades, and rows of sewing machines operated mostly by women. Lunch hour in a garment factory "would find many of the workers absorbed in Tolstoy, Kropotkin, or Heine. . . . While Broadway was receiving Ibsen coldly, the East Side was . . . applauding Nazimova in [Ibsen's] *Ghosts*. The ghetto has produced a remarkable Jewish literature of its own, much of it mirroring the harsh life of sweatshop and slum." The guide notes the influence of Lower East Side culture on American speech and through entertainers ranging from George and Ira Gershwin to Al Jolson, Fanny Brice, Milton Berle, and the Marx Brothers.

For the WPA life histories, interviewers would talk with Lower East Siders who were not very different from Anzia in her youth. Bessie W. asked to withhold her full name: "I grew up too fast; I didn't have much of a childhood. At eleven, I was almost as tall as now, well-built, and I was going around with fellers already. We were living on 9th Street near Avenue A. Five of us in two small rooms. . . . I was very unhappy then! I'll tell you something I never told anyone. I used to stand in front of a mirror and practice suicide scenes with a knife. . . . I just wanted to get away from my home in the worst way."

There were many Project workers who agreed with the public perception of WPA as a handout, but others saw their work as legitimate. The writers were digging for the truth of their local history, neighborhood by neighborhood.

Yezierska made her way to work from Morton Street south through the Village to the office at 110 King Street, near the city's huge dairy freight terminal with its trucks coming and going. Beyond were the piers

A Greenwich Village cheese store, 1937.

on the Hudson where freighters and riverboats docked. She wrote in
Red Ribbon:

> Each morning I walked to the Project as light-hearted as if I were
> going to a party. The huge, barracks-like Writers' Hall roared with
> the laughter and greetings of hundreds of voices. As we signed in,
> we stopped to smoke, make dates for lunch and exchange gossip.
> Our grapevine buzzed with budding love affairs, tales of salary
> raises, whispers of favoritism, the political maneuvers of the big
> shots. There was a hectic camaraderie among us.

On payday after work, a number of them celebrated at a place nearby
called Tony's Bar. "I followed, swept along by the wild elation. . . . Men
who hadn't had a job in years fondled five- and ten-dollar bills with the
tenderness of farmers rejoicing over new crops of grain."

Her cohorts included Joe Gould, an eccentric personality who claimed
to be writing the most complete history of the world ever attempted. One
of the last bohemians from the period before the Great War, Gould had
grown up in a blue-blooded New England family and graduated from
Harvard in the Class of 1911. After traveling among Native Americans
in North Dakota and doing field research for a study, Gould returned to
the East Coast and devoted himself to writing his oral history of civili-
zation. In the 1950s, *New Yorker* writer Joseph Mitchell would explore
in *Joe Gould's Secret* the man's ambition and failure. Yezierska seemed to
recognize, before others did, that Gould had little, if any, of it written,
and she empathized with his failings. (In *Red Ribbon,* she changed his
name to Jeremiah.)

Failures among the Project's higher ranks would soon become clear. One
morning Yezierska opened the newspaper and was stunned to read that
Orrick Johns, her boss, was embroiled in a scandal, having been attacked
by the boyfriend of a WPA worker with whom Johns was having an affair.
The jealous boyfriend, a sailor, had set Johns's prosthetic leg on fire. "The
tabloid story of a 'drunken illicit tryst' was such a shock that I couldn't eat
breakfast," Yezierska wrote in *Red Ribbon.* "WPA was again under fire,
lampooned as 'counterfeit work, supported with taxpayers' good money.'"

Johns, the New York director, was forced to resign, and a young replacement was named, who would exert more focus on producing the long-awaited New York City guide.

The shift involved dramatic reassignments and writing quotas. Although bored by the tasks, Anzia was energized by the company. "I feel like a bit of withered moss that has been suddenly put into water," she told her daughter, "growing green again."

Vincent McHugh grew up in a blue-collar Rhode Island family and moved to New York in the 1920s to live as a writer. He wrote several well-received novels and short pieces for the *New Yorker*. Then in late 1936, the WPA called. Even before the dismissal of its previous director, the New York City guide had stalled under the weight of about eight million words of hodgepodge, a fractured staff, and sit-in strikes. Henry Alsberg asked McHugh to take a job that required a political animal. That was not McHugh's nature, but he accepted the challenge and became the technical director. He visited Washington, D.C., to get guidance from headquarters but left as soon as he could.

"I never wanted to move to Washington," McHugh said later. "HQ was middle class and since I came from a working-class family I felt much more comfortable with the New York crowd."

After he returned to New York on the train from Washington (a passage in his 1942 novel describes the scene with a surrealism that could have echoed McHugh's own sense of disbelief), his first task was to retrieve the only copy of the manuscript guidebook from the mayor's office. It was being held hostage there by Mayor Fiorello La Guardia, who was so worried by the warts-and-all picture of the city that he threatened to pulp the manuscript. McHugh managed to cajole him into returning it, but within a day it was stolen by one of the Communists on staff, who were bitterly divided between Trotskyites and Stalinists.

"Political factions had sprung up," Anzia Yezierska noted in *Red Ribbon*, with the Communist Party organizing the lion's share of the Manhattan office staff, followed by "America Firsters, anti-Stalinists, pro- and anti-Roosevelt groups."

McHugh recovered the draft once again and set about giving it a coherent shape. He arranged the guide to reflect the city at the street level. For this, he laid out a plan based on neighborhoods and sent the writers out to gather information. McHugh himself got caught up in the treasure hunt for the city's stories and hit the pavement along with his staff to do fact-checking.

He delved into nooks and crannies of the city's inner mechanisms, including the Weather Bureau perched on top of the Whitehall Building overlooking Battery Park. He absorbed the sleepy, bureaucratic interior ("rather like the offices of an old-line shipping firm in the 1890s. . . . Heavy oak furniture. Slant-top chest-high mercantile desks, long tables, and leisurely men in shirt sleeves and gray alpaca jackets"), the weather instrument shed on the roof, and the thrilling view outside, which he later used in his 1943 novel *I Am Thinking of My Darling*:

> I looked out the high windows, under the overhang of the bow roof. . . . There was no land in sight under us. Like the view from a clipper's main truck. Governors Island in its eighteenth-century neatness of a fortified place, the Brooklyn shore, the hump of Staten Island in the blue. A quarter mile off the Battery, a middle-sized liner was being pushed in circles by three merry tugs, her siren going like a wounded bull.

McHugh got so deeply immersed in the workings of the city for the guidebook—the bus routes, the bridge load statistics, the neighborhood shops—that he proposed a book called *New York Underground*, a non-fiction account devoted to the subterranean labyrinth of sewers and subway lines.

McHugh didn't shrink from demanding any detail, however small. Yezierska struggled with the mind-numbing research tasks. She viewed the assignments as "some bitter medicine we had to swallow." Joe Gould took it harder, reacting to "his assignment to write up the Fulton Street fish market as if he had been asked to break the tablets of the law." Another staffer, a poet, melodramatically threatened suicide. He declared, "I, who have dedicated my whole life to poetry, would rather die than go on working on a street map for the Bronx."

One morning Yezierska went uptown for her new assignment: to catalog the trees in Central Park.

"I waited half an hour outside an office of the Park Department and got a list of the 253 varieties of trees in Central Park," she wrote in *Red Ribbon.* The rest of the day she spent wandering around the park, tracking down the trees. The guide would eventually include notes on the wisteria arbors and the inscriptions on statues throughout the park. Near an underpass on the park's east side, a bronze figure of an Alaskan husky was honored with these words: "Dedicated to the spirit of the sled dogs that relayed antitoxin over six hundred miles of rough ice, across treacherous waters, through Arctic blizzards, from Nenana to the relief of stricken Nome in the winter of 1925."

Other days, Yezierska's assignment sent her burrowing into the stacks of the New York Public Library on Fifth Avenue for a minor character in New York's eighteenth-century history.

> The circulating department of the Forty-second Street library was a book traffic center as bewildering to me as a foreign country. . . . I opened the first drawer of the catalogue, and then another. Smiths peopled the world. They crowded about me. . . . Down the endless rows of Smiths, my eyes blurred. . . . It was getting late. Lamps were being turned on at every table and my assignment was still undone. The whole day's work at those files gone to waste. . . . Still no words for the wordage machine.

Richard Wright arrived in New York in mid-1937, hoping to get on the Writers' Project as a foothold into America's literary capital. Before that, Wright had worked for the Chicago office, where he had edited essays for the Illinois guide. He had to wade through red tape over residence requirements and certification, but, ultimately, he got a position. For the New York City guide, he wrote about black history and introduced readers to Harlem (which included Spanish Harlem). He described the neighborhood as a community packed with old apartment buildings and brownstones where half of the residents had no jobs and where

The scene on Harlem's Lenox Avenue, 1938.

poverty sprouted gangs: "In summer the sidewalks are crowded . . . ; the unemployed move chairs to the pavement and set up cracker boxes for checker games. On Lenox Avenue soapbox orators draw crowds nightly . . . , one of the speakers being, inevitably, a disciple of Marcus Garvey, leader of the back-to-Africa movement, now in exile in England."

Wright was working furiously, grinding out essays by day and his own fiction after hours. He fueled discussion by recruiting a smart young man from Oklahoma City, a sharp dresser named Ralph Ellison, who would soon be taking assignments downtown in the public library and interviewing Harlem residents for the evolving folklore division. In general, African Americans were underrepresented on the Project, making up only 2 percent of the staff nationally.

At one point, WPA writer Harry Roskolenko observed, you could find John Cheever in the cafeteria elbow to elbow with Richard Wright.

Yezierska described her own lunchroom talks with Wright in *Red Ribbon on a White Horse*, saying that in his drive and appearance, he "stood out among the white-faced men drained by defeat." Yezierska saw in Wright an avatar of her youthful self: ambitious, oppressed, and talented.

In the Old Custom House at Bowling Green, WPA writers described the "somewhat ponderous" neoclassical architecture and identified the sculptures in all of the rooms, even as WPA artist Reginald Marsh was painting murals on the ceilings there.

On the Upper West Side, WPA researchers walked Morningside Heights between the Hudson vista of Riverside Drive and the striking Renaissance architecture of the Church of Notre Dame de Lourdes, where sermons were delivered in French and a grotto appeared to be scooped out of Morningside Cliff. They listed the colleges of Columbia University and its range of scholars, from the New Deal's "Brain Trust" to its law school graduates and leading anthropologist Franz Boas. (Boas's students in the 1920s included Zora Neale Hurston, who on his advice returned to her native Florida to collect African American folktales.) On Central Park West, field-workers combed exhibits in the American Museum of Natural History and remarked on the gables and the oriel windows adorning the tony apartments in the Dakota.

Richard Wright in 1938.

At Riker's Island, WPA workers wrote up notes on the new penitentiary, its inmates, and the prison farm's pork production, as well as the nearby North Brother Island, where the city hospital's most famous resident had been Mary Mallon, a hospital cook who unwittingly caused an epidemic as "Typhoid Mary."

A twenty-two-year-old high school dropout named John Cheever had been surviving in the city on raisins and the mercies of Yaddo, the artists' colony, since he had arrived from a Boston suburb two years earlier to make it as a writer. In his journal he recorded scenes, the odd juxtapositions of an impoverished New England with its incongruities and cold humor. His entries from that time include sharp, perfectly framed daguerreotypes of stoic Yankee poverty, like this sad roadside family vacation in the White Mountains:

> The pines on Mount Washington are about the oldest things on the face of the earth. People in the early evenings sat in their cabins, watching the traffic pass. A family from Massachusetts had set a card-table up on the sandy road shoulders and were having their supper there, between the smell of pines and the dust and the fumes from the traffic. "I love to sit on the piazza and watch the traffic." Looking for out of state license plates. They are a less neurotic people, perhaps. The desire for privacy has not been developed. What does this express: sitting complacently at a card-table on the shoulders of a main traffic artery on a holiday evening, eating a supper of pickles and cold beans and eggs.

Because his fiction hadn't yet gained traction among New York editors, Cheever reluctantly took a position with the Writers' Project. The junior editor job required that he move to Washington, D.C., so he packed his belongings and trundled southward on a slow train, a new New Yorker unhappily displaced by hard times.

3

CHICAGO AND THE MIDWEST

Lots of speakeasies helped to serve the jazz art. . . . In 1927 the place to go was Kelly's Stables. Respectable girls had to go there on the q.t. . . . We'd always be stopped by the cops and searched for machine guns.

—MUSICIAN BUD JACOBSON, IN A WPA INTERVIEW WITH SAM ROSS

LOUIS TERKEL ENROLLED IN THE UNIVERSITY of Chicago's law school partly to please his mother with the prospect of stability. At that point, Chicago's unemployment rate had reached 50 percent. On his walk to and from campus, Terkel often dawdled in sidewalk music shops and paid a nickel each for "race records," the term for African American music. He already had suspicions that he wouldn't enjoy law school, but the alternatives weren't good. His father had died in 1931 when Louis was in college, and the family business—a boardinghouse—was struggling. The Wells Grand—a posh-sounding name for a place at the corner of Wells and Grand on the Near West Side—catered to workers. Now, with everyone out of work, there

The Chicago skyline at night, mid-1930s.

were often empty spaces in the ledger. (For decades afterward, seeing a Vacancy sign in a motel window evoked a personal terror for Terkel.)

Terkel had first seen Chicago from the window of a train in 1920 when he was eight years old. He and his mother had come west from the Bronx and had gotten off at Chicago's La Salle Station, where his older brother Ben, who had traveled ahead with their father, ran up and spun Louis's cap around backward. They had made it to a new home.

Their father, Sam Terkel, was a gentle man who enjoyed listening to his homemade crystal radio set. He wasn't much of a businessman, but his interest in the radio was forward-looking. In the early 1920s, radio was new, and the notion that you could pick voices out of the air on a contraption you built yourself was revolutionary. Schools in Chicago saw enrollment skyrocket for courses in electrical theory and shop, where students built radio cabinets. On the radio, the Terkels heard the voice that made Louis want to become a lawyer: that of Clarence Darrow, who defended Tennessee teacher John Thomas Scopes in 1925. Chicago listeners heard Darrow's closing arguments in the Scopes trial live (along with those of his opponent, William Jennings Bryan) because the *Tribune's* radio station, WGN, paid wire charges of $1,000 a day for the show.

Instead of the drama and idealism of Darrow, however, Terkel found in law school the harsh glare of torts. He loathed it. "I wasn't cut out for it," he later said of the law. After suffering as much as he could, he dropped out at age twenty-two, into one of the worst job markets in history. He helped his mother run the boardinghouse, working the front desk and listening to the residents' cautionary tales about their lives. He heard them argue politics over cribbage in the lobby. Upstairs, one lodger, an old coppersmith who suddenly found work again after Prohibition was repealed (breweries needed his services to get back in business), had a "new heterodyne radio set, in a baroque cabinet that occupied half his room." It boomed throughout the boardinghouse, Terkel wrote in *Hard Times*. In the lobby, the night clerk kept the dial tuned to Father Coughlin's weekly program from Detroit.

With the Depression deepening, Father Charles Coughlin's national audience had grown to around thirty million. As Coughlin became more rabid in his tirades against bankers and Jews, he grew more popular.

Under the el in downtown Chicago, 1940.

From initially supporting the New Deal, he turned against FDR and charged that U.S. monetary policy was being shaped "for the benefit of the one billion Orientals who from time immemorial have identified their trade and commerce with Gentile silver." *Orientals* was a code word for Jews. Coughlin's voice must have upset Terkel's mother, who had fled pogroms near the Polish-Russian border at the turn of the century. But the bitter night clerk ignored requests to "Turn the Roman off."

When Terkel left law school, he was getting small parts in stage productions and as a supernumerary in operas. In 1935, he landed a speaking role with the Chicago Rep Theater as a cabbie in Clifford Odets's play *Waiting for Lefty*, about a cabdrivers' strike. He found a day job doing clerical work at a relief agency and sent out letters to hotels, requesting work as a concierge.

The distance from the Terkels' boardinghouse to Richard Wright's family apartment on Indiana Avenue on the city's South Side was nine miles and a world away.

The Near West Side neighborhood of Chicago, 1941.

African American residents in the South Side's Black Belt were forced into a narrow channel of housing options by discriminatory real-estate practices. Many worked in the meatpacking plants just to the west. Wright's family had left the segregated South, coming north from Mississippi by way of Memphis, where Jim Crow laws had limited blacks' access to services so much that Wright once forged a note to a city librarian over a white man's signature: "Dear Madam, Will you please let this nigger boy have some books by H. L. Mencken?"

In books, Wright found refuge from a hostile world. And in Mencken's books, he first encountered language that had the power of a weapon.

Wright arrived on the South Side in late 1927, not yet twenty years old. Already he was the main breadwinner for his mother, aunt, and younger brother and was under heavy pressure to find work in Chicago. He managed to land a part-time job at the post office and had hopes for stability when, walking to work one winter day, he passed a newsstand where headlines read STOCKS CRASH—BILLIONS FADE. Wright didn't give it much thought: "Most of what I had seen in newspapers had never concerned me, so why should this?"

Before long, the post office faced cutbacks, and he was out of a job. He walked the streets looking for work but found only other despairing job seekers. Wright sold burial insurance for a while, then grew disgusted by the way the industry preyed on the poor. He and his family moved to a cheaper apartment, a dismal place with falling plaster and sagging wooden stairs. His mother cried when she saw it for the first time.

With their pantry nearly empty, he resigned himself to signing up with the city relief agency. "I rose, put on my hat and coat, and went out. As I walked," he wrote in *Black Boy*, "I knew that I had come to the end of something." For the city relief wage, he dug ditches, cleaned hospital operating rooms, and cared for lab animals.

"I rode in zero weather for miles in open trucks, then spaded the frozen earth for eight hours, only to ride home again in the dark," he wrote of that time. "I knew that my life was cast with the men with whom I worked: slow, plodding, inarticulate men, workers all."

When he joined the Writers' Project, Wright gained a license to delve into South Side life. A letter dated January 1936, addressed "To Whom

It May Concern," declared Richard Wright "an authorized representative of the American Guide" and urged the recipient to "give any information or suggestions that will help to make our Guide more authoritative and accurate," for the benefit of all Illinois.

The young man with a seventh-grade education soon found himself an essays editor for the Illinois WPA guide. Later, he described it as the time when "I tried to earn my bread by writing guidebooks." The salary allowed him to support his family and connected him with others who were as committed to words and writing as he was, the type of people Wright had been seeking out since he arrived in the city. People like Nelson Algren.

The Chicago office was an exceptional version of what Henry Alsberg could scarcely have hoped for when he said that WPA writers "will get an education in the American scene": a community of talents that would absorb the local culture in each place with fresh eyes and imaginations. Algren and Wright provided alphabetical bookends to a startling roster that included Saul Bellow (in his first paid writing job), novelists Arna Bontemps and Jack Conroy, choreographer Katherine Dunham, Terkel, and poet-novelist Margaret Walker.

Most were in their twenties. Wright was twenty-eight when he joined. Algren was twenty-seven. Terkel was a few years younger. Bellow was twenty-two. Walker was twenty. Wright had met a few of his colleagues in 1934 at the John Reed Club, a feeder group for the Communist Party that gathered in a second-floor apartment on South Michigan Avenue. Wright, outwardly affable but somewhat aloof, had deep ambitions that he rarely showed. He wanted a group of writing peers, a public voice, and recognition for untold stories.

"If 1929 became a symbol of despair and ruin," historian Michael Denning observed in *The Cultural Front*, "1934 stands as one of the lyric years in American history," when mounting public sympathy for labor reached a kind of critical mass. The line between the working class and artists was dissolving. The Writers' Project and Communism in Chicago saw a good deal of overlap. According to *Black Boy*, many of Wright's coworkers on the Project were members of the Communist Party.

In his essays and descriptions for the Illinois guide, Wright captured South Side life on a large canvas, covering entertainment from its tearooms and nightclubs to barrooms and sports halls.

[T]he most attractive place of entertainment is the Grand Terrace Dine and Dance Café at 3955 [South Parkway] . . . one of the most popular and best known of all Black Belt night clubs. . . . It possesses a splendid dance floor, accommodating about two hundred. . . . The most distinctive feature of the Grand Terrace is Earl Hines' NBC orchestra which is known the nation over. . . . Four floor shows are given nightly; it is an all-Negro revue.

The Poro Tea Room, Wright noted, served "the best food to be found on the South Side at very reasonable prices." It was a quiet and clean retreat for customers who wanted privacy. Wright, an avid filmgoer, described the Metropolitan Movie Theatre, which specialized in first-run movies

Musicians in a South Side tavern, 1941.

like *G-Men, Top Hat,* and *Imitation of Life.* With tickets at 25 cents for adults and 15 cents for children, it was a good place to be on a hot summer day ("there is a cooling system"). Wright continued his description of the neighborhood:

> In the late twenties [the Savoy Ballroom] was the most popu- lar dance hall on the South Side. Louis Armstrong used to play here to huge crowds. . . . Next door to the Savoy Ballroom is the Savoy Outdoor Boxing Arena, seating about five thousand. Here on Tuesday nights are given boxing bouts, mostly amateur. . . . This amateur boxing is followed by the athletic-minded on the South Side. The usual "card" consists of ten boxing bouts and two wrestling matches. Adjoining the arena is a training headquarters. Joe Louis, contender for the World's Heavyweight Championship, trained here for his bout with King Levinsky. It is also used by Joe Louis for training when he is in the city.
>
> Walking southward along South Parkway we pass the homes of wealthy Negro publishers, doctors, bankers, lawyers, and business men. . . . It is not until we reach Garfield Boulevard that we see the heart of the Negro Rialto district. Along Garfield Boulevard . . . are dozens of beer gardens, restaurants, shops, . . . "chicken shacks," horse racing, bookies, pool rooms, and small hotels. Here is the center of gambling, prostitution and "high-life." . . . Walking still further west on Garfield Blvd. Till we reach State Street, we find a night club of the old 1920 variety—the Club Delisa at 5516 S. State St. There is an average bar and a huge dance floor. The place is Italian owned and caters, it is rumored, to "gangster trade." It is very popular with the more daring "nighters-out." . . . the dance floor opens around 10 PM.

Beyond the legwork exercise, the Project authorized Wright to research the history of black life in Chicago, which he laid out in an essay titled "Ethnographical Aspects of Chicago's Black Belt," intended for the Illinois guide. In it, he forthrightly describes the violence in the city's past:

A form of organized resistance to the moving of Negroes into new neighborhoods was the bombing of their homes and the homes of real estate men, white and Negro, who were known or supposed to have sold, leased or rented local property to them. From July 1, 1917 to March 1, 1921 the Negro housing problem was marked by no less than 58 bombings. Arson, stoning, and many armed clashes added to the gravity of the situation.

From the very beginning the Negroes were outspoken in their indignation over these conditions, but their protests had no apparent effect.

Wright knew the context for the black migration and the loaded emotions that complicated simple daily routines for the new arrivals:

From an extremely simple set of rural relations in the South, Negroes were transported to more complex relations based on more elaborate distribution of responsibilities. Thus . . . contacts in the public schools, politics, business, industry, sport, colleges, clubs and housing were points of contact making for friction, comment, antagonism, resentment, prejudice or fear.

From that intimate focus, Wright then resumes the sweep of his historical account with a journalist's eye for key events:

On July 27, 1919, there was a clash of major proportions between white and black. It began as a brawl at a bathing beach and resulted in the drowning of a Negro boy. This, in turn, led to a race riot in which 38 lives were lost—23 Negroes and 15 whites—and 537 persons were injured. After 3 days of mob violence . . . the state militia was called out to assist the police in restoring order.

Besides gaining a historical perspective, Wright found in the Project a model for his own South Side Writers' Group.

Nelson Algren's father was a Jewish auto mechanic and machinist; Nelson was born in Detroit and grew up in Chicago. After studying journalism at the University of Illinois, Algren found himself jobless in 1931. He got temporary work as a door-to-door salesman and a truck driver. When those jobs ended, he hopped a southbound freight train. He spent time in New Orleans and then headed west through Texas, listening to the stories of his fellow hoboes. One day, on a freight going east from El Paso, he scanned the landscape from the train's roof and, aching for a typewriter to get those stories down, spotted what might be a college campus. When railroad bulls pulled him off the train ninety miles down the line, he hitchhiked back to the town. His hunch was right: the Sul Ross State Teachers College had a room full of unused typewriters. Algren asked to borrow one and became a hobo-in-residence for the fall. When he left, he tried to take the typewriter, a theft that landed him in jail for a month.

He returned to Chicago and met Wright at John Reed Club meetings. They grew closer on the Writers' Project, which set up an office in a warehouse near Lake Michigan. The big open room where staff members met between assignments held nearly a hundred people.

Margaret Walker in 1942.

On Margaret Walker's first day on the job, she stepped off the elevator and bumped into Wright, whom she had met before. In her view, the Project ended the isolation of African American artists. The political climate in the warehouse changed her writing markedly, from the "very romantic and sentimental" poetry of her university years to a more "realistic" style. She later told interviewer Judith McCray, "I was very conscious of making that change."

Born in Birmingham, Alabama, Walker had moved to Chicago with her parents. Her father, a Methodist minister, had brought his family to the city from the Deep South to ensure that his children got an education. When Margaret was twelve years old, he gave her a notebook in which she could write all of her poems. "That motivated me to fill the book," she said in *Conversations with Margaret Walker*.

Now she had her degree from Northwestern University but no work. She fudged her age by a year because people needed to be twenty-one to qualify for the Writers' Project.

In after-hours gatherings over cold cuts and cheap wine, the staff members flirted with one another and debated politics. Walker recalled in her book about Richard Wright a party during which, one moment, a conservative colleague cautioned her about Communists in the office, and the next minute, Wright pulled her aside to warn her against a lesbian coworker. "Don't let that woman put an arm around you," he told her. "And don't take candy from her."

The assignments varied; many were boring. Saul Bellow, a son of Russian émigrés on the Near West Side and also, like Walker, fresh out of Northwestern University, started in the filing room and moved up to writing short biographies of Midwestern writers. His twenty-one-page manuscript on Sherwood Anderson shows Bellow's piercing eye: he described the author as out of fashion and his questioning style as "old-womanish and querulous," but he did respect Anderson's knowledge of the Midwest as "acute and full of truth."

Nelson Algren started as a field interviewer, and through a series of firings and rehirings he eventually became a supervisor. He first was paid $87 a month, then $96. Eventually, he was earning $125 a month, as he said, "the most money I had ever made." His rent ate up only a fifth of his paycheck, "so I had a hundred bucks and I was going to the race track. It was a kind of affluence . . ." At least as important, he said, it "put me in touch with people again."

As in other states, the main goal was completing the state guide; people pursued their own projects on the side. Algren and Wright both composed their fiction after hours since the Project work wasn't too demanding. According to Algren, "Everybody used [the Project] to the extent that it was a place where you could report at ten in the morning and then leave at two and then you had the rest of the day to yourself."

Nelson Algren in Chicago.

He was writing poems and stories and ambling toward a novel, while Wright put together the stories that would become *Uncle Tom's Children*. Jack Conroy, a mutual friend, had already published two proletarian novels, *The Disinherited* (1933) and *A World to Win* (1935).

For the folklore division under Ben Botkin, Conroy and Algren interviewed bar patrons, prostitutes, and boxers. Botkin's life-history program pushed writers to find ever more personal stories. Conroy called their assignment a matter of visiting sleazy bars with incongruously "grandiose royal names" like the King's Palace, Queen's Paradise, and Duke's Castle and catching patrons at happy hour. In the King's Palace, it was called the cuckoo hour, and bartenders shouted "Cuckoo!" to signal the time when patrons could get another shot of whiskey for a penny more.

Algren immersed himself in people's voices, intent on their rhythms, syncopation, and repeated phrases, as in music. He captured these qualities in his life-history interview with Ellen O'Connor, a prostitute, in which she stresses the importance of deception:

When you live like I done, people give you a line all the time, all day long wherever you're at. All day long, everybody's givin everybody else a line, and after a while without thinkin much about it one way or another, just trying to get along you know, there you are givin somebody a line just like everyone else. . . . So you got to be real careful. You got to lie to *everybody*, you can't believe *nobody*—but still sometimes you got to believe *something* that *somebody* says, but most of all you got to lie to yourself. That's the main thing. Sometimes you can take a chance and talk straight to somebody *else*—but when you live like I done you can't *ever* stop kidding yourself a *second* or you're through. It'd just take all the heart out of you, you'd get blind drunk and blow your top. So you got to be more careful. What you say to yourself even more than what you say to cops and doctors.

The Project's mandate to record people's lives, suggested Denning the historian, echoed the John Reed Club's call for writers to study industries and trades. And in their fiction, Algren, Conroy, Walker, and Wright were distilling a synthesis of fictional invention, autobiographical reflection, and urban fieldwork.

After several months on the Project, Wright started the South Side Writers' Group, adapting the supportive atmosphere of the Writers' Project and the Communist Party to a writing group for black writers. He invited Margaret Walker to join, a prospect she found nerve-wracking, as she recalled in a 1973 essay on Wright.

I received a penny post card inviting me to the first meeting of the South Side Writers' Group. Twice I left the house and turned back, the first time out of great self-consciousness because I felt I looked abominable. I had nothing to wear to make a nice appearance and I was going to the far South side where I felt those people would make fun of me. But my great desire to meet writers and end my long isolation conquered this superficial fear. I made myself go.

The group members gathered and discussed their manuscripts regularly throughout the year. It was an exciting time. By mid-1937, however,

Wright was eager to try his luck in New York. It was a leap of faith and a plan he withheld from friends until the last minute. Margaret Walker was puzzled by his nervousness on what turned out to be his last day in town. They had always gone together on paydays to cash their checks. But that Friday afternoon in May was different. After Walker got her pay, she looked around and saw that all the young white girls were mobbing Wright with loving farewells. He was leaving Chicago.

"We got on the El, and got seats," she wrote later. "He said, 'When I go tonight, I will have forty dollars in my pocket.'" Wright wanted to get on the Writers' Project in New York. "I hope I'm not making a mistake, going this way," he said. But he had told her more than once, "I want my life to count for something."

"His stop came and suddenly he grabbed both my hands and said goodbye," she wrote.

Louis Terkel applied to the Writers' Project while he had another job gathering statistics for the Federal Emergency Relief Administration (FERA). (Although 90 percent of Writers' Project slots were reserved for those who met the pauper's oath, 10 percent of the positions in most offices were reserved for qualified professionals.) Terkel's FERA job involved tracking certain sectors of the economy in cities where unemployment was especially dire: for example, meatpacking plants in Omaha and Chicago and shipping wharves in San Francisco. Terkel led a group of six women who gathered data on Omaha. That year, 1935, a racehorse named Omaha emerged as a favorite for the Triple Crown. Leading the Omaha table at work, Terkel took it as a lucky sign and decided to bet a couple of bucks on Omaha. It wasn't hard to do: there was a bookie shop one floor below his mother's boardinghouse.

When his coworkers heard about his bet, they wanted in, and each put up four bits (fifty cents). Then the Saturday of the Derby came, and Terkel felt guilty for taking their money. He thought, "I talked them into it, those six girls." So he placed his own bet but held back the $3 they'd given him. Instead of watching the race, he and a friend went to see *Bolero*, starring Carole Lombard and George Raft.

"I come out, the headline is OMAHA WINS DERBY AT EIGHT TO ONE. And that means I won $16. But what about the $3 of the girls?"

His conscience got another flogging, as he imagined the women hearing about Omaha's victory on the radio and thinking they'd won. "They're jumping up and down, 'The horse won, eight to one!'" He had to pay them what they would have won, so he went around and borrowed $24. "I paid the girls their 8 to 1 odds," he said with a laugh, "four bucks apiece. And they were jumping up and down embracing me. Winning the Derby *cost* me money."

Soon after that, between taking gangster roles in radio plays, Terkel found a way onto the Writers' Project. He had written pieces for radio but had few other writing samples, so for his application he wrote an essay about Tecumseh. Then he found out that the Project required typing skills, so he learned how to use a typewriter. He got the position.

"That's where I met Nelson Algren, who was an outsider too," Terkel recalled. The friendship shaped Terkel's work profoundly, he said at one point, "more than anybody" he knew.

In the Project's Radio Division, Terkel and others researched and wrote profiles of famous artists and scientists for a weekly one-hour broadcast. He went to see curators at the Art Institute of Chicago and, with their advice, scripted profiles of Daumier, Van Gogh, Matisse, Eakins, George Bellows, and others. He often did his work at the Wells Grand and went into the office once or twice a week to meet the others and discuss the scripts. "We were critical of one another," he said, "but there was a comradeship there." They revised the scripts and coached the actors for the Friday night broadcast. Some afternoons, Terkel slipped out with Algren to the Arena bowling alley down the block to knock down pins at 20 cents a line. But the work got done. Listening to the shows at home on the radio, Terkel recalled, "was very, very exciting."

"Everybody felt alive," remembered Sam Ross, one of Terkel's friends there. The Radio Division had real deadlines, direction, and immediate production of the work, Ross told interviewer Al Stein. "We were linked to the community."

"I'm on the Writers' Project," says the main character in Ross's novel *Windy City*. "I write radio scripts that are produced at WBBM and WGN." The young man confidently uses this as a pick-up line with girls. For him, as for Ross, the Federal Writers' Project "renewed his hope, his optimism, his vitality."

Ross was not an intellectual; he was a star swimmer from the Near West Side, loved music, and knew his way around Chicago's nightclubs. This earned him the task of escorting the national folklore director to jazz clubs on the city's South Side during one of Botkin's visits to Chicago. Hearing great musicians in the settings of their 1920s heyday put Botkin in heaven. He was thrilled by the experience, and by the end of the night he was handing out cigars. Later he gave Ross the assignment of interviewing the older Chicago jazzmen for their life stories; they included Muggsy Spanier, Richard Voynow (who had managed Bix Beiderbecke's group), and clarinetist Bud Jacobson.

Ross would go hear the musicians play and then hang around afterward to talk with them. He also jotted down the exchanges between band members during rehearsals to capture the way they hammered out ideas and even the story in a tune. "After the clarinet, play four bars soft," one would say. "Get it real clean before the bangout."

"Right after that soft clarinet you gotta beat it right out," another told the drummer. "I'm startin' to feel it a little bit now . . . ah-ha, that's it."

"We gotta get something to keep that rhythm solid," said another. "See what else you can get out of them drums."

"Aw play it, ah-ha, aw play it."

"You might say I was born in a trunk," Bud Jacobson told Ross. "My mother was the first lady sax player in the world, and I can remember there were always horns around the house."

He and other white musicians described what they had learned from the black musicians from New Orleans and Kansas. For sax players, Jacobson said,

Coleman Hawkins was the guy. . . . Up till then nobody knew what to do with the sax in the orchestra. At White City, Bud Freeman kept apologizing all the time for his playing. . . . Bud played very ordinary sax until he heard Hawkins. And from then on, Bud's rise was perpendicular. He'd play those Hawkins things and then let that develop out of himself until he played about the best sax in the business.

Jacobson, like some of the other white musicians, "thought it'd be a wonderful idea to make some recordings with some of these colored artists" with their "two styles mixed up and coming out like one and like real jazz." But in the 1920s, musicians were strictly segregated. "The union knocked the idea out. Said it was a national ruling that whites and colored couldn't play together on jobs. But if it had gone through, it would have been an awful big thing for us."

Muggsy Spanier, who started as a teenager on drums and later switched to cornet, told of learning the parts to Joe "King" Oliver's Dixieland band from their records. Eventually, Oliver let the young man sit in with them.

"That was unheard of in those days up North here, a white person playing with Negroes," Spanier said. "I learned how to play from listening to Joe Oliver a lot. Joe would play with that little mute and get some wonderful effects and I decided I'd do that too, which I'm still trying to perfect."

Ross was mining a uniquely rich deposit of stories at the seam between the modern age in the Radio Division and the backward-looking life histories in the folklore unit. As a jazz buff, Ross felt lucky to have a chance to document this national treasure and hone his own talent.

"I learned my dramatic craft there," he later told author Ann Banks. Ross eventually became a Hollywood scriptwriter.

The work in the folklore division immersed many interviewers in their own neighborhoods. That was true for Hilda Polacheck. Born Hilda Satt in Włocławek, Poland, the eighth of twelve children, she came with her parents to America when she was about ten years old. Her father was a master stonemason who carved gravestones and did ornamental work and whose abilities in five languages put him in demand in Chicago. But he died soon after the family arrived, and they had no social network to help them. Hilda had to leave the fourth grade and work in a series of knitting factories.

From 1900 to 1910, when she was in her late teens and early twenties, Hilda spent every evening she could at Jane Addams's Hull House, taking classes. Soon she was writing plays and stories and getting some published in the *Sentinel*, which was published by Hull House. She married, but in the late 1920s her husband died. She faced hard times with two children and no reliable means of income.

"The fact that my father died relatively young," said Polacheck's daughter, Dena Polacheck Epstein, in an interview, "was a thing she had to cope with for a very long time." Depressed, Hilda often paced around the dining room table, crying. "It took about two years before she really recovered." Polacheck struggled to find hotel jobs and other work in the 1930s. She kept involved with Hull House and its social causes and always managed for her children to see plays or opera or to read a book. Dena's brother acted in radio plays with Louis Terkel, who recalled Hilda Polacheck as his friend's earth-mother parent.

The children would not know the depth of her need to write until much later. "As a child and even as a teenager," Dena admitted, "I was more impressed with Hilda's cooking and baking and making wine than with her writing, which I felt was sort of a hobby."

When Polacheck learned about the Writers' Project, she spent a month queuing up in a dilapidated building, waiting to be certified for relief work. This was a big admission of failure that took years for many people to make. Those years saw a gradual shift in the people signing up for relief work, as Arthur Schlesinger Jr. noted: after a first wave of unemployables, there followed the working-class jobless and then white-collar workers whose savings and self-respect finally vanished. "I simply had to murder my pride" to sign up, one engineer said.

"Finally my certification came through," Polacheck wrote later in *I Came a Stranger*. "I was now a member of the Illinois Writers' Project of the WPA."

She tried her hand at short radio scripts, but her main task was conducting life history interviews, most of them in her Near West Side neighborhood. She captured firsthand recollections of landmark Chicago events, as well as immigrant stories that otherwise would remain hidden. She transcribed blues songs, steelworker yells, and children's stories, sitting beside a school playground across the street from her home and listening to the kids as they played games.

She interviewed an old peddler named Morris Horowitz, who had lived in a rooming house on what is now Federal Street at the time of the Great Fire in 1871:

We used to go to bed early, because the two roomers had to go to work very early. We were getting ready to go to bed, when we heard the fire bells ringing. . . . So I went out into the street. I saw the flames across the river. But I thought that since the river was between the fire and our house, there was nothing to worry about. . . . The next thing I knew my two bed-fellows were shaking me. "Get up," they cried. "The whole city is on fire! . . . We are going to Lincoln Park."

I jumped out of bed and pulled on my pants. With my clothes under my arm and my pack on my back, I left the house. . . . Everybody was running north. People were carrying all kinds of crazy things. A woman was carrying a pot of soup, which was spilling all over her dress. . . . No one slept that night. People gathered on the streets and all kinds of reasons were given for the fire. . . . [A] minister said the fire was sent by God as a warning that the people were wicked. He said there were too many saloons in Chicago. . . . Many people left the city. . . . There were thousands of men walking from farm to farm with heavy packs on their backs.

Polacheck did not have dreams of becoming a best-selling author, recalled her daughter, but Hilda was proud of her work and felt that she earned her pay. She had mixed feelings about the job—satisfaction tainted by the belief that her work was not acknowledged or appreciated. "The time spent on the Writers' Project were days and weeks and months of deprivation. A time of heartbreak and constant worry as to whether the money would stretch to buy the needed food and pay the rent. But it was also a time of hope and even some satisfaction. I was living in a country where the government cared enough, at least, to give one a chance to earn the bare necessities of life."

She didn't know what happened to the manuscripts she submitted, though. "They were filed and forgotten," she wrote in *I Came a Stranger*. Although everybody later knew the WPA guides, Hilda said, "I do not know what part I had in the writing of these guides. I was never told."

In July 13, 1939, the folklore unit in Chicago held a staff meeting with all hands present: Nelson Algren, Hilda Polacheck, Jack Conroy, Margaret Walker, Sam Ross, and a few others. As folklore supervisor, Algren announced a new tack in collecting industrial folklore (which Conroy once defined as the jokes that factory workers tell one another). Algren said that headquarters was planning a volume of urban stories along the lines of a recently published collection of rural life stories, *These Are Our Lives.* Algren was most excited, though, to see a new style of documenting these stories coming in publications from New York. The new stuff had less editorial interference from the interviewer and more exact quotations, more direct expression of character through dialogue. Like fiction.

"The people on the New York Project are doing almost straight dialogue," said Algren, holding up an example from a recent writers' conference. "It's the feeling of the New York writers that realism in American letters will become increasingly documentary." Sam Ross then read aloud the life history "I'm a-Might-Have-Been," which was documented by a WPA writer in New York, Clyde Partnow, and published in *Direction* magazine. It was filled with colorful phrasing but was almost aimless, seemingly following the jobless man's every tangent: "Which reminds me—ain't it time for me too? Here I'm riding a whole cavalry of ideas and I ain't got enough to buy doughnuts. If I had my life to live over again I'd choose an existence of plenty. Otherwise it's better for us to shut our eyes, the undertaker downtown got a special this week. Which means this, this whole spiel: It's an explosion, I mean an explanation, of one thing. . . . Brain I got plenty, but the will power of a Chinese Eskimo."

The examples "reveal a new way of writing," Algren said, "which we'll attempt here."

That caused a lively debate, evident in Bessie Jaffey's notes of the meeting, about the role of the interviewer. Should he aim for an engaging narrative for readers? Or let the informant discover a potentially "truer" and more surprising story that the interviewer couldn't anticipate? Stuart Engstrand argued that the interviewer should go into the interview with a theme in mind. If you didn't have any idea of a goal, the informant was likely to "ramble all over," and the interview would go nowhere.

Yet a more open-ended approach could yield better material, Algren countered. "Sometime if you just let them ramble, they might say more than if they feel you've got an idea" about what you want to hear. Margaret Walker agreed. "If they have [your] one thing in their mind," she said, "they'll just go back to it and keep repeating it."

The other point of contention, at a time when the Project was under intense scrutiny from Congress and the press, was the role of the editor. Another staffer got to the nub of it: headquarters asked for unedited interviews, but were they supposed to write it straight or censor it?

Algren, the smart aleck uncharacteristically put in the role of a cautious supervisor, hedged. "You've got to use discretion," he said, especially on obscenity. "This may be naturalism, but we aren't working here as individuals: we're working in a group observed by the society. . . . Let's not stick out our necks for a fetish."

The focus was contemporary folklore, a long way removed from the traditional tall tale. In other words, the method of using straight dialogue, the preferred style in new novels, was also becoming the modern way to record folklore. To close the meeting, Abe Aaron read from his interviews with post office workers, and the staff filed out.

Hilda Polacheck went on to interview many more people, including her niece's husband, who worked at a fish store. In explaining how he had come to America, he was so uncomfortable about having entered the country illegally (from Cuba, with no visa, on a rumrunner's boat) that Polacheck gave him a pseudonym, Louis F.:

I sell fish. I begin to sell fish the day I come to Chicago. . . . I was born in a small town in Poland. . . . I knew a fellow who used to take people across the border, so I fixed it up with him. . . . In Berlin, we took a train for Amsterdam. Then we took a boat for Cuba. . . .

I wanted to get to Chicago where I had three brothers. . . . The only way that I could go to Chicago was to be smuggled into America. . . . I met a fellow who said he would take me to America for $150. . . . One very hot night in March, this fellow came and told me to get ready. He said I could not take anything, that it would take all night and all next day, and that I would have nothing to eat and nothing to drink. Not even a drink of water. . . . That day was the worst day I ever spent in my life. I am ready to go to hell, if I have to. It cannot be any worse than was that day in the boat. About nine in the evening we got to Key West. The man pulled us out of the boat. We were more dead than alive. He took us to a dirty boarding house near the ocean where we got something to eat. . . . We slept on the floor, but the floor was heaven because we could move our arms and legs.

The next day we took a train. . . . I'm telling you, when I saw my brothers and uncles when I got off the train in Chicago, I cried like a baby.

In these interviews, Polacheck and the others balanced their role as public historians with the private truths of their sources. She and Sam Ross were channeling these individual experiences into America's story. Later, Terkel would say, "You got Hilda doing that," alongside other WPA interviewers, and the work was reconnecting them to the community. "And they suddenly become oracles of it, in a sense."

In New York, Richard Wright finally got on the Project after months of bureaucratic red tape and began to make his name. He published an essay in a 1937 anthology of Project writers' after-hours work titled *American Stuff.* Wright's essay was "the first piece of writing to hit me squarely between the eyes," reported a *New York Times* reviewer. Then his story "Fire and Cloud" won a short-story contest for WPA workers organized by *Story* magazine. It brought him a $500 prize and a publishing contract for *Uncle Tom's Children,* his collection of stories. Wright began to work on a novel based on a murder trial in Chicago.

Algren remained in Chicago, working off and on for the Project, and was having less success getting published. A note of friction entered their correspondence, as seen in his postcard to Wright dated February 18, 1939:

Dear Dick,

Heartiest congratulations on your winning of the Story contest—and more power to you. Or, as the Irishman says, may yer shadda niver grow less. . . . I hate to knock down that $500, needing it as I know you do—but you will recall that you intended to send along a couple bucks I loaned you, when you could spare it. So you see I have a long memory, and besides we live here pretty much on the grim verge ourselves. Let's hear from you. Best, Nelson

At the same time, Wright's success buoyed Algren and his other friends in Chicago with the hope that they, too, could make it.

Informal mentors came and went. Turnover at the WPA office was high as the economy started to improve. Margaret Walker was working on a new poem and wanted feedback on it, but Wright, the person she'd normally ask, was gone. So she took the poem to Algren's house, and they talked through it.

"I think it was just after my twenty-second birthday and I felt it was my whole life gushing out," she explained later. "'For My People' was

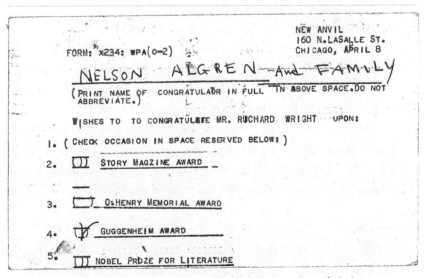

Nelson Algren's 1939 postcard congratulates Richard Wright and spoofs the bureaucracy.

just the way I started the poem." The poem gives a sweeping view of African American life, from Harlem's Lenox Avenue to New Orleans's Rampart Street. "But at the end of six or seven stanzas I didn't know how to finish it. I kept wondering what the conclusion should be." Algren read the poem. And he asked her simply, "What do you want for your people?" She went home and wrote the powerful last stanza of "For My People":

Let a new earth rise. Let another world be born.
Let a bloody peace be written in the sky.
Let a second generation full of courage issue forth; let a people lov-
      ing freedom come to growth.
Let a beauty full of healing and a strength of final clenching be the
      pulsing of our spirits and our blood.
Let the martial songs be written, let the dirges disappear.
Let a race of men now rise and take control.

Walker was also clipping articles from the papers about the murder trial that Wright kept asking her about. She sent those clippings to him in New York, where he arranged them on the floor of his apartment and set to writing the novel that became *Native Son*.

Success was taking Wright even farther from Chicago. With a recommendation from Henry Alsberg, he received a Guggenheim fellowship that enabled him to go to Mexico. Algren sent Wright a postcard in April 1939, a satire of soulless WPA bureaucratic forms.

In early 1940, Wright's *Native Son* became a Book-of-the-Month Club sensation. Algren received a copy inscribed "To my old friend Nelson. Who I believe is still the best writer of good prose in the U.S.A. Dick." Algren was stunned and fell back on wisecracks in his reply:

Dear Dick,

   Native Son arrived this morning. I haven't begun it yet because I can't get past the autograph. I hope you meant it all the way, because it did something to me. . . . I'm now hoping I can do something—just a little—toward earning that inscription. . . .

I'm looking forward to moving so I can get settled and get some work done before I'm totally bald (three years away) and I hope you won't wait till I'm bald to write.

All the best, Nelson

Algren wrote again a few days later with a more considered response to the book.

Dear Dick,

I really hadn't planned on writing you about *Native Son*, because I'd assumed it was just one more good book in America. . . . But I'm honestly hit so hard I have to get it off my chest. . . . I don't feel any need to tell you how well-thought out or how well-sustained it is and all that, you'll hear all that all over. . . . What does get me is it's such a threat. I mean a personal threat. At first I felt it was just a challenge, but it's more. You've done a very, very smart thing: I don't think any white person could read it without being either frightened or angry at the end. My own reaction happened to be anger more than anything else. I mean when someone's threatened out of a clear sky, he starts getting sore.

After offering his gut response, Algren continued, "I don't mean I'm angry now. I don't see how anyone could stay angry, assuming he's got a notion of what it's all about, because, of course, you're right. . . . You can't stay angry at patent truth." Algren shared the self-doubt and anguish of anyone who is first confronted with his innate racism. He continued, "I have the feeling that I've been going around with that surface-look"—the look Wright described on the face of a white character. "And of course anyone resents suddenly seeing himself as a dope, especially when it's so true. "

Then Algren turned to the novel's merits. It's a reader's appreciation and a friend's expression of love, complete with a doodle in the margin. The cartoon shows a stick figure of Algren, knocked out with a book near his head like a spent weapon. "I've never read anything more psychologically convincing than *Native Son*. I wouldn't want to. . . . You've hit me with something you've been holding behind your back . . . [but I'll be] grateful for being slugged out of a coma. Sincerely, Nelson."

"I think you reacted more honestly than anybody I know," Wright replied. "But really, I wasn't trying to frighten anybody or make anybody angry. I just wrote as I felt. . . . I just threw shame and fear and pride out of the window."

Algren's letter and Wright's reply offer a rare, unguarded exchange— rare for any two writers, especially those two—and reveal the unambiguous tones of a friendship, despite the reticence of two introverts. Like any two members of a writing group who have swapped manuscripts, their focus is on the work, and they can discuss race as an element of that and navigate very personal feelings across treacherous terrain.

Native Son's success encouraged Algren to pursue his own work. By May, he had moved into the Polish neighborhood around Milwaukee and Division streets, which has been described as "an old-time proving ground for Chicago hoodlums." Algren was working on a novel about a boxer that became *Never Come Morning.* His marriage was falling apart, and his sister, the only family member who had encouraged his writing, was dying of cancer. He told almost no one how her illness rattled him, but he did confide in a 1940 letter to Wright: "Trouble and tribulation. Economics and death. My sister, age 37, died last week leaving two little kids, 10 and 6. Trouble, trouble. "

As the decade ended and Wright became further distanced from his old life in Chicago, the two men still traded personal plans, including what to do if the United States entered the war. Despite the miles between them, they had many shared reference points. Algren wrote to update Wright on the Project firings and the staff moves well into 1941, as if he were relaying family news: "Ran into Bob Davis and he told me that Margaret Walker got sick and had to go back home. I suppose you know that. He seemed anxious that people write to her. Scotlandville, Louisiana, Box 3."

In Cuernavaca, Wright relied on such letters to relieve his isolation. He spoke little Spanish but enjoyed the break from the racial prejudice at home. Still, he told a friend, "One becomes bored to death at times." From New York, Ralph Ellison sent clippings about black domestic workers in Brooklyn, the subject of Wright's next novel.

Algren stayed with the Writers' Project, fitfully, even as it grew more controversial. It still gave him perspective on his muse, Chicago, and sent him out to locations such as the Davey Day Luggage Shop on East Forty-seventh Street. He describes his sense of the city in a letter to Wright, while commenting on Wright's essay "How Bigger Was Born":

What I liked best in it was a paragraph that was just a by-product, describing "that fabulous, roaring city," etc. I've always thought of Chicago as such a place—like the Petersburg of Dostoyevsky—a place of extremes of heat, a sort of sprawling chaos of men and women, taverns, els, trolleys, markets, brothels, poolrooms, with no two persons going in the same direction and no meaning to the whole insane business of milling and elbowing and clutching until you stop to look at just one person, any one. . . . In other words it's a town with a wholly inhuman aspect taken in bulk and from a rooftop, but understandable when approached in human terms.

Algren was still awkward expressing gratitude. "The above lines indicate an effort to thank you," he wrote, "for the plugging which laid a contract and five Cs on my doorstep."

Wright helped Algren gain entrée with New York editors, provided crucial suggestions for improving the structure of *Never Come Morning*, and wrote a glowing introduction for it. Algren was touched and wrote to Wright in 1941: "[T]he introduction gives me the feeling that you know better than I do what I'm up to, and will afford me an explanation which I've never tried to articulate myself."

Even with growing acceptance among publishers, Algren was reluctant to give up his spot on the make-work Project. He joked to Wright that he would need a few more well-paid magazine assignments before he'd "quit the W.P. & A.," giving it the ring of a steady railroad job. He urged Wright to come back to Chicago to renew his own creativity.

Algren groused about battling his old typewriter and how his novel was stalled for lack of a better machine. In July 1941, he wrote Wright that he finally "got the boot off the Project, among some twenty other supervisors and over a hundred field workers. Conroy got it also."

By then, Algren was making forays into drama, with "Louis Terkel—I'm not sure you know him," he told Wright, "the rep group kid they call 'Studs' adopted the part of Biceps which appeared in Southern Review for radio, so it'll be over NBC Wednesday evening on the program called *Author's Playhouse*."

Neighborhoods opened up to other WPA writers. Anna Kenny noted that Rabindranath Tagore, the Indian writer and Nobel laureate, had lived in Illinois while his son was studying agriculture at the University of Illinois. The Illinois guide features Chicago's Chinatown, its importance as America's third largest Chinese community and as a commercial and social center for six thousand Chicagoans. The guide ventures

Studs Terkel (far left) in a 1950s photo.

past its sidewalks and storefronts and grocers with bitter melons, birds' nests, "thousand year" eggs, and lotus roots. The WPA writers got a look inside the Chinese City Hall at the shrine room, with framed portraits of George Washington and his counterpart Sun Yat-Sen and teakwood chairs lining the walls. They passed the smell of burning joss sticks and the dim light of oil lamps on their way to meeting halls, a courtroom for business disputes, and a schoolroom where children learned Mandarin and traditional customs. At the Chinese New Year, "tables of the many good restaurants in Chinatown groan under the weight of 27-course dinners."

The Illinois guide was published in September 1939. Reports hold that Algren wrote most of the text on Galena, an old town perched on the western edge of the state overlooking the old Fever River (also called the Galena River) before it joins the Mississippi. Galena was a town with three hotels and one cinema, where houses clung to the hills "like chalets in an Alpine village" and empty warehouses lined the old shore.

Later in life, Algren would stress the importance of the Project work for him. "My most successful poetry, the lines people threw back at me years after they were written, were lines I never wrote," he said. "They were lines I heard, and repeated, usually by someone who never read and couldn't write."

The blend of documenting place and people, arguably most pronounced in Chicago, infused the WPA writers' work elsewhere in the Midwest. In its calendar of annual events, the WPA guide to Wisconsin includes a rutabaga festival associated with Scandinavians, Norwegian Independence Day, and Menominee ceremonials in August. The tour routes note annual lutefisk suppers in the Norwegian churches in Stoughton, where "people come from miles around to eat the flaky fish." The Wisconsin guide also contains an essay about conservation by Aldo Leopold, a wildlife ecologist whose 1933 book on wildlife management was the first to suggest that hunters think about population dynamics and stewardship, food chains, and habitat protection. His essay opens with a bleak assessment of people's impact on Wisconsin's environment and mourns the loss of the virgin forest that had covered the state ("Today those woodlands are all but gone"). He recalls the Peshtigo fire of 1871 that swept six counties and killed more than a thousand people.

Leopold later wrote *Sand County Almanac*, published after his death, which put forward a land ethic that "simply enlarges the boundaries of the community to include soils, waters, plants, and animals, or collectively the land." His thinking, and the Wilderness Society that he founded in the 1930s, laid a foundation for the environmental movement and Earth Day, which Wisconsin senator Gaylord Nelson helped to establish in 1969.

In the Wisconsin guide, tales of gangsters and the outlaw John Dillinger, who had been shot down by FBI agents just a few years earlier, crop up in the driving tours. The entry for Little Bohemia on Tour 7 combines the public's fascination with outlaws and fantasy. It describes how Dillinger and his gang hid in a local lodge until FBI "G-men" came to flush them out. The outlaw's father, John Dillinger Sr., managed a cabin nearby that displayed belongings of some of the decade's most notorious gangsters, including Baby Face Nelson. The guide wryly notes the site's advertising and that it drew more than fifty-one thousand visitors in 1937.

One part of the Writers' Project in Wisconsin was dedicated to gathering stories of the Oneida, as mentioned in chapter 1. Ida Blackhawk was one of a few Oneida women on staff. Born in 1884, she had seen her people lose nearly all of their lands and timber.

When the Depression started, the Oneidas were usually laid off first because so many white people think that all Indian people have some other income from the government. The residents of Oneida were beginning to feel the Depression. About 40 percent of Oneida homeowners lost their land and homes. Families crowded in small houses together, two or three families together.

My youngest brother died in the winter of 1929 when he was about 30 years old, and my oldest brother died the following summer. So my father had to pay two funeral bills. It was a blow to him to lose two grown-up sons within four months. He kept on farming as it seemed the only thing for him to do. My mother was sickly and so I came home from Nebraska to help them out. My mother died in January 1931. My father asked me to stay, and I did.

Despite pockets of such pungent material, nationally the Writers' Project did an inadequate job of infusing contemporary Native American voices and portraits into the WPA guides. Alsberg and his staff made an effort to note tribal cultural events in the guides and to reverse the habitual denigration of American Indians. When Franz Boas was asked for his suggestions, he recommended a former student who oversaw the Project's material on Native Americans. But in practice, the Project produced broad overviews of the tribes from an outside perspective, rather than portraits of their communities from within. In this respect, the Oneida experience was an exception driven by the local knowledge and contacts of linguist Floyd Lounsbury. In Montana, Assiniboine and Gros Ventre tribal members on the Project staff around Fort Belknap, two hundred miles north of Billings, crafted narratives that portrayed the realities of their lives as they were changing in the 1930s. Although the community prized these representations and used them for decades afterward in education, they were overlooked by headquarters.

Oscar Archiquette was an energetic, outspoken man in his thirties when he joined the Oneida Language and Culture Project. His grandmother was a chief's daughter, and his father had volunteered with the Union Army during the Civil War at age fourteen.

Archiquette was hired as an interviewer, the youngest member of the Oneida staff. At that point, he had lost two previous WPA jobs for misbehavior, one when he lost his temper and struck his supervisor. This was his third chance. He received training with the others in writing Oneida, using a new transcription system. The Oneida community came to accept the WPA interview program in large part because of Archiquette, the most fluent member on the Project. After writing up interviews with elders, he told his own story in Oneida. "I was born," he wrote, "at the time when raspberry blossoms, June fifteenth."

As a small boy, I would run away when I saw a white man coming, the reason why I was afraid of them is that I used to hear conversation about how bad the white people were and that they kidnap children. At that time I did not know one English word. . . . I was fourteen years old when my father gave me the responsibility of managing the farm. I was able to work as much as a grown man. At this age I started to chew tobacco and also started to like girls, I mean their looks. My father noticed. I was surprised when he said, "You go to West DePere and buy yourself a suit at Risdon's store." It was just what I wanted.

Archiquette's father died in 1919. By 1920, the nineteen-year-old Oscar was on the bum. He worked winters "up north in the lumber camps, cutting trees of all kinds." In 1924, he turned up in Oklahoma; in 1927, Texas; and later he lived in Milwaukee:

> I married my wife at the time when Colonel Lindbergh's son was kidnapped in 1932. I thought maybe we would die of starvation. . . . I was the first Indian to become a foreman on the WPA in 1934. About two years later I was demoted, because I shook a WPA official by the collar. In 1937 I was foreman again but I lost that job too. . . . Then I got a job as a stone driller. On February 6th, 1939, I was transferred to the Oneida language project, carried on by Floyd Lounsbury. He is very ugly but what keeps him down is that he knows us Indians scalp a person if they make us mad. It is through the first-class training by Mr. Lounsbury—Ad^ná*tsle—[Lounsbury's name written in Oneida] that I am able to write my own language.

Oscar Archiquette, in the late 1930s, on the Oneida staff of the Writers' Project in Wisconsin.

In time, Archiquette would become a noted orator and a strong advocate for revitalizing the Oneida language. He translated his father's diary, published a hymnal in Oneida, and was prominent in tribal politics, becoming the tribe's chairman.

In Saint Paul, Minnesota, a young Meridel Le Sueur was writing about how the pressures of poverty pushed law-abiding women across the line of criminality. Le Sueur had published several pieces in *Anvil* and other leftist magazines before she got a slot on the Writers' Project.

The Minnesota state director, Mabel Ulrich, was also a strong woman, a physician and a novelist. Ulrich had not voted for FDR, and she was by nature skeptical. "But the Depression screwed up the emotions to an almost unbearable tension," she wrote in a 1939 issue of *Harper's*, and made a person feel that something must be done. So when a Project official came from Washington in October 1935 and asked her to direct the writers in Minnesota, working with "white-collar workers caught in the wreckage," Ulrich agreed.

She interviewed hundreds of applicants and "heard again and again of closed avenues of work and prolonged illnesses that had eaten up a lifetime's savings." Ulrich hired a staff and threw herself into the task. The first phase was thrilling. Then came the withering bureaucracy and officiousness from Washington, with editorial memos that bore little relation to the situation on the ground. Ulrich finally asked Katharine Kellock, the tours director, if she had ever been to Minnesota. "No," Kellock replied, "but I have been to Maine!"

Quotas for workers went up and down, personality problems on the staff emerged and were handled, workers' grievance committees protested rules from headquarters over which Ulrich had no control, "chiselers were terminated and midnight telephone threats shrugged off." Ulrich's biggest problem was the guide's tour section, which required that 6,586 miles of road be covered for visual description and mileage. The office had only three cars for the job.

Over time, Ulrich was most disturbed by the change in attitude of the Project staff, from initial gratitude and hard work to a sense of entitlement and apathy. "Fear receded, but boredom took its place." She concluded that nothing is as destructive to morale as continuously being paid for substandard work.

"On the whole I was inclined to welcome communist truculence as a healthier symptom than the apathy that had descended on so many." Ulrich was surprised to find that one young typist, whom she named Miss L., was organizing women during work hours for the radical Workers Alliance. Others considered Miss L. "a violent communist" and a

Meridel Le Sueur in Minnesota, 1940.

public threat. Ulrich took a personal interest in the young woman and tried to get her to open up. Whenever the conversation turned to social injustice, Ulrich wrote, "this bored, colorless little typist became the flaming incarnation of all the revolutionary women of history."

Whether Ulrich's Miss L. was Meridel Le Sueur is not known. Le Sueur was then participating in regular meetings with women in the Workers Alliance and writing to raise their "miserable circumstances to the level of sagas, poetry, cry-outs." Le Sueur wrote the stories of the other women because some of them could not write well, and she felt that the function of the writer was "to mirror back the beauty of the people, to urge and nourish their vital expression." In her novel *The Girl*, she created a composite portrait of a woman forced by family and poverty to work first at a speakeasy, then as a prostitute, and finally as a getaway driver in a bank holdup that goes wrong. She is eventually rescued by a group of homeless women who are evidently Communists.

When the novel was published forty years later, Le Sueur was known as a pioneering author of the women's movement. In the afterword,

Women living in a Saint Paul, Minnesota, rooming house, 1939.

she called the book a "hosanna" from a past generation of women to a new one, a shout of joy and strength to "those wonderful women our mothers ourselves who keep us all alive."

"It was a white culture up to then," Le Sueur said at a reunion of Writers' Project members in the 1980s. "There was no black movement, no Indian culture, no women's culture," she said, meaning that no one had asked them about their histories before. It was unmapped terrain.

4

GATHERING FOLKLORE, FROM OKLAHOMA TO HARLEM

It was this way: Sweet could make hisself invisible. . . . He was the boldest black sonofabitch ever been down that way. Hell, he had everybody in that lil old town scaird as hell; black folks and white folks.

—LEO GURLEY, IN A WPA INTERVIEW WITH RALPH ELLISON

IN THE SUMMER OF 1937, CHANGE ELECTRIFIED the air in the normally placid halls of academia. At the American Writers' Congress in New York City, the topic was not textual analysis but engagement. Ernest Hemingway, straight from the front lines of the Spanish Civil War, took the stage and urged writers to join the fight against fascism. He had no patience for writers who lived in an ivory tower. Martha Gellhorn, a young war correspondent (and Hemingway's paramour), spoke of writers who had gone to Spain not to describe local color but to enlist in a cause worth fighting for: democracy. The *New*

York Times declared that the theme of the congress was "all must take part in political and social war."

Another speaker there, overshadowed by Hemingway and mentioned only in the last line of the roster of participants, was Benjamin Botkin, who was a folklore professor at the University of Oklahoma. Botkin's talk, "Regionalism and Culture," was not rousing, but it was equally insurgent. Writing on folklore should well up from the grassroots, he said, and not be orchestrated from above. The United States had a culture rich with life and imagination that should be freed from theoretical attempts to pigeonhole it. "Regional writers do not make the mistake of identifying culture with *a way* of life," he said, "they describe *ways* of living." Furthermore, the writing he championed would do more than *describe*, more than *report*. It would help change how people related to one another.

"Realistic regional literature can serve as an organizer," Botkin said, "as well as an interpreter of social thought . . . by helping us to understand and respect one another, and by showing the failure and breakdown of old patterns and the growth of and hope for new ones."

One unlikely example of such a regional literature had appeared a year and a half earlier in the pages of *True Detective*, a crime magazine. The writer, Botkin's friend Jim Thompson, had interviewed Robert Norwood, a young hobo in Oklahoma who had been shaken by the murder of his friend, another transient. Norwood had set out to solve the mystery of his friend's death and bring the killer to justice. His story had the elements of a WPA life history, but for *True Detective*, Thompson had leeway to shape the story. He used all of the storytelling techniques at his disposal—what he called his "little bag of tricks"—and made the hobo detective's tale not only a gripping read but a window into the existence of the homeless in the Southwest. "The Strange Death of Eugene Kling" is an unsparing glimpse of human nature and at the same time a sensitive picture of young Norwood's trials: lonely freight rides through Texas and Oklahoma, hard landings, privation, and hopes of becoming a real detective one day.

A month before the national writers' congress, Thompson had organized a lead-up to it, with Botkin's support. More than 150 writers from

Oklahoma, Texas, and New Mexico gathered at the YMCA in Oklahoma City for the Southwest Writers Conference. They were pioneering the kind of regional literature that Botkin advocated. Jim Thompson gave a talk that described his work for both the WPA and the true-crime pulps, and he argued that writers were really workers. Not surprisingly, the gathering drew suspicions. The next day's headline in the *Daily Oklahoman* ran WAS WRITERS' MEETING RED OR WASN'T IT? After another such episode, Thompson told Botkin in a letter, "Everyone was accused of being a communist but the party members."

It was after the 1937 American Writers' Congress that Henry Alsberg approached Botkin and asked him to lead the folklore division of the Writers' Project on John Lomax's departure. Alsberg needed a trained researcher who could manage the troops that were documenting a broad spectrum, from modern city life to rural folktales. He made the case that it was an unprecedented opportunity to chart the country's localities and regional flavors. Folklore studies, a branch of academia stuck awkwardly between anthropology and literature, seemed to be the right vessel for collecting and sorting all of this.

The fact was that Alsberg needed help with the flood of material pouring in for the guides. He was already parrying press accusations that the Project was way behind schedule and riddled with incompetence. He pointed to the strong sales of the first WPA guides, about Idaho, Washington, and Lincoln, Nebraska. But it was true that the Project, which started with a six-month mandate, was after nearly two years a long way from completing the task of a cultural inventory. Beyond the guides, such an initiative—what Botkin would call "the greatest social experiment of our time"— was tremendously ambitious. Botkin believed that the WPA folklore division's duty was nothing less than to show a living culture and understand its function in a democracy. The job held more risks besides ambition, however; the WPA was a bureaucracy, an uncertain new agency, and not as stable as a university.

Botkin would influence the WPA writers not merely by leading the folklore division, but also in the WPA guides' coverage of culture (he drafted and edited essays on folklore for several of the guides). This chapter looks at that work through two WPA writers who happened to come from Oklahoma, where Botkin had spent much of the previous decade. One was Jim Thompson, for whom an Oklahoma worldview would provide the soil for the dark dramas of his later fiction. For Ralph Ellison, whose work flowered primarily in New York, Oklahoma City was the starting point of a journey that linked him to millions of other African Americans who had migrated north from segregated towns and cities in the South and the Southwest.

Botkin was not much better suited than Alsberg was to lead a national project. The thirty-six-year-old professor preferred reading and research to administration. His hobbies included walks in the country, gardening, and field trips to gather folklore. He had spent most of the previous fifteen years in Oklahoma and Nebraska, far from his youth in the big cities back east. Most of that time, he'd lived in Norman, Oklahoma, a town of about eleven thousand people, where the shops on the main street catered to farmers and the only off-campus points of interest were the church, the hospital, and the city park with a WPA-built amphitheater. But Botkin understood the national challenge and grasped the difference between nostalgia and a dynamic exploration of the regional patterns affecting people's lives. As he said in his speech at the American Writers' Congress, geography—where a person comes from—doesn't determine a person's character, but it does shape the "social structure that underlies individual character and action."

By chance, two people who would take forward very different forms of that kind of writing came from Oklahoma City, a town of sixty-four thousand residents. Jim Thompson and Ralph Ellison could have passed each other on the street during their childhoods, yet they lived in separate worlds. You would not expect to find a common thread, much less a mutual acquaintance, between them. Thompson was born in Anadarko, southwest of Oklahoma City, in 1906, and his parents moved to the city when he was a small boy. When Thompson was seven and a half years old, Ralph Ellison was born in the city's black neighborhood of East First Street. Both families struggled with financial and personal troubles. Both boys grew up with a strong empathy for the disadvantaged. Thompson later created the con men and the serial murderers who populated novels like *The Grifters* and *The Killer inside Me*. Ellison would write the

epic *Invisible Man* and the unfinished race-spanning odyssey that was
ultimately published as *Juneteenth*. They both would spend years steeped
in folklore on the Writers' Project and be changed by the experience.

In 1934, Jim Thompson returned to Oklahoma City's west side after
shuttling between Texas oil fields and Nebraska, where his mother's family lived. Oklahoma was not a destination. Before the term *Sooner* was
a nickname for Oklahomans, it was a reproach, referring to impatient
whites who jumped claims in Indian Territory before they had a right
to them. From the first, Oklahoma was a place where the swift and the
mighty prevailed.

Thompson's family had absorbed a series of shocks after his father, a
once-prosperous lawyer, made and lost a fortune in oil-drilling invest-
ments. When Jim was born, his father was the sheriff of Caddo County,
and the family lived in an apartment above the county jail. But by the
time Jim was a teenager, he was forced to get a job to help make ends
meet. He worked nights as a bellboy in a rowdy Fort Worth hotel, after
going to high school during the day. At the hotel, he witnessed haunting
scenes and began to form his impressions of human nature.

An Oklahoma oil rigger, 1939.

WPA interviews with residents of Fort Worth hotels echo the darkest of Thompson's later creations. Mrs. Robert Lindsey, who ran the Donna Hotel with her husband, told a harrowing story about how powerful ranchers, "prominent men in the county," had driven her grandparents from their farm:

> [S]everal ranchers were always deviling grandfather to sell out. He wouldn't do it because that was his home, and if he sold it, he wouldn't have a home. [So] a bunch of men bunched up and tried to run other ranchers out of the county. They called that gang "The Mob." . . . Why, they killed Shorty Brown, my grandmother's brother, after they'd told him to leave and he wouldn't. The whole county turned out to hunt him when he come up missing, and they found him hung to a tree in his pasture by the creek. . . . Why, two different sheriffs, one by the name of Hawkins, and the other Atkinson, were the leaders of the "Mob.". . . They killed old Hartman's son over some little something or other, and buried him in the sand.

At home, things for Thompson weren't much better than at work; he bore the weight of his father's disapproval, and not only because he was working in a seedy hotel with whores and bootleggers. Another problem was that Big Jim Thompson was a burly, boisterous man, and his son was thin and quiet. According to young Jim's sister Freddie, the old man "could not understand where this boy came from, who blinked his eyes a lot and was shy, withdrawn."

Thompson wasn't planning on college when he finished high school in 1925. He joined his father in the West Texas oil fields and worked there for three years. He liked oil-field workers and learned a lot from them. His first stories, "Oil Field Vignettes" (February 1929) and "Thieves of the Field" (June 1929), took place in the oil fields and appeared in *Texas Monthly*. The editor there encouraged Thompson to go to college, so he enrolled at the University of Nebraska in Lincoln, near his mother's relatives. Thompson left Oklahoma City just ahead of the law. Police wanted to arrest him for selling twenty cases of bootleg whiskey at the hotel where he worked.

Thompson funded his education in Lincoln with moonlighting jobs in a funeral parlor, as a movie projectionist, and in a bakery. He fell in love with a girl whose family disapproved of his prospects as a writer and made them end the relationship. Soon after their breakup, he had a blind date with Alberta Hesse, a slender, smart, and earthy young Lincoln woman. They eloped in September 1931. He was still taking classes in agriculture, but with the Depression, his college days were numbered. He kept writing, and in Lincoln his layered stories caught the attention of Lowry Wimberly, the professor who edited *Prairie Schooner*, a leading literary journal. Thompson became a regular at the casual gatherings at Wimberly's home every other Sunday, when they each read from their writing. That's how Thompson, the only member from the College of Agriculture, found himself in a writing circle described as "avant-garde" and how he made friends with a literature PhD student named Ben Botkin.

The Depression deepened, and by 1934 Thompson had moved back to West Texas. He lived with his father and worked as a doorman at the Texas Hotel in Fort Worth. Still, he nursed his dream of becoming a writer and began to publish stories in pulp magazines: *True Detective*, *Master Detective*, and *Daring Detective*.

Thompson enlisted his mother and his sister to help with research on the crimes that appeared in the newspaper, which he then wrote up. The gory details always upset him as he typed them, his sister recalled. His descriptions reached toward victims like the homeless Eugene Kling, who

> had been struck eleven times across the head, apparently with a heavy blunt instrument. And, apparently, by an assailant of some strength. Each blow had left a gaping wound in his skull, and the smallest of these was two inches long. Then, as if that were not enough, he had been left to lie face down, exposed to the rain on one of the coldest nights of the year. . . . There were signs of a terrific struggle . . . and . . . evidence of long hours of writhing.

"The Strange Death of Eugene Kling" appeared in *True Detective*'s November 1935 issue and may still be the only story with a hobo sleuth hero who hops freight trains to track down his friend's murderers.

The piece showcases Thompson's abilities as an interviewer and a storyteller who can get inside the head of his hobo protagonist. Norwood realizes that finding the solution to his friend's death will require someone who knows the routines a poor homeless man might have, the psychology of people in homeless shelters, and the route a hobo would likely travel out of town. In Norwood's hunt for the killers, readers learn what it's like to jump from a moving freight: "as any 'bum' can tell you, it's pretty hard to get out of a boxcar when a train is going very fast. I ploughed up the cinders for a good many feet when I jumped, skinning the hide from myself, and making a few new holes in my clothes." Readers also taste the isolation and fears of the homeless:

> That was another long lonesome old ride for me. And for the benefit of those boys who are planning to go on the road, I'll say it wasn't any fun. I got to thinking about Kling and it made me nervous. I didn't want to die like that, beaten to death in some dark corner, miles away from home and friends. I tried to tell myself that that sort of thing could not happen to me; but I knew that it could, very easily.

Transient men in the soup kitchens and shelters of Fort Worth stare out from the photos that accompany the article. Next to them, ads pitch remedies for dying gray hair and getting profitable jobs through correspondence courses. (The same issue included an installment of the five-part "Exposing Soviet Plot to Overthrow U.S.A.") "Kling" has elements of Thompson's later noir style—a murder victim writhing in the mud, a "viciously thorough" killer, a conflicted protagonist—together with a social conscience.

In *Master Detective*, Thompson paints the oil field southeast of the city as a place of black-slickened slush pits and creeks, half-starved dogs, tangles of abandoned drilling equipment, and shacks. A place "where great wealth is contrasted with deplorable poverty" and where "evil overshadowed the good." The case involved copycat crimes, false allegations, thefts in a black neighborhood on the northeast side of town, and the horror of lynching ("The murder of one man by another is ordinarily left to the courts. . . . But the murder of a white woman by a black man frequently instigates a lynching party").

The pulps might seem an odd place to find social realism, but in 1930s Oklahoma, where outlaw Pretty Boyd Floyd was buried in 1934 after being gunned down in Ohio, reality didn't look much different from the inky shadows of *True Detective*. Every issue had a guest article by one state governor or another, urging greater vigilance against crime. But with all the black-and-white morality, what troubled Thompson most were the twilight grays—the injustices of bad gambles like his father's and conspiracies like the Mob. These cast idealism in a different light, one that might be called noir.

The magazines and the hotel work paid poorly. Now with a wife and a child to support, Thompson applied in April 1936 for a job on the Oklahoma Writers' Project. His position was tours editor with a half-time wage of $60 a month, which enabled him to move his family to a slightly better apartment. His job for the WPA tours section meant driving all over the state to "visit Indian mounds, bat caves, fields of wildflowers," in the words of one coworker.

A thriving downtown Oklahoma City in the 1930s.

An Oklahoma City family in front of their shack in "Stringtown" in 1939.

In the first paragraph on Oklahoma City, the WPA guide paints a panorama of skyscrapers, fine hotels, a "fabulously rich oil field with drill rigs reaching up out of the backyards of many fine homes," parks and university campuses, and elm-lined residential streets. It also takes in the city's huge slums, a "Stringtown" of shacks near the river "occupied by victims of poverty but also by nomads who know quite well how to contrive for themselves." Flush with oil money, the city juxtaposes fur coats, oil derricks, and threadbare overalls. The list of traveler details for the city notes that only two of its nineteen hotels accommodated blacks and two of its twenty-seven movie houses allowed blacks. Thompson wore no rose-colored glasses about his hometown. He called Oklahoma City "a big town built upon the ideas of still smaller men" and a place "whose cultural life is wrapped in the rusty hide of [a lean, long-dead] steer."

At the WPA office, Thompson was promoted to full-time guide editor, which doubled his salary. He and Alberta now had a son and a second daughter, and the two younger children would grow up hearing that they were born in Oklahoma because their father was on the WPA.

In the guide, Thompson introduces the world to Oklahoma's combination of brutality and humor with a folklore essay, which contains little nostalgia for the frontier:

> According to an imaginative early historian, a pioneer settler in Oklahoma ran amuck on a visit to town and, in the course of a few minutes, killed a representative of each of five races. The historian adds that it was possible because they were found within the space of a city block. Considering the diversity of sources from which the state's population was drawn, the story is not so farfetched.

Guns, the essay explains, "hold an important place in [Oklahoma's] folklore." Back when the state was Indian Territory, the only place where a dreamer was safe was in bed.

The folklore essay punctures the idealized notions of academics, while at the same time spinning discredited tales, including "the story of the outlaw who lined his family up against a barn door and traced their silhouettes with six-guns." Thompson unspools what may be an essentially Oklahoman ambiguity of good and evil when he describes a long-standing interplay between law and outlaw: "Some of the officers were reformed outlaws, and some of the outlaws had been officers; there was understanding between the two classes even though there was no compromise." All of it made for a peculiar concoction, a "light-hearted disregard of life and death," in which a buddy's hanging could be described as a "string around his neck." (The chorus of one song goes: "A little piece of string / it seems a tiny thing. . . . When my friend I last did see / he was hanging from a tree / With a little piece of string around his neck.") The essay also ably explains the role of square-dance musicians and the challenges and the familiarity of a caller with his audience.

That part of the guide offers a lot of tall tales, but it also does a remarkable job of clarifying *how* Oklahomans used these stories to tease newcomers or youngsters by heaping more and more outrageous lies into a yarn as it went along, testing the newcomer's credulity and polite willingness to believe his or her host.

For Tour 11, Thompson follows US 81 and its course along the old Chisholm Trail of cattle drovers, along the same route his own family had shuttled over between Nebraska and Fort Worth. The tour starts at the Kansas line and goes south to where the road crosses the Red River into Texas, just north of Ringgold. That meant sifting through tall tales to unearth the facts of the trail's origins with a trader named Jesse Chisholm. At the top of the tour in Osage country, Thompson notes the story of the tribe's "mourning parties," a macabre double entendre. An old Osage custom had been to bury a tribe member with the scalps he had taken, but since peace had been established between the Osage and other tribes, scalps were scarce. So "the custom arose of sending out secretly what were called mourning parties to bring in a scalp," with the result that "scalps of isolated white men were in demand."

In truth, as Calvin Roberson told a WPA interviewer, white renegades were more likely than Indians to harass people. Roberson had moved to Osage country with his parents in the 1880s when he was five years old. He worked for years as a cowhand on a ranch near Chickasha and told a WPA interviewer:

> Rustlers gave us our worst trouble, stealing the cattle and burning the brands. . . . A few people believed that the Indians were doing this but . . . the Indians that we knew were fairly well civilized and seemed to want to be friendly. . . . the gamblers and desperadoes who came through the country crooking every one they could was what made it so tough. The Indians were easier swindled out of their cattle than the white men were and that was one cause of the rough element coming to the Territory in such great numbers.

Farther along the trail, the town of Duncan, south of Chickasha, was dominated by the oil industry and its satellites. The guide notes,

> To serve the oil industry, six supply houses have quarters in the city, and there is a refinery with a daily capacity of 6,500 barrels.

The Halliburton oil well cementing process for safeguarding wells, which is used throughout the world, was originated and developed here. The processing plant employs some 1,650 workers. . . . Branches are operated in eleven other oil-producing states, in South America, and in several European countries.

Thompson gives a sense of how a wildcatter felt about the oil fields in a narrative he wrote for Botkin titled "The Drilling Contractor." Presented as an interview, it channels his father's boom-and-bust experience under a different name and includes everything from the Teapot Dome Scandal of the 1920s to his son's job at a disreputable hotel. The piece strikes a reader now as a curious blend of personal history and fiction—the kind of "impure folklore" that Botkin liked. The narrator says that most of their oil wells were shallow, but he knew them by name. "You could drive along there at night and see a dozen of our little rigs running, the white signs on the walking-beams winking under the lights as they bobbed up and down . . . Markham and Carey, Maggie Jones Number One."

Regrets, especially about how he had shortchanged his family, haunt the narrator. "I'd let my son become a bootlegger and an alcoholic," he says. "And it had been a point of honor with me—all those years he was killing himself to support my family—that I'd never asked a friend for as much as a dime." It was probably the only apology Thompson ever got from his father, and he wrote it himself.

As an editor, Thompson complained that making sense of his staff's manuscripts was "like trying to work with a ball of yarn that a cat has been playing with."

Meanwhile, a young man who was born Louis LaMoore, from North Dakota, joined the project. He claimed a huge amount of experience from his travels to Africa and Asia. He and Thompson became friends, and LaMoore visited the Thompsons' house from time to time. As a staffer, LaMoore helped organize the Southwest Writers' Conference in May 1937 and sent out the invitation letters. After a while, though, Thompson tired of LaMoore's tall tales about himself. A coworker recalled entering Thompson's office one afternoon while he was on the

Louis L'Amour (center) and Jim Thompson (right)
on the Oklahoma Writers' Project.

phone and watching him get more and more angry. "I went up to Jim's desk to turn in some copy," said Gordon Friesen. Thompson was shouting, "You goddamn phony!" into the receiver. "After he hung up he turned to me and said, 'That's the biggest fraud in the world. That was Louis L'Amour.'" LaMoore soon changed the spelling of his name to L'Amour and went on to become one of the best-selling authors of Western novels of all time.

By this point, Thompson's mother and sister had returned to Oklahoma City from Nebraska, but things were bad for the family. In 1937, Thompson's father lost his janitorial job and felt, as Thompson later wrote, "useless and cast aside." Thompson continued that his father's "distress saddened and worried me as nothing else could." Thompson poured his concern over his father's decline into a story about an old man's self-doubts and incipient dementia and the little swindles in diners and drugstores that nickel-and-dime him out of his family's money. "Time Without End" appeared in a local pamphlet titled *The Economics of Scarcity: Some Human Footnotes* and was compiled from the after-hours creative work of the Oklahoma Writers' Project staff. Thompson's story delves inside the forgetfulness and the regrets that descended on his father "like a cloud of locusts." By the end, what is happening in the old man's own mind is as frightening as any murder story.

As Botkin reconfigured the Writers' Project folklore division to give greater emphasis to life-history interviews, he found that Thompson was on the same wavelength. Thompson liked the samples of the American folktales that Botkin sent him, especially "the one about the fool-killer." Soon Thompson was submitting his own interviews and encouraging his staff to do the same. He directed one staff member, Dan Garrison, to devote his time to oil-rigger stories. Those included an interview with a man named Joe Haskins, who engaged in the kind of one-upmanship and outlandish tales that Thompson described in the state guide's folklore essay. Haskins said his father was a Pennsylvania bootlegger named Joe, who named each of his four sons Joe ("all the men in our family from way back was named Joe"). He said all four brothers looked so much alike that "a gal could date all four of us, and think she was going steady with a fellow." Then he stretched his tale further: the only way you could tell the four boys apart was by the difference in how well they could hold their pa's whiskey: "Joe could drink a pint, Joe could drink a pint and a half, Joe could drink two pints, and Joe could drink two pints and a half." This set up the kicker: "Paw and maw was always getting us boys drunk to find out which one to scold."

"If you want a true life story of a rigbuilder, you've just got to put up with the lies," Garrison wrote. That narrative also conveyed an oil-field hand's respect for loyalty and views on religion. ("Going to church never kept a man from sinning. . . . If there's sin in a man, it's coming out despite heaven, hell, and plain old dust.")

That spring, Thompson's experience with the Project began to sour. He was working feverishly ("till 10–11 at night," he wrote to Botkin) and submitted a *Dictionary of Oklahomaisms* that his staff had painstakingly assembled and revised. "Throw it away, or edit it, or do whatever you want to with it," he told Botkin. But by May, he was discouraged by all the meddling from Washington editors on the state guide, which he felt rendered all of his work "wasted." He complained that they were cramming the guide "into a mold" and described himself and his staff as a martyred platoon "marched into the valley of death. All of our literary training may have taught us that interest and originality should never be sacrificed for brevity and simplicity, but we have learned to follow orders no matter how wrong we know them to be." The friendly tone of Thompson's letters to Botkin cooled, and their correspondence appeared to have tapered off. By December, Thompson felt he was finished with Oklahoma City, too. "You're fortunate in being away from this God-forsaken place," he wrote Botkin. "Best wishes for the holidays."

When Ralph Ellison was born in 1914, he was named for his father's favorite writer, Ralph Waldo Emerson. Lewis Ellison ran a small delivery business in Oklahoma City and didn't have much education, but he loved to read and had great hopes for his son. He would tell people, "I'm raising this boy up to be a poet." Ida Ellison's hopes for their son were just as high: in the 1920s, she imagined Ralph as a great bandleader and composer.

When Ralph was three years old, he rode with his father on the bench of the horse-drawn cart as Lewis went on his rounds, delivering ice to grocers and homes. (Before refrigerators, ice was sold in large blocks and kept in iceboxes.) One hot summer day at Salter's grocery, Lewis Ellison told his son to wait in the cart. As Lewis shouldered a huge slab of ice and started down the steps to the cellar, he slipped. Ralph heard his father fall and the ice thud on top of him. The sharp edges sliced into Lewis's stomach. He was taken to a hospital, bleeding badly. Ida, who was pregnant with their second child, rushed to be with him. Lewis died several days later from infections.

The medical fees and funeral costs wiped out the family's savings. Ida took jobs cleaning white people's houses to provide for her two small sons, and as she struggled to keep the family together, she gave the boys life lessons. The Oklahoma City zoo became the site of Ralph's first lesson in challenging injustice. When he was four or five years old, he pestered his mother to see the animals, and although the city had banned blacks from visiting the zoo without a white escort, Ida gave in and took the boys on the streetcar. They walked through, and the boys marveled at the animals. As they were leaving, a guard strode up and demanded to know which white family they were with. Ida Ellison replied that she was a taxpayer and had a right to visit the zoo with her boys. "I don't need any white folks to show me the way," she said. The guard shooed her away. On the streetcar home, she urged Ralph to remember that.

Ralph then joined the band at school and took trumpet lessons from a teacher and bandleader named Zelia Breaux. "Mother Breaux" came from the most educated black family in Oklahoma and taught the children classical, as well as popular, music. Duke Ellington's grace and elegance personified Ida Ellison's hopes for her sons, so she was pleased when Mother Breaux recommended Ralph for the music program at Booker T. Washington's Tuskegee Institute in Alabama. He was accepted in 1933. The Ellisons couldn't afford the train ticket, so Ralph, still a teenager, prepared to hop a freight and traverse four states.

An Oklahoma City resident amid segregation signs, 1939.

Hundreds of thousands of young people were riding the rails then, looking for work. Ralph got a lesson in freight hopping from an older man named Charlie, who suggested the best route: go north to St. Louis and east, taking a longer route to avoid Arkansas. A black man caught riding a freight in Arkansas would get a merciless beating. Ralph took the advice. As it happened, railroad bulls in Alabama pulled him and several others from the train and beat them with blackjacks anyway. His enrollment photo at Tuskegee shows a young man still bruised and bandaged.

Ellison dedicated himself to his music studies, read voraciously, and dressed sharp, considering his budget. He studied composition, served as a student concertmaster, tuned the band for concerts, and led it at football games. His classmate Albert Murray recalled finding Ellison's name in almost every book he checked out from the library.

At home in Oklahoma the family's situation became insufferable, so Ellison's mother took her younger son, Herbert, to stay with relatives in Ohio. There, she fell and cracked her hip. Without taking X-rays, doctors at the segregated hospital said she was suffering from arthritis. Infection soon set in, and by the time Ralph arrived, his mother was in so much pain she could barely recognize him. She died the next day.

Ralph stayed in Ohio for several months to care for Herbert and take stock. It was a terrible winter. From time to time, he found warmth in the public library, where he immersed himself in books. But he was sick with grief and unable to afford college tuition. With no job, he foraged for food and tried his luck at hunting:

> February is climbing up a hill into the full glare of the early sun, alone in all that immensity of snowscape with distant Dayton drowsing wavery to my eyes like the sound of distant horns. . . . I descended into a little valley in the windless quiet and the smell of apples. . . . I bent forward and knelt within the circle of the fruit-fall, searching out an apple missed by the birds. . . . I had lived through my mother's death in that strange city, had survived three months off the fields and woods by my gun, through ice and snow and homelessness.

That spring of 1938, he left Herbert with relatives and ventured to New York City. He spent nights on a park bench in Harlem but was confident that things would change. New York was thrilling, and in Harlem a black person had options. When he first arrived, no longer bound by segregation's rules, he savored choices as simple as which seat on the bus to take. At the Apollo Theater, he could hear Duke Ellington and other great musicians.

Here the self-confidence Ellison had learned from his mother paid off. On his second day in the city, he strolled into the lobby of the YMCA and joined a conversation with two men. One of them was Alain Locke, whom Ellison recognized from the poet's visit to Tuskegee. The other man was Langston Hughes. When Locke excused himself, the kid from Oklahoma kept talking with Harlem's poet laureate across a full range of cultural topics, from T. S. Eliot's "The Waste Land" and musical structures to his plans to study sculpture at a nearby art studio.

Harlem had many writers, sculptors, and thinkers for Ellison to meet. Hughes introduced him to Richard Wright, who was just a few years older but already publishing stories about black people's lives. Wright urged Ellison to read Ernest Hemingway to learn how to convey realistic action and Henry James for showing how people think. Reading them could show a writer how to make characters live on the page. Ellison was still a musician, but he had always felt that writing, too, was powerful and important.

In Harlem, even politics was jumping. As biographer Lawrence Jackson noted, the Communist Party there was in fact a party, and its high spirits appealed to young people. Being a Party member in Harlem, said one Young Communist League leader, "was like being the swinging present and the swinging future simultaneously . . . you were enjoying all the boogying and boozing and everything in the present, while you had your socialist perspective to give you the inspiration to continue."

Wright helped Ellison get his first articles published in *New Masses* and the *Daily Worker*. He suggested that Ellison join the Writers' Project and helped him get on the roster in 1938, as a way to pay the rent. The Project was even more chaotic than the Communist Party, but it held its own opportunities and connected Ellison with other writers and material that grounded him in New York. He researched black life in the city and conducted interviews with Harlem residents. According to Jackson, "Ellison saw the WPA, with all of its shifting political ground, contested hallways, and cross-purposes, as a model for interracial antagonistic democracy in cooperative action."

Wright showed Ellison the ropes at the Project office. When Ellison reported to work in the big, busy Manhattan building, he found hundreds of people there. He was assigned to go to the library and research facts about the history of blacks in New York City.

When the guide work ended with the book's publication in mid-1939, Ellison's assignments changed. His task for Botkin's folklore division was to interview people in Harlem about their lives. He met them on street corners, in tenements, and on park benches. Having no recording machine, he quickly wrote down what people said or memorized it until he could jot it down later. And he began to find that he had things in common with those people. The migration from the segregated South to the complicated North was a shared theme. Mastering the art of making a life and not choking on bitterness wasn't easy.

Ellison met a young dancer and actress named Rose Poindexter, and in September 1938 they married and moved into an apartment on 150th Street. On the front steps of their apartment building one summer afternoon, Ellison talked with a young drummer named Jim Barber who was disgusted with the hypocrisy of whites who asked him to show them around Harlem but would never think of inviting him to their neighborhoods in the Bronx. "Jack, I'm just sitting back waiting," Barber said. "Hitler's gonna reach in a few months and grab and then things'll start. All the white folks'll be killing off one another. And I hope they do a good job!"

In another interview, Ellison asked an older man he met on a park bench in St. Nicholas Park (the same park where he'd spent several nights on a bench when he first arrived) how he had come to the city. The man had arrived from Virginia when he was young, and he took solace in his faith.

God made all this, and he made it for everybody. And he made it equal. This breeze and these green leaves out here is for everybody. The same sun's shining down on everybody. . . . I breathe the same air old man Ford and old man Rockefeller breathe. They got all the money and I ain't got nothing, but they got to breathe the same air I do. . . . The Lawd made all men equal and pretty soon now it's gonna be that way again.

Ellison listened to people whether they told him the truth about their lives or concocted tall tales, whether it was children's chants or old men's journeys. And as he listened to how folks talked and worked on getting that down on paper, he found that their stories had a certain music.

5

RISING UP IN THE WEST: IDAHO

Slowly, deliberately, curiously, he began to walk around me as if trying to tell whether I was a human being or a New Dealer. . . . Then a dozen file clerks left their desks and joined the parade, and round and round me they walked, and like an owl I turned my head to keep an eye on the director, not knowing what he might be up to.

—VARDIS FISHER, "WRITERS ON RELIEF" (1941)

IN PARTS OF THE WEST, THE DEPRESSION experience was made more difficult by the environmental damage to farms in the Dust Bowl, which made for an often harder path out of poverty. Couples seriously discussed the possibility of one spouse committing suicide in order for their children to have enough to eat. The government was truly a last resort in the land of the pioneers, where self-reliance was a fact of life. But the dire circumstances also stirred strong reactions against the system. During the bleakest days, the dismantling of small farms advanced steadily as families lost their land and homes to mortgage banks.

In Nebraska on October 6, 1932, widow Theresa Von Baum was forced to put her farm and equipment on the auction block. On the day of the auction, her neighbors showed up in force. More than two thousand Nebraska farmers faced the bank's receiver, as one of them declared, "We don't intend to have that woman sold out." They offered him $100 for the mortgage. When he balked, they took over the auction themselves; livestock, horses, plows, and equipment went for pennies each. All of the items were then returned to Mrs. Von Baum, along with a collection. That first "penny auction" was a farmer's Bunker Hill, a stand against the disastrous shifts in the American economy. Penny auctions spread quickly. By the following spring, legislatures in Nebraska and eight other states had passed a moratorium on farm foreclosures.

WPA writers in the Western states faced a tough audience. In the Southwest, as mentioned earlier, far from being seen as fellow citizens and sufferers, they were known as *el Diablo a pie* ("the devil on foot"). The writers were stuck between the burden of presenting their home states to the nation through the filters of Washington editors and representing that system to the people of their states. It was often a no-win situation.

Vardis Fisher grew up in eastern Idaho, far from schools, a post office, or any other landmark of a town. Born in 1895 to Mormon parents, Fisher often said that he was born on a real frontier, in a one-room shack made from cottonwood logs, with a dirt floor and a dirt roof.

A loner and a fiercely free thinker, Fisher rebelled against his religious upbringing. After an isolated childhood during which he was home-schooled up to age sixteen, he pursued education more out of dogged tenacity than from any interest in academic institutions. He graduated from the University of Utah, did a stint in the military during World War I, then completed a PhD in literature at the University of Chicago. He lived in New York City for a few years in the 1920s, sharing an office with Thomas Wolfe, who later wrote the best-selling novel *Look Homeward, Angel*, while both men taught English at New York University. The two instructors also shared a prodigious ambition to tell stories on a large scale.

By the late 1920s, the crowds and the high cost of living in Manhattan sent Fisher back west. He was hired to teach at the University of Montana but was an indifferent instructor and soon lost the job. Yet he did not hold it against his boss, H. G. Merriam, who was one of the few people Fisher respected. In a letter dated September 9, 1932, Fisher admitted that Merriam's support helped him keep going as a writer. To Merriam, Fisher confided his fears with acid humor: "My last novel sold fewer than a thousand copies and I don't know where my next dollar is coming from, but I'm getting a lot of fun out of being isolated here in the mountains, with the snow deep and the wind hard and the appetite keen."

Fisher had published three novels about Rocky Mountain pioneers by then, but they were for the most part ignored and gave him little income. Many later critics considered Fisher's series of novels a remarkable achievement, although readers can find his style rough-hewn. Wallace Stegner, from a later generation of Western novelists, said of Fisher's novel *Children of God* that it was a good book but not elegant. "It hurt my ears, it seemed so blunt," Stegner said. "It was made with an axe."

Fisher returned to Idaho after losing the Montana teaching job, angry at the mainstream culture and its arrogance. Like many Westerners, he was skeptical of government and any "authorized" view of America.

Vardis Fisher, director of the Idaho Writers' Project, at his Hagerman home in the 1940s.

In the fall of 1935, Merriam wrote to Fisher that some kind of project for writers was on the horizon. Maybe Fisher's wife, Margaret, could head the Idaho office, he suggested, allowing Vardis to keep writing fiction. Fisher was grateful for the suggestion. "Thanks a lot for giving Margaret and me a boost toward the four billions," he replied. With a good word to "the director of indigent writers," as he referred to Henry Alsberg, Fisher was recruited to head the Idaho office. By October, he was joking with Merriam: "Yes, I'm a Roosevelt man now! I'm going to try to make a cultural survey of Idaho with assistants chosen from relief rolls! Well, I'm going to try, with Margaret's help, to make a job of it."

Fisher sounded more sheepish in telling his literary agent, Elizabeth Nowell. "It looks now as if I shall accept supervision of WPA writers' project in Idaho and that will mean I shall have less time for writing than I intended," he wrote her. "I feel absurd in going into this work but when a man is financially against a wall and has two sons soon ready for college he does absurd things." Within a month, Fisher would be complaining to Nowell that the WPA job was "one infernal round with starving persons and red tape."

That winter the Fishers moved into Boise, a hill city of squared-off blocks. Vardis loathed the bureaucracy and administrative chores. Other New Deal projects had already staked out office space, so, for a while, he had to work out of a box in a hallway of the Sonna building. Finding qualified staff was difficult. "I'm scouring the hinterlands for Roosevelt to see if any unsung Miltons are out in the Idaho sagebrush," he wrote Nowell. He was both inspired by the task of wrestling Idaho into a book and driven to rages of frustration, just as he had conflicted feelings about the frontier where he had grown up. ("I both liked and detested it," he told interviewer John Milton later in life. "There were so many, so many things . . . that terrified me . . . but there were also many beautiful things there.")

At first, Alsberg was thrilled with the drafts that Fisher sent in and called the quality of writing "an unexpected windfall." Vardis threw himself into the work since he wanted to use the guide to dispel myths about the Rockies and the pioneers who settled the region. "The frontiers were conquered by neither saint nor villain," he wrote in the opening essay. "The men and women who pushed by thousands into the West were quite like the people of this generation. . . . They were trying to make a living, to survive."

The Boise landscape in the 1930s.

What the generation of pioneers did have, Fisher felt, were the energy and the will to create their own worlds: "The men and women who blazed the trails and built forts and laid open the mines and the forests had zest and vitality, and there are no virtues more indispensable than those."

Fisher had another agenda for the Idaho guide. He wanted it to be published first among the state guides and thus snag the national spotlight. And he hoped to be able to deliver the state to readers across America in his own voice:

Topographically, Idaho is one of the strangest states in the Union. . . . It has no logic in its present boundaries except the Bitterroot Mountains and the Continental Divide between it and Montana, and the Snake River between a part of it and Oregon.

A farm for sale in Boundary County, Idaho, 1939.

Fisher had taken the WPA job thinking that it would be a serious effort under the stewardship of taxpayers' money. He soon began to feel that others didn't share that view, and he bridled in letters to Washington headquarters: "I don't like all this bewilderment of orders that rescind orders or contradict orders. The discrepancies in the various instructions we have received leave our finance administrator throwing up his hands. What I want is explicit and irrevocable orders to go ahead as I was first instructed to, or an invitation to resign."

Another bone of contention for him was the guide's tours section. Headquarters dictated that every guide narrate tours north to south, but Fisher argued that this was ridiculous. In Idaho, most traffic ran in the opposite direction.

Fisher insisted on researching the tours himself, not entrusting the task to his staff. He often mistrusted locals' information, too. "Going to opinionated old-timers for information," he griped, "has proved only that old-timers don't know half as much as they think they do." Given his on-the-ground experience and the isolation of many of his mountain contacts, he probably had a point.

Tour 3b of the Idaho guide starts in the southeastern corner of the state in Pocatello, nestled up against a handful of rust-colored mountains. In the guide, Fisher called it "the ugliest of the larger Idaho cities." Outside of town, he noted a trout farm worth visiting, although visitors had to leave by sundown to avoid "several huge savage dogs" that roamed the property at night. From Pocatello, the route to Boise curved west, passing through long desertlike expanses. The road in 1936 was rough, and Fisher probably would have punctured a tire or two on the route.

Southeastern Idaho has a singular tradition of storytelling and history. According to Susan Swetnam, a professor at Idaho State University in Pocatello, that area's Mormon history included a writing tradition built on the idea that life in a hard land held rich rewards. The land seemed to encourage a wide range of people to ponder and express themselves, and the truth-telling tradition fostered that. Fisher, who grew up a few hours' north, fits within that heritage. Others working in that vein in the 1930s included Juanita Brooks, another Mormon who worked for the Writers' Project in Utah, and Annie Pike Greenwood, who published *We Sagebrush Folks* in 1934. In this, Fisher can be seen as a sort of counterpart to James Joyce, whose work reflected the influence of the Jesuit tradition, except, as Buck Mulligan says of Stephen Dedalus in *Ulysses*, it's "injected the wrong way." Fisher's unsparing eye invoked the Mormon view of the land, in his own way. Of the Snake River's passage through that area, he wrote, "In the upper valley here it goes too lazily to achieve much, but beyond Milner it gathers speed and anger and has been most impressively busy."

Heading west for Tour 3b, Fisher passed through the wide flats and sullen hills in low brush. Bearing south from the main road about an hour west of the town, he rumbled over a rough gravel road into a vast emptiness. There he encountered the soaring ruin of stone known as the Silent City of Rocks, a geological sentry from pioneer days that stretched nearly six miles long. He wrote in the guide that the Silent City

is a weird congregation of eroded cathedrals and towers and shattered walls. Because formerly it was the junction of two famous trails—the Sublette Cutoff and the California Road—it has recorded upon its walls one of the largest chronicles known of transcontinental travel. There are thousands of names and dates, as well as messages left for persons who were soon to follow; and it is evident that some of the more spectacular and foolhardy scribes must have been suspended by ropes from the tops of the cliffs, so high and remote from human footing are the records which they left.

The pioneers' cryptic axle-grease graffiti from the 1880s and the haunting landscape affected Fisher. As a ground-level version of first-hand history, written on the land like ancient paintings on cave walls, their messages may have struck him as a precursor of the Idaho guide itself.

Around that time, a WPA researcher in New Mexico was gathering the story of Samantha Foley and her mother, who had spent punishing winters in southeastern Idaho in the 1860s. Samantha Lake (the mother) came west with her husband, a missionary to the Indians on the Salmon

Register Rock at the Silent City of Rocks.

River. He was killed in the course of his work. She later married Noah Brimhall and took her two small children to Spanish Fork, Utah, where they stayed with friends while Brimhall joined an army expedition to Baho Canyon. Her daughter, Samantha Brimhall Foley, wrote for the WPA in 1936:

When peace had been restored and Noah Brimhall returned to Spanish Fork, the young widow of Bailey W. Lake became a member of the family of her sister-in-law. They all returned to the north and settled in Hiram [Hyrum], Cache County, Idaho [now Utah]. In the year of 1864 the family moved still farther north some 40 miles away, where there were no families within miles of them. It was a wild, lonely spot. The native verdure had grown in undisturbed splendor since the morning of creation. It seemed to these two women so far from human habitation, where everything was so wild it was appalling. The all-pervading silence of the valley was unbroken except for rushing mountain streams by day and the roaring wild animals by night and these two women . . . felt this isolation so keenly.

Samantha Lake Brimhall's life story unfolds in the pattern of hardships overcome, with the same beautiful, relentless backdrop:

During the months of January and February the snows seemed to fall instantly. Their road was blocked, and they were indeed alone. [They] had to chop ice in the streams. . . .

It was a hard winter, but at length Spring appeared, and when the deep snows were melted, people from the settlements below came to look over our location, which resulted in several families settling near us. This gave the two lonely women the human companionship which they craved. The new settlement was located near a widened part of the mountain stream where it was shallow enough for the oxen to ford it easily. And they named the settlement just that—Ox-ford—or Oxford [about 55 miles south of Pocatello]. A small school was started that summer, by Mrs. Mary Anna Brice, under the willow porch of her home. She had no school books, but among other things, she taught them that there were seven days in a week, twenty-four hours in a day, and sixty minutes in an hour. Also demanded that each child learn the day of his or her birth. . . .

Samantha Lake Brimhall was expert and she did much of the weaving for the settlement, in order to help out in a financial way, and to procure the necessary things of life. She wove many different kinds of cloth. She also became an efficient gardener, and her beautiful rows of cabbage and other well cultivated vegetables were the marvel of the village. This she could do without leaving her home. She was strictly a home woman and seldom left her doorstep. She created her own enjoyment and employment within her home, all in service to her family. . . . At harvest time she stored away an abundance of fine wheat straw, and this she wove, during the winter months, into hats for men, women and children. And she found ready sale for the products of her industry.

Fisher traveled on, continuing to probe the landscape westward on Tour 3b. Along the way, he explored a valley that enchanted him and that he would eventually call home:

North out of Buhl on US 30, . . . on the left is the mouth of Salmon Creek, the gorge of which is a fantastic wonderland. . . . The highway now drops down into the lovely Hagerman Valley. . . . Long a source of mystery to both laymen and geologists, it is now believed that the Thousand Springs are the outlet of buried rivers that get lost in the lava terrain 150 miles in the northeast. . . . At points through this valley a person can put his ear to the ground and hear deep and troubled rumblings as if a mighty ocean rolled far under. . . .

Throughout Hagerman Valley, marine fossil remains are abundant. . . . There are also survivals of mastodons, wild hogs, and a rare species of ancient horse.

Back in Boise, Fisher's marriage was failing as he struggled to maintain and shepherd a small staff of fifteen to twenty workers. One was Julia Conway, who had graduated from the University of Idaho in 1934. She had been working in the state capitol building, collating training materials to mail to CCC camps "for the boys to improve themselves," when she read a notice in the *Idaho Statesman* that a government-sponsored writers' project was hiring. In the CCC effort, she felt that her skills were being underused, yet jobs were hard to find. Her father was recovering from a mining accident in which he had lost an eye and contracted pneumonia. The family had no insurance, so every dollar counted. Conway wrote to Fisher, asking about the work and mentioning that she had grown up in Silver City, an old Idaho "ghost town." To her surprise, Fisher showed up at her office in person and hired her.

Conway's WPA salary never exceeded $65 a month, but it helped. She spent most of her time in the library doing research for Fisher. This was also when she met her future husband, Jim Welch. "I'm afraid that being in love," Conway wrote later, "I was not a good worker."

Fisher ordered a great deal of research on the state's population (the 1930 census showed that most Idahoans came from a Scandinavian background, along with English, German, Scottish, Swiss, Irish, Russian, Italian, Welsh, Spanish, Japanese, Mexican, Indian, African American, Chinese, Korean, Hindu, and Filipino backgrounds, plus five Hawaiians). He also explored Idaho's Basque community:

> The largest and by far the most significant colony in Idaho is that of the Basques in Boise, said to be the second largest in the world. . . . Because they were highlanders, they ventured inland, seeking the mountains, and one body of them established a colony at Jordan Valley, Oregon. . . . The center of the colony drifted to Boise. . . . Loving solitude and the hills, the early Basque men here became shepherds. . . . Aloof rather than gregarious, they still preserve in Boise the outlines of their native culture. . . . Their chief game, jai-alai or handball, is still their own, and admission to their special functions is still by invitation only.

The Basque midsummer festival, the Idaho guide notes, "is a genuine Romeria, similar to fiestas in Spain, with Basque food, costumes, dances and music."

To achieve his goal of a national publicity coup, Fisher worked with his publisher at Caxton Press in Caldwell, a small town west of Boise. They assembled the Idaho guide as fast as possible for the presses.

Henry Alsberg had his own ideas about the Project's public relations, however. He intended to launch the American Guide series with the *WPA Guide to Washington, D.C.* because he considered national fanfare appropriate for the nation's capital (as well as a politically savvy offering to Congress). When Alsberg learned that Fisher was close to having the Idaho guide completed, he set up obstacles in Fisher's way and insisted on a blizzard of changes. Editors deleted Fisher's references to tensions between truckers and railroads, for example, and Fisher's disparaging comments about the popular novelist Zane Grey, the state of Wyoming, and Idaho's former governor. (They let stand his barb at academic historians and "their own anemic and stultified lives.") On the publishing schedule, though, Fisher was intractable. A heated phone call with headquarters ensued, with members of Fisher's staff gathered around him in the office. They were sure that his obscenity-filled outburst would get him fired.

Alsberg sent a deputy editor to Boise to set things straight. Fisher, by his account in the thinly veiled fiction of *Orphans in Gethsemane*, took the man to the publisher's office in Caldwell and got him drunk. Then Fisher put him back on the train east and sent the guide to the printer.

The Idaho guide appeared in January 1937, the first in the series. It was dedicated "to all Idahoans who helped to make it," an openhanded salute that is, in another sense, possibly Fisher's wry salute to himself. He said he had worked himself to exhaustion in the process of putting Idaho first and to "bring honor to this small segment of a national boondoggle." Reviews called the Idaho guide "more than a mere guidebook to the state" and "an almost unalloyed triumph."

Despite the ups and downs, Fisher stayed with the Writers' Project for four years, taking on added responsibilities. Fisher even made peace with Alsberg, who in turn jokingly called Fisher "the bad boy of the Project." When Fisher visited Washington, basking in the Idaho guide's fame, Alsberg's staff gave Fisher a reception that he himself called "the red carpet treatment."

In the summer of 1939, Fisher traveled to Santa Fe to help complete the New Mexico guide. Lorin Brown, a member of the New Mexico Project staff, recalled that "Fisher would show up at the office, peruse finished material submitted for his inspection, make revisions of same, or offer suggestions as to deletion or expansion." Fisher offered pointed observations about the work and then spent the afternoons in the city park in the town center, where he sat and wrote furiously in a notebook, presumably working on his fiction.

Lorin Brown himself was a hard worker and composed nearly two hundred documents for the New Mexico office: sketches, translations, folksong transcriptions, and field reports. Brown was born in a mining camp in 1900 and grew up in Taos, where his mother's Latino parents lived. His father was an Anglo newspaperman, and his mother, born Cassandra Martínez, taught school in rural villages in northern New Mexico. His maternal grandmother was a *partera* (midwife) and a *curandera*, or folk healer, and little Lorenzo (as Lorin was called in Taos) went with her on house calls. She taught her grandson remedies from her Mexican and Native American heritage, practices and beliefs that he would use all his life.

Brown's bicultural background and his sharp observational skills made him valuable to the Project's Santa Fe office, but they also pitted him against its more glaring flaws. Brown's boss objected when he translated lyrics of a popular song ("*vente chinita conmigo*") as "come away with me, my little curly-haired one." She insisted on her own translation: "come away with me, my little Chinese lass." Another time, Brown was asked to transcribe a conversation of local men around a bonfire for the folklore division. He wrote down the dialogue more or less verbatim, with the archaic patterns of village Spanish. The piece came back with a high-handed editorial comment that it was, at best, very poor pedestrian Spanish. After that, Brown preferred assignments that kept him out of Santa Fe.

After several separations, Vardis and Margaret Fisher divorced in 1939. On the Project he had grown close to a young WPA researcher, Opal Holmes. She was drawn by his forceful mind and his presence, which she found handsome, as she said, "in a manly sort of way." In 1940, they built a home on land he had bought in his paradise of Hagerman, and they settled there.

6

NAILING A FREIGHT ON
THE FLY: NEBRASKA

The writers' project was a challenge greater than nailing a freight on the fly. It was to introduce me to a heterogeneous group of people, constantly changing.

—RUDOLPH UMLAND, THE EDITOR OF THE NEBRASKA WPA GUIDE

[I]f you were to see our oldest and youngest girls together you would think they were as different as day and night. The youngest is typically American—she looks like an American, her manners and all. The oldest girl likes the old-country Japanese.... [W]e want our girls to live the life of the country, as they are Americans.

—MISAO WADA, IN A WPA INTERVIEW WITH RUBY WILSON

WHEN RUDOLPH UMLAND DROPPED OUT OF college in 1928 and bummed his way to the West Coast, he did not expect to miss Nebraska. Born on a farm in Cass County, southeast of Lincoln, Umland was eager to see the world and write novels, having published several stories in *Prairie Schooner*. The last place he expected to be eight years later was back in Lincoln, chronicling Nebraska's old-timers. By the time he reached California to look for work as a deckhand on a freighter, though, there was none to be found. So for three years during the

Depression's darkest days, Umland led a hobo's life and logged twelve thousand miles by boxcar. He scraped by as a janitor, a farmhand, a dishwasher, a logger, a longshoreman, and a day laborer. In 1932, along with an estimated two hundred thousand other youths on the rails that year, Umland hopped one more freight and returned to his father's farm outside of Lincoln.

It was a hard homecoming. Umland spent several years there "fighting drought, chinch bugs, depression, and dust storms." He saw his neighbors reduced to surviving on rotten apples and worm-eaten corn. In February 1933, he joined other farmers and marched on Lincoln to protest farm foreclosure policies. He also frequently met with Lowry Wimberly, the editor of *Prairie Schooner* and an English professor at the university. Back when they first met, Umland had discovered that he and Wimberly "both shared the same birthday, had slept in jail, and liked Chaucer. . . . We both hoped to write a novel that would shock the world." Wimberly gave the young man encouragement. "Wimberly made the putting of words on paper the most exciting thing a person could do."

Umland worked on the farm in the morning and on his fiction at night, by kerosene lamp light, bundled in an overcoat:

This was my Russian Period [when] I tried to write in the style of Dostoyevsky, Chekhov, Gorky and other Russian realists. I wrote gloomy pieces about social injustice and death and similar miseries. I wrote . . . on derelicts and hungry people in the slums of New York and San Francisco.

He called his novel *Journal of a Floater*, and an excerpt of it appeared in *Prairie Schooner*. The short bio there described Umland as "raising swine on a Nebraska farm, thoroughly disillusioned and *unzurfrieden* [unhappy] with the Powers That Be." After suffering through more Dust Bowl deprivations and drought, Umland was ready to wander again by the spring of 1936. Only his discussions with his mentor stopped him.

Wimberly urged Umland not to leave. "It's too damned cold to ride in a boxcar," he told Umland and pointed the young man toward the Writers' Project and its downtown office. So Umland joined the Project, despite never having done any editorial work. More than a dozen of

Wimberly's *Prairie Schooner* contributors would end up working for the Nebraska Writers' Project at some point.

The Project office in Lincoln didn't escape the cronyism that was rampant in larger states, according to Jerre Mangione's book about the Project, *The Dream and the Deal.* A Nebraska senator appointed his friend's ex-mistress as state director, and she proved to be not up to the job. Politically, however, it was impossible to completely remove her. Her desk was eventually relocated from the office to her home, where she continued to collect a salary.

Within a few months, editorial responsibility for the state's new project would fall to Umland, a twenty-eight-year-old former hobo. Members of the shifting cast who passed through the office ranged from unemployed teachers and typists to bankers, housewives, insurance agents, and an osteopath. There were a few able writers and many poor ones, all packed into a crowded warehouse near the train station. "The staccato rat-tat-tat of over a hundred typewriters, voices barking out dictation, clerks opening and closing metal filing cabinets, ringing of telephones, scurrying of workers to and from restrooms," Umland later wrote in a 1997 issue of *Nebraska History,* "was little conducive to writing."

The first drafts of the Nebraska state guide were a disaster. After plowing through an especially appalling manuscript about early Nebraska travelers, Umland moaned, "I was ready to fight several wolves." He strove to create order by setting up an editorial board with rewrite editors, a tours editor, a cities editor, an essay editor, and a managing editor.

As in other states, Umland and his staff debated the story that the Nebraska guide would tell. Would local legends get the benefit of the doubt? Nebraska had been settled for barely a generation, and its history was riddled with hearsay. Yet few on the

Rudolph Umland, editor for the Nebraska guide, in 1937.

staff felt capable of questioning it, particularly where it concerned local leaders. It didn't seem right that out-of-work teachers, who were used to drilling morality into students with rote memorization, should be exposing scandals about prominent citizens. One researcher was dumbfounded to discover that a prominent Lincoln churchwoman had had an illegitimate child.

"They accepted, in complete seriousness, the assertion that Lincoln was the Bethlehem of America," Umland wrote. Getting writers to document the city's wild frontier days with a clear eye, he found, demanded "editors who did not 'lean on their shovels.'"

In Nebraska, as elsewhere, Project workers faced the stereotype of shiftless "pencil leaners" and boondogglers on the dole. Conservatives complained that all WPA programs were a huge waste. Introducing yourself as a WPA writer could end an interview on the spot.

The staff worked hard but paused at moments to register the absurdities of the times. "Lord, we had laughter in those years of economic depression!" Umland later recalled. Laughter was sometimes the only possible response to the hardships. Umland had watched foreclosures roll over farm families like a juggernaut, then witnessed an environmental nightmare in the Dust Bowl. America's economy and landscape were broken and were threatening people's lives. When the Communist Party held meetings to suggest alternatives, Umland tagged along a few times.

After its editing, fact-checking, and polishing, the WPA city guide to Lincoln hit the streets in 1937 with a price tag of twenty-five cents. To everyone's amazement, it became a local best seller and sold more than ten thousand copies. It was praised even by Republican newspaper editors, who had expected to skewer it. The reception gave Umland encouragement for the state guide, and the process that produced the Lincoln guide served as a template: newspaper archive research fueled interviews with older residents and eyewitnesses to key events. These interviews and the background research helped to shape the local histories in the guide and provided an insider's perspective of each town.

On a map, the tour routes in the guide appear to rip down through the state. Tour 1 follows US Route 75 south along the western bank of the Missouri River and its own seam of history, through the Winnebago and Omaha reservations, Lewis and Clark landmarks, the Underground

An unemployed man in Omaha, 1938.

Railroad, farm life, and the Dust Bowl. The tours research also turned up a history of dissent. In Dakota City, at the northern end of the tour, Umland and his staff found a roman à clef of local politics. In the late 1800s, Father Martin, a resident journalist and a part-time missionary, became so disgusted with local politics that he took revenge on town leaders by writing a thinly veiled fiction titled *The Conflict: Love or Money?* He serialized it in his newspaper for nearly a decade. Martin's real-life rival Atlee Hart became Atlee Heartless. "There were no libel laws," the guide reports, "and the editor died of natural causes."

The tiny hamlet of Union, founded during the Civil War, consisted of two short rows of buildings that faced each other on the broad plain. According to the guide, in frontier days one Union resident was particular about spelling ("he killed a man because he did not like the number of *d*'s the man wrote in the word 'peddler'") and liked to stage fake gunfights.

The WPA writers' descriptions of the sites along most of Tour 1 held up remarkably well for decades. Omaha has changed more than any other place on Route 75, having more than doubled in size since the 1930s.

Gone are the *World-Herald* building, where William Jennings Bryan ruled as editor before his four bids for the presidency, and the Omaha Club building, which according to the WPA guide served both as executive mansion for President McKinley (briefly) and as a posh jail for two cattle barons arrested in 1905. But tumultuous change suits the boomtown air that Omaha had from its start, when newspaper editors settled their differences with horsewhips. In the beginning, the WPA writers found, Omaha was a place of fast deals, dubious land claims, and gambling. In the paragraphs about Capitol Hill, where once stood Nebraska's first state capital, the writers describe the first July Fourth celebration, in 1854:

> The anvil salute consisted of ramming the hole in the top of the anvil with powder, inserting a fuse, turning the anvil upside down and lighting the fuse. The resultant blast sent the anvil more than 100 feet in the air. To the consternation of the party, the report of the anvils attracted a band of Indians who were camping at Sulphur Springs. The women and children were frightened and the entire party hurried to their wagons and drove pell-mell to the ferry landing. They escaped unharmed.

A few blocks away in Jefferson Square, at Chicago Street and 16th, the Nebraska guide describes a scene of modern hardship, calling the park "a rendezvous for the idle men who crowd its benches." The guide states, "The personnel changes from day to day, but the scene, with its air of frustration and despair, remains the same." One of the drifters whom WPA interviewer George Hartman met near there was A. L. Gooden, who recalled first arriving in Omaha back in 1882. "My first night in Nebraska I slept in a big elm tree in Omaha," Gooden said. He spent twenty-five years in Nebraska before moving on to California. Hartman described Gooden as tall, willowy, graying, and stooped. "He is old and passed [sic] his best days," yet still drifting. "Informant came to Nebraska in a freight car and likely to go out in a freight."

Another landmark gone from Omaha is the building that stood at 912 Douglas Street. Its elaborately carved stone columns had distinguished a brothel managed by "a notorious queen of Omaha's underworld," the guide writers note, until she bequeathed it to the city for use as a

An Armistice Day parade in Omaha, 1938.

hospital. The city elders argued at length about whether they should accept such a gift. Ultimately, they did but removed the carvings of naked women.

Umland's staff interviewed Fredda Smart, who had once managed an Omaha house of ill repute. Her views unfold on race relations in Nebraska, how she made a living, and the regrets of her life. "Because of my color, the large Omaha stores will not allow me to study in their free classes," she told the WPA interviewer.

> I became a hostess or landlady of a house on Fourteenth Street. The lady on the corner of Fourteenth and Cass Street had to give up her place [and] I took over. . . . Others took care of the payoff to the authorities. . . . As the landlady I took in plenty of money. Times were good. I also sold beer and whiskey. I figured as long as I was in the game, do it right.

Smart regretted not having set aside some of her "easy money" to "pay my way through some university or college to make myself a real artist."

If she had done that, she said acidly, "I would be far happier today, and no WPA questioner would get into my house."

In the course of the research, Umland and his staff corrected many mistakes on local historical plaques. A stone marker on the city's Military Road proclaimed that the site marked "one of the Oregon Trails." There was just one Oregon Trail, Umland knew, and it didn't pass through Omaha. The city's Bohemian Cafe and the Sokol Auditorium recalled the thousands of Czech immigrants who were drawn by jobs in the meatpacking plants. Until a decade ago, you could wander the stockyards' unloading area, where a receiving agent prodded each truckload of pigs toward the gate, crying, "Yessa! Yessa!" The catwalks above the cattle pens passed over ghostly stalls. The old brick livestock exchange towered over the pens.

"There is an atmosphere of incongruity about the Stock Exchange Building," the WPA guide says. "Talk of the range is heard in the ornate lobby, and bronzed cattlemen frequent the bar." After operating continuously since the 1800s, the sea of livestock pens—once the world's largest stockyard—is quiet.

Umland traded hobo stories with Loren Eiseley, another of Lowry Wimberly's former students who joined the Project and who had spent time on the rails. Umland then assigned the job of writing the guide's essays on Nebraska's natural setting and prehistory to Eiseley, who would later gain fame for his writings on natural history.

The Nebraska staff interviewed all kinds of people for Botkin's life history program, from new arrivals to old-timers who were suspicious of modern technologies. They interviewed bootleggers, lawyers, blind musicians, and a Buffalo soldier recruited from Jamaica to fight the Indians.

"There were some good, lovely little towns in those days that the automobile ruined," mourned one Plattsmouth resident. An Omaha handyman was more optimistic and laughed to recall crusty old farmers pulling on the reins to calm their horses as a car passed. "They would swear plenty at the autoists," he said.

No interviewer was more prolific than Ruby Wilson of North Platte. In a town of twelve thousand, she interviewed more than 1 percent of the population, ranging from Mexican beet farmers and Japanese American hoteliers to elderly pioneer wives and railroad men. She talked to a retired federal marshal who had escorted Theodore Roosevelt across

Wyoming at the turn of the century. Wilson was in her late thirties and had worked as a nurse in the 1918 flu epidemic. When her husband lost his job because of an injury, she returned to nursing to support her family, but in the 1930s, when all other work dried up, she joined the WPA. The typescript interviews she compiled reveal how absorbed she became in people's stories. "Some marvelous tales!" she wrote at one point.

"I came about 1917 from Old Mexico to work in a coal mine," John Valdez told her and explained how Mexicans lived in cities throughout New Mexico, Colorado, Kansas, and Texas. "They rent their homes and some buy, just like other people." He discussed the economics of clearing the land and how they get paid for harvests. For Mexican dances, he said, the community would "borrow the halls at Hershey or Sutherland and the hall at North Platte. . . . Everybody comes but the old people do not dance. . . . For weddings there is a big dinner and a big dance. . . . I'm going to have a big grand wedding when I get married."

One summer day in 1940, Ruby Wilson paid a visit to Mrs. Misao Wada, whom she described as an attractive "young Japanese matron" and "a remarkably smart woman." At the Gateway Café, which Wada and her husband managed at 215 South Jeffers Street, she told her life story: about her girlhood in Hawaii, her father's work on the Union Pacific Railroad in Nebraska, and how she and her husband had returned to Nebraska to run a diner and raise their daughters. Misao Wada shared her mother's advice and marveled at how her daughters were as different as night and day: her oldest liked "the old-country Japanese"; her youngest was typically American.

Many of the more than three hundred Nebraska life histories that are now included on the Library of Congress Web site tend toward pioneer-day recollections and tall tales. Recalling the grasshopper plague of 1873, Plattsmouth old-timer Ed Grantham said that the bugs devoured his family's fifty acres of high corn to stubble in hours while everyone was at church. In a neighboring tobacco field, he claimed, the grasshoppers "added insult to injury by sitting on the poles of his corral and spitting tobacco juice in his face."

Grantham talked about Wild Bill Hickock as if he'd just seen the legendary lawman the day before. "I got quite well acquainted with Wild Bill," he said. "I have seen Bill at target practice many times.

I have thrown up bottles and empty cans for him to shoot at." (Wild Bill was a quiet fellow and vastly preferable to Buffalo Bill, whom Grantham also got to know in the 1880s.) Grantham complained that in Cecil B. DeMille's movie about Hickock, Gary Cooper got the draw motion all wrong. Cooper did a slick "crossdraw," but that was bogus. Wild Bill drew his gun straight up, right-hand gun from his right side.

The WPA writers gathered these stories against a backdrop of changes in the wider world. From time to time, Umland visited a Lincoln tavern near the office with a friend who had recently returned from the Far East, where he had reported on the atrocities following Japan's invasion of China. Americans knew that war loomed across both oceans, and that their own hometowns were changing as the modern world came closer.

For some of the younger staff members, including Weldon Kees, the past was tedious. "He had a brain that didn't like to go back at all," Umland said of Kees. "The future was always yawning ahead, and Weldon was furiously impatient to get into it." Wimberly thought that Kees might be a new kind of person whose mind could *only* face the future.

An office Christmas party for the Nebraska Writers' Project in Lincoln, 1936.

Kees joined the Writers' Project in 1937. Another Wimberly recruit, Kees grew up in Beatrice, a town less than thirty miles from the Umland farm. A year earlier, he had been living in Los Angeles, trying to break into Hollywood—acting, playing in a studio orchestra, scriptwriting, and doing anything that would support him while he worked on his novels and short stories. Writing fiction was his passion. But he couldn't find work, and a fire gutted the house where he was living and destroyed his manuscripts. So he returned to Lincoln. He told Wimberly that he needed a job that would allow him time for his writing. Wimberly called the WPA staff, and the state director hired Kees and asked deputy editor Norris Getty to show him around.

Kees and Umland had met a few months earlier; they were both writing fiction for *Prairie Schooner*. One night, the two sat on the lawn beneath the apartment of a girl Kees was mooning over and talked a long time. "It was a starry spring night," Umland wrote later, and they talked about girls, dance bands, their stories, and books. "About 3 A.M I left him there on the grass and went back to my own furnished room. I was twenty-eight and unmarried then; Weldon was six years younger."

Kees, the only child of a prosperous hardware manufacturer, upset his parents with his decision to join the WPA. But the Project surrounded him with like-minded writers from a mix of backgrounds. He gained a reputation for being a spoiled and brilliant adolescent, according to biographer James Reidel, someone "who had read too much about art, novels, poetry, movies, and jazz and who also remembered everything that he had read." Although he had no interest in the state guide (he couldn't imagine anyone seriously using the book or wanting to go to any of its out-of-the-way places), Kees performed his work dutifully. For Kees, the Writers' Project was a stopgap until a better opportunity arrived. Later, he was glad that his name was left out of the credits.

Stories that Kees wrote back then for *Prairie Schooner* testify to Nebraska's icy winters and the ironic observations of youth. A frustrated character in "So Cold Outside" worries about his heating bills and escapes into newspaper comics. Everything annoys him: his neighbors' inane greetings ("Cold enough for you?"), the licorice-smelling liquid soap in the men's room, and the paper towel dispenser that sanctimoniously asks

WHY USE TWO WHEN ONE WILL DO? The protagonist "used four, wadding up the damp sheets and throwing them at the wire basket under the washbowl. Only one of them went in."

One of Kees's tasks for the guide was the section on his hometown, Beatrice. "Originally *Be*atrice, the name is now pronounced with the stress on the *at*, a deviation attributed by some to brass-voiced railroad conductors," he wrote. The description of his father's hardware business shows uncharacteristic restraint:

> The F. D. Kees factory, open 8–5 weekdays . . . , is a low red-brick building. . . . The odd-shaped machines . . . are used for a wide range of processes—from the shaping of curtain rods to the count-ing of ball bearings for roller skate wheels. The founder developed one of the first practical cornhusking hooks.

When Kees's father visited Lincoln to see his son, Umland recalled him as a quiet, gentle man, "like a character in a Sherwood Anderson story. He still clung to the hope that Weldon, his only child, would develop an interest in his business."

Beatrice also had some well-traveled residents, such as I. B. Smith, whom Albert Burks interviewed for a life history. Smith was born in Rhode Island, the son of a Seminole mother from the Florida Everglades and a father from the West Indies. "I left Providence when I was about twenty one," he said. "I taught . . . and spent much time going to prison farms throughout the south, preaching to the inmates. I delivered a sermon before three thousand inmates at the Federal Prison at Atlanta, Georgia. I came to Nebraska in 1901 and settled at Beatrice."

Umland came to love the stories that they uncovered. He liked to go into a Lincoln tavern, order a beer, and watch the other patrons and imagine their stories. While "writing the WPA guidebooks, I became deeply conscious of local history, the drama played by Nebraska pio-neers, and the passing of the generation of the old bearded men," he wrote later. "The tavern encompassed it all."

The Writers' Project was likely the only welfare project that had a following among successful writers. John Steinbeck tracked the Project's work closely, along with that of the Farm Security Administration workers, as he did research for *The Grapes of Wrath*. Mari Sandoz was probably the most successful of Lowry Wimberly's former students. She was a daughter of Swiss immigrants raised in the hardscrabble Sandhills of western Nebraska. She had earned a university degree despite not having a high school diploma and had won a $5,000 prize from the *Atlantic Monthly* for *Old Jules*, her 1935 biography of her complex father. Sandoz was a candidate to lead the Nebraska Writers' Project, and although she declined that role, she provided valuable counsel to her friends there. She gave Kees advice on his fiction and met Rudy Umland often for coffee in the Lincoln bus depot to discuss the Project's work and its staff.

As Sandoz worked steadily on her historical novels, she conducted WPA-style interviews and often traveled west to the Sandhills to meet with ancient veterans of Little Big Horn and other battles. Those interviews turned up information for her biography of Crazy Horse that no academic historians had previously found. Her 1939 novel *Capital City* would kick up dust in Lincoln for what residents regarded as an unflattering portrait of their town.

Umland remained with the Project beyond the publication of the Nebraska guide in 1938 and beyond the collection of many of the WPA life histories, until the Project's budget was slashed in 1939. By then, he was married with a child on the way. At his daughter's birth, he made a gift to her of a spoon he had found while he was a lumberman in Canada during his wandering years. Its inscription, "Yvonne," marked the first time he had ever seen that name, and he was enchanted by it. It was an unusual choice for a girl in their family, but for Yvonne Umland in later years it summed up her father's sense of whimsy.

Umland was surprised to be summoned for military service when World War II began (he thought that being in his thirties put him past the age of recruitment). He was assigned to a post in the South, where he met other WPA writers. After the war, he moved his family to Kansas City, wrote stories for literary magazines about Nebraska life and book reviews for the *Kansas City Star*, and worked for the Social Security Administration. He never realized his dream of having a writing career, but he kept in touch with Sandoz and continually received her encouragement. When his daughter, Yvonne, was in her last year of high school, she visited Sandoz in Greenwich Village. Yvonne remembered the woman's stylish hair and clothes and her wit. Most vividly, though, she recalled Sandoz's hands—big, weathered hands that had clearly done farmwork.

Weldon Kees left the Project for life in Denver ("like rats deserting a sinking ship," he said of himself and his colleagues). He had more of his stories published in literary reviews and in *Best Short Stories 1941*, but his breakthrough came when he began to write poetry, with encouragement from his WPA coworker Norris Getty. Biographer James Reidel believed that Kees would not have developed into the poet he became without his experience on the WPA guide. For a while afterward, Umland stayed in touch with Kees and even visited him in Denver.

One of Kees's most bitter poems from that time, "For My Daughter," paints vividly the dangers that faced children who entered the world in that time of fascism's global advance. Kees had no daughter, as the poem makes clear at the end. In later years, Umland was convinced that the news of his own daughter's birth had inspired the poet's fearsome vision.

7

POETIC LAND, PUGNACIOUS PEOPLE: CALIFORNIA

Us Floaters had America and the World to talk about. . . . We were gambling like we had an income. We made an agreement not to break each other, all of us had been broke once. No one could lose any more than three dollars of his money on that train.

—WPA WRITER ELUARD LUCHELL MCDANIEL

IN THE LATE 1920S, KENNETH REXROTH was twenty-one years old and recently married when he and his wife, Andrée, made their way from Chicago to California. The West Coast did not welcome their arrival. They caught a ride with a traveling salesman and on their first day in California stopped at a roadside restaurant. For two pieces of pie and two cups of coffee, the restaurant's owner charged them three dollars, about five times the usual price.

Rexroth thought the man was joking. "You mean sixty cents, don't you?"

"No," the proprietor said. "I mean three dollars. A dollar apiece for the pie and fifty cents for the coffee."

Rexroth recalled in his *Autobiographical Novel* that he stood there in disbelief with his wallet in his hand. He told the man to stop kidding.

"Listen, you son of a bitch," the man said, "fork over the three dollars. We don't want bastards like you in this country."

He came around the corner and hit me full in the mouth and knocked me down. As I went down I kicked him in the nuts and as he fell backward Andrée hit him over the head with a bottle of ketchup. The salesman grabbed us, threw us into the car, and tore off down the road. At the first gas station we asked where we could find a sheriff. "Down the road half a mile, the first house on the left." He was sitting on the porch, muddy logger's boots up on the railing, reading a newspaper and spitting tobacco, a star pinned to his greasy vest. We went up and made a complaint. He didn't even take down his feet, but drew a pistol and said to the salesman, "Get off down the highway and get those sons of bitches out of the country or I'll lock you all up." We had arrived in California. Episodes like this were the common thing in the northern three counties of California in those days.

Rexroth nonetheless quickly fell in love with San Francisco, which he found "a truly Mediterranean city" for its setting and the rich heritage of its Italian population. It reminded him of the bohemian Chicago of his boyhood, before he was orphaned at thirteen. His father, a pharmacist, had been drinking pals with Theodore Dreiser and other writers, and his mother had been a suffragette.

"San Francisco has always cherished its eccentrics," the WPA guide notes. "It has been inclined to regard graft with a tolerant eye; it has always prided itself on the international flavor of its food and drink, and its cosmopolitan tastes in feminine beauty; it has always been a 'good' town for the actor and the musician." Despite daily morning fog, earthquakes, political scandal, and labor wars on the wharf, the city "remained unmistakably itself" amid the neon lights and the skyscrapers that were replacing the rambling old buildings of the Embarcadero and Market Street.

San Francisco in the 1930s.

Nearly a decade after Rexroth's arrival, the city's crowning achievements were its two great spans, the Bay Bridge and the Golden Gate. The latter was the world's longest suspension bridge when it was finished in 1937. But what kept Rexroth in California for many years was the natural environment, he wrote in his *Autobiographical Novel* (the publisher added *Novel* in the title to avoid libel suits; Rexroth insisted that it was all true). For Rexroth, who had once considered becoming a monk, hiking in the Sierras to Yosemite was a rejuvenating spiritual experience. In the mountains, he could spend a morning "botanizing and writing" and then hike old lumber roads. There he might meet with a group of convicts building a road across the valley and learn from them about a trail covered in timber and brush, hidden to preserve a secret, pristine fishing lake of the upper valley.

Rexroth joined the northern California office of the Writers' Project, located at 717 Market Street in San Francisco, as editor of its natural history articles. He and Andrée had worked on a predecessor to the Project since 1933 and had proposed that the federal government hire artists to paint murals on the walls of Coit Memorial Tower on Telegraph Hill. (Rexroth appears in one of the murals in the tower: in Bernard Zakheim's fresco of a library scene, the poet-painter is climbing a ladder.) By the mid-1930s, his marriage with Andrée was breaking up. Andrée suffered from epilepsy and was showing increasingly erratic behavior. When she wanted to pursue an "open" marriage, Kenneth balked. "I got a new furnished room—a large drawing room in an old Victorian house on Post Street," he wrote, and "began quietly to separate myself from all organizations dominated by the Communist Party."

At the WPA office, Rexroth did much of the editing. According to his autobiography, he also influenced hiring policy with Alsberg during a visit to San Francisco. When Alsberg demurred on a request to hire a PhD candidate, Rexroth exploded.

"Bullshit. What the hell is the project for if not to help people get back into decent jobs?"

"I guess you're right," Alsberg conceded. "We can make an exception for her because you know perfectly well that most of these people could never get decent jobs in their lives."

Rexroth settled in Potrero Hill with the woman who would become his second wife, Marie Kass, a nurse and a poet with an "ironic and frisky" sense of humor. Potrero Hill at that time had a large Russian community, full of recent refugees from the Soviet regime and older émigrés who had escaped the czar. The latter gathered at the Russian Orthodox church on Green Street and held an elaborate ball every year, dressing "in faded regimentals of the Imperial Army to pay each other elaborate respects over vodka, tea, and caviar."

Weldon Kees and his wife visited Rexroth around this time, having left Nebraska. The two poets had little in common, noted Kees's biographer: Kees said that Rexroth's work was "lost in a fog of private sources," and Rexroth regarded the younger poet as not yet free from T. S. Eliot's shadow and the Jazz Age. Yet as Reidel notes in *Vanished Act*, both enjoyed abstract painting and music, and they each saw that the other had a certain authenticity. Both were pacifists. Kees described Rexroth as "volatile, anarchistic, and very witty." (Rexroth later would

First Russian Baptist Church in Kenneth
Rexroth's neighborhood of Potrero Hill,
San Francisco, 1939.

enlist Kees in his political activism for Japanese Americans, and he once
added in a 1942 letter's postscript, "If a chubby gentleman calls on you
unexpectedly and says his name is Abraham Lincoln Kanai—take him
in—bed him and feed him—he is a pearl without price, the real saint
of the 'evacuation.'") San Francisco impressed Kees with its compact-
ness. Telegraph Hill was just a few minutes' walk from Chinatown. "You
grunt and puff climbing the hills," Kees wrote, "but you do not really
mind because the weather is fine and cool."

When he tired of the city, Rexroth often set off backpacking in the High
Sierras with Marie. His backpack was so big that it required both of them
to lift it onto his shoulders. "I would put it on a stump or a downed timber,
adjust the shoulder strap and the tumpline around my forehead. She would
pull me to my feet, and we'd start off," he wrote in his autobiography.

Kenneth Rexroth and an unidentified girl in 1955.

Rexroth's love for the mountains comes across in the WPA guide's section on the Sierras. Tour 3 down US 99 (now coinciding with I-5 on the northern part of the tour route) starts at the Oregon line and works southward to Sacramento, Fresno, Bakersfield, and Los Angeles before moving on to Mexicali. Rexroth's typed manuscripts of his research for portions of the route read almost like poetry:

> US 99 presents a complete cross section of California. From the rugged wall of the Siskiyous on the north, it winds down barren river canyons, round Mount Shasta, and along the twisting Sacramento River between steep, evergreen-forested slopes. . . . Its course . . . turns southeast through the sagebrush reaches of a desert trough . . . past the Salton Sea, into irrigated farmlands of the sun-scorched Imperial Valley. The highway passes smoking

lumber mills among bare, stump-dotted slopes; mines and quarries on scarred mountain sides and dredges scooping river gravel; herds cropping broad pastures and far-spreading acres of hay and grain; fruit-laden orchards around packing houses, truck garden plots, and groves of date palms.

Mount Shasta was a special place for Rexroth, who describes it in the guide as "the most striking of the many extinct or dormant volcanoes in the northern California mountains." Making his way toward the peak, he follows the winding road over hills and brush. He notes how the thick groves of conifers that had covered Mount Shasta's lower slopes before 1880 had been "recklessly denuded." The lumber companies had cut the most accessible timber and burned off the land to destroy the piles of brush and debris.

The hike up Mount Shasta could take as long as ten hours. Rexroth advises climbers to "wear calked shoes, heavy clothing, colored glasses and carry food for three meals and water, an alpenstock, and a gunny-sack or piece of carpet for sliding the mountain in descent," as well as black greasepaint to prevent sunburn.

> The trail, narrow, rough, and dusty, but compensating for its discom-forts by ever changing vistas, winds through stretches of chaparral, in springtime fragrant with wildflowers. Then it ascends through stands of sugar and yellow pine and, at higher elevations, through whitebark pine and Shasta fir. . . . A start from the lodge at 2 A.M. allows time to reach Thumb Rock to watch the sunrise.

Rexroth shows no hesitation in urging readers over "stretches of bare, rough, brown lava" to reach the "snowfields and ice of the summit . . . where a vast panorama of tumbled mountains and valleys spread on every side."

In the guide's praise of the mountain, Rexroth invoked California's "poet of the Sierras":

> "Lonely as God and white as a winter moon," wrote Joaquin Miller, "Mount Shasta starts up sudden and solitary from the heart of the

A view of Mount Shasta.

great black forest. . . ." Sixth highest mountain in California, it is more impressive than the highest, Mount Whitney. The Indians looked upon it with awe, believing it to be the abode of the Great Spirit. Even among whites a latter-day legend persists—that high within the snow-mantled crater dwells an ancient white-robed brotherhood, descendants of the Lemurians, inhabitants of a vast mid-Pacific continent.

The guide entry includes an account of naturalist John Muir's treacherous venture when an April blizzard near Shasta's summit trapped him and his companion in the cone of the hot spring. They lay there for thirteen hours, "scalded on one side, all but frozen on the other." Muir called Shasta a "fire mountain."

Rexroth's draft for the Mount Shasta tour shows his visceral reactions to the mountain's beauty and man's ravages. He calls Shasta's vistas categorically "the finest views in America" and bemoans the fact that loggers have eliminated most of the magnificent forest of its slopes and replaced it with thickets of ceanothus, manzanita, and chinquapin brush. His assessment of any mine operator who would leave the landscape that way is scathing:

> He is most often a stranger to the country in which he operates, with no interest in its well being and no care for the conservation of its resources. . . . He is interest[ed] in the immediate exploitation of the irreplaceable commodity. The effects of that exploitation on the surrounding country and its population, or on the workers . . . are the least of his cares. Former mining areas are littered with abandoned machinery, the streams are polluted, the forests are destroyed, and the aboriginal population murdered or enslaved.

The passage ends with a withering indictment: "This, due to its history, is still the prevailing ideology of the state of California. . . . Most of the top soil of Northern California is in San Francisco Bay."

The draft shows the influence of Eastern thought on Rexroth: "This is the region in which, appropriately enough, the Living Buddha of Public Opinion has chosen to take his last stand."

"From the summit of Mt. Shasta . . . sometimes Thor and Odin can be glimpsed, descending the rainbow to visit their disciple, and the spirit of the master is more than manifest over a landscape of thousands of square miles." The published version cut these comments and replaced them with the observations of Joaquin Miller and Muir.

Farther along the route, Rexroth expands on the Kings River Valley and California Route 180:

> Connoisseurs of mountain scenery have long exalted this route as one of the most beautiful in the world. Everything that the Sierra can offer in the way of breath-taking contrast and dramatic beauty is here—tiny peaceful meadows below towering polished domes, dozens of cascades, any one of which would be considered a crowning glory in an Eastern State, and multi-colored crags against skies unbelievably blue.

Continuing south, he pauses at the hamlet of Mineral King, at the base of Sawtooth Peak, "founded in 1873 by three spiritualists" who pursued

> the White Chief Lode silver claim, named in honor of the Indian spirit control who they said had guided them to it. By 1875 they had interested enough capital to enable them to build a toll road to the claim. There was a brief inrush of miners but the silver could not be recovered in paying quantities and in 1883 a snowslide destroyed much of the property.

> Now located in Sequoia National Park, the town's scenery "is magnificent, in early summer the profusion of wild flowers passes belief, and Mineral King at the end is the best of all outfitting points for trips in the high mountains." Just beyond, the Tagus Ranch erected a billboard advertising itself as the "World's Largest Peach, Apricot and Nectarine Orchard." The fruit warehouses, cotton gins, and loading platforms were piled high with cotton along the railroad sidings.

These travels through rugged passes gave Rexroth and Marie a taste of life, love, and nature, as he describes in *Autobiographical Novel*:

> One day we climbed up to Desolation Lake and went swimming. Afterwards we lay on the granite sand and speculated on how difficult Mt. Humphries would be to climb. It certainly looked difficult. Suddenly I said, "Look, somebody's climbed it, there's somebody on the top. And there's something else there I can't quite make out." Finally we were able to tell what it was—a fox terrier. So we decided the mountain could certainly be climbed and up we went. It was not easy. It is still considered one of the most difficult west faces in the Sierras (the steep climbs are mostly on the east face of the Sierra fault block). Near the summit we came on the High Sierra polemonium—dense clusters of deep blue flowers with the most beautiful floral odor I know. And just before we had passed through five hundred feet of almost equally beautiful Sierra primrose. In the twilight we passed through clouds of perfume. It was quite dark when we got back to the lake, and we picked our way off down the plateau

in the moonlight, ate our supper of golden trout, risotto, and dried fruit, made love, and slept till the sun woke us up.

Rexroth explored the Sequoia National Park, with its high mountain lakes created from glaciers, and "mountainsides of exposed rock and the great, irregular granite ridges, cleared of their earth and vegetation by ice thousands of years ago." There, WPA researchers uncovered the 1885 history of land claims filed by a socialist group who planned "a Utopia in the wilderness," and who pledged not to cut the great Sequoias. They "named the outstanding big trees after the heroes of the Paris Commune and of American socialism." The largest one they called Marx. The government launched an investigation and eventually expelled the group. The majestic splendor endured:

Moro Rock is climbed by a winding rock and concrete stairway. The view from its summit is magnificent, particularly at sunset. A sheer 4,000 feet below is the Kaweah River, a shining thread. In the east a pale moon rises above the slowly darkening, irregular ridges of the Great Western Divide. Westward miles of hilltops reach toward the San Joaquin Valley, and in the far distance the red sun sinks behind the Coast Range.

Rexroth would gain fame two decades later as a mentor to the Beat poets. In October 1955, he emceed the Six Gallery reading where Allen Ginsberg first recited his epic poem *Howl.* Later in life, as California's leading poet, Rexroth recalled in his autobiography his ventures into the Sierras as the clearest memories of his youth:

Ski touring and mountaineering have given me some of the happiest moments of my life. It's not just swinging long turns down a steep mountainside, or traveling through the snow-bound forest where the tree tops stick up like little Christmas trees, but even crawling out at night to piss under the black sky full of billions of stars shedding a pale grey light in the infinite expanse of snow. One is tempted to write one's initials doing this, while realizing under planets, stars, and nebulae, and surrounded by peaks heaved up in the Jurassic, that like Keats "Here lies one whose name was writ in water."

As I look back on the period between the wars, with all its busy work and endless meetings in the labor movement, mass strikes, police attacks and killings, and all the other seemingly eventful activities, what I remember clearly are stones and trees and flowers and snow, and the companionship of my wife. "Tout passe, ils demeurent."

Another member of the California Writers' Project deeply affected by Eastern literature was the avant-garde composer Harry Partch. The son of missionaries to China, Partch grew up in Arizona and realized early that he was gay. He looked to ancient cultures as bastions of freedom and resolved to live without compromise. Frustrated by the conformity of music studies in Los Angeles in the 1920s, he adapted the viola to a new microtonal scale and composed music to the poetry of the eighth-century Chinese poet Li Po. Partch studied in Europe for a year and returned in 1935 to find that he had lost sponsorship for his music, so he turned to hoboing for most of the next decade.

Harry Partch in 1943.

"Life is too precious to spend it with important people," constantly fighting for position, Partch said later in life. He found hoboes and other people he met on the road warmer and more open-minded. "In little ways," he said, "there was a tremendous amount of creativity in everyday living."

"Hoboes are extraordinarily individualistic people," Partch explained in a BBC documentary. "That's why they're hoboes."

In 1936, he asked Ross Santee, the director of the Project in Arizona, for a proofreading job. Partch acknowledged that he was mainly a musician, but he had proofreading credits from the *Los Angeles Times* and the *New Orleans Times-Picayune*, among other publications, and he showed Santee his journal of hobo life. Santee sent the journal to George Cronyn in Washington headquarters (the same official whom Vardis Fisher had gotten drunk before sending back East). Partch got the job and worked for months rewriting the tours section of the WPA guide to Arizona, for which he won admirers in Washington.

"Your essay style, combining color with detachment, is a rarity," Cronyn wrote to him. "There are few enough people in America with a shrewd and observing eye. . . . An outsider might consider you maladjusted; that's the penalty of looking clearly at a maladjusted world."

Partch's tenure didn't last long. By May 1937, he was bristling at authority and ready to move on. He appreciated Cronyn's encouragement and may have even considered moving toward writing rather than music. But he took to the road again, heading north from Phoenix. In September 1937, he spent some time in Boise and by October was back in California, staying with a friend in Glendale. In one of his few documents from this time, a satirical sketch dated April 26, 1938, he contrasts the speech style of bums on the road with that of a group of musicologists in New York City. "The bums' courage in remaining stoically humorous in the face of even the gravest misfortune was a value Partch treasured," noted Bob Gilmore in *Harry Partch: A Biography.*

Other members of the California Project were hoboes, too, including Eluard Luchell McDaniel, who had bummed up and down the West Coast. Born in 1912 on a small farm in Mississippi, McDaniel had run away at age ten and worked his way across the country as a newsboy, a farmworker, an auto mechanic, a machinist, a photographer, and a hotel clerk. In the early 1930s, he settled in San Francisco and began to take writing classes at night. He published fiction in *Story* in 1935, then volunteered to fight with the Abraham Lincoln Brigade of Americans against Franco in the Spanish Civil War. McDaniel returned to San Francisco and became a WPA writer for lack of other work. He recounted his experiences as a black teenage hobo in "Bumming in California," a piece that appeared in the *American Stuff* anthology. He was tossed off a train by railroad bulls near Los Angeles, ate grapes and apricots from a ranch

An anti-Nazi street meeting
in San Francisco, 1936.

near San Bernardino, made breakfast of raw sugar beets on a freight car
in Fresno, and performed farmwork south of Oakland.

In the fall of 1938, Harry Partch was also doing migrant farmwork again, following the harvest up to Spokane, Washington. By early
1939, he was back in Los Angeles and staying at the YMCA on South
Hope Street. He reconnected with a musician there who had written an
article for *Pacific Coast Musician* about Partch and the new instruments
he'd built. The article described Partch's innovative music as accessible
and remarkably American, having "the immediate appeal of lyric Irish
speech, the charm of spontaneous Negro music, the power and emotion
of Hebrew chant." Decades later, composer Phillip Glass agreed and
called Partch's music "profoundly American."

WPA workers in San Francisco protesting
cuts in WPA relief, February 1939.

Partch joined the California Writers' Project in 1939 for another
stretch of gainful employment. He is one of only four credited on the
WPA guide's editorial staff for Southern California. He stayed on the job
through the summer, fall, and into winter, leaving in January 1940.

When the WPA California guide appeared in May 1939, it received
glowing reviews and became a national Book-of-the-Month Club selection, the only WPA guide to do so. The *New York Times* called it comprehensive and "more than a guide book." Reviews called attention
to its social history descriptions, from the conditions of farm labor to
the brutal repression of union organizers. The guide took readers
to Yosemite's glories, Edward G. Robinson's Hollywood home and his
collection of modern French paintings, and behind the barred gates of
San Quentin, describing the prison's rules on solitary confinement (one
meal a day and no visitors, tobacco, mail, or reading material) and its
prize-winning dahlias.

By 1941, Harry Partch was at a creative standstill. He left California
on a freight bound for Chicago, and his composition *U.S. Highball*

Okies looking for farmwork in California.

evokes the hardship and freedom of the hobo experience on that trip. It remains the most evocative musical depiction of that lifestyle: the harassment by railroad bulls, the patronizing rules of shelters, the alienation and defiance, and the occasional tender welcome.

"Leaving North Platte, Nebr-ass-ass-katte!" the singer cries in *U.S. Highball.* "To hell with Nebraska. And the hell with Idaho, Wyoming, Colorado, California, Nevada, and Utah!"

8

RAISING THE DEAD IN
NEW ORLEANS

Let it rain. Little old water never hurt a mighty Zulu. With all the dignity he could summon, King Zulu mounted his "Pink Elephant." Then a signal, and the parade was on. Out Poydras Street they rolled, the thirteen-piece band swinging. . . . Finally the parade reached the City Hall and paused. The white mayor wasn't present, but his representative received coconuts and a bow from His Majesty. The band played "Every Man a King," Huey P. Long's song, and the dancing was wild. It was King Zulu's day.

—*GUMBO YA-YA*, A BOOK OF LOUISIANA FOLKLORE

FOR LYLE SAXON, MARDI GRAS WAS THE DAY that once a year lifted his soul. He celebrated his first Mardi Gras when he was twelve, with his family's young black hireling, Robert. The two boys wore masks and went together from event to event. With their faces covered by the masks, they passed unbothered from the black Zulu parade to the whites-only Rex parade. It gave the privileged Saxon a magical sense of a broader society and a tiny glimpse of how light-skinned African Americans "passed" in white society.

"Southern art, music, and literature have been enriched by a century of Carnival," Saxon wrote in the *WPA Guide to New Orleans*. The guide

A New Orleans shop advertising Mardi
Gras costumes in 1941.

devotes four pages to the preparations for Mardi Gras, including a visit
to the two companies that built all of the Mardi Gras floats in old warehouses on Calliope Street near South Claiborne Avenue. "It is a location
which few people know, and even fewer ever see," since a special permit
from the manager is needed to visit.

All of the advance work pointed to the day of the parade. In the early
afternoon of that Tuesday, hot dog stands, peanut wagons, cotton candy
sheds, and souvenir vendors would appear along the streets. Cars gathered along the side streets off St. Charles Avenue. By five o'clock in the
afternoon, the sidewalk crowd would be so thick that pedestrians had to
walk in the streets: "Children form human chains to whip through the
crowd, and there is much laughter and noise." Then Saxon places
the reader in the roiling mix:

Suddenly a glow spreads in the sky, and there is a rumbling sound as a squad of motorcycle policemen approaches. You back out of the street to the sidewalk. You press closer and closer to the people already there. The thundering motorcycles pass, only to give place to mounted policemen four abreast, who are determined to clear a passageway. The horses' hoofs terrify and succeed in their purpose; you are well out of the street.

The scene unfolds: the parade marshal, the masked captain, the black dancers carrying torches, the float of maskers greeted by people jumping up and down, eager to catch the trinkets that bring good luck. There are mermaids, clowns, Indians, a man dressed entirely in macaroni. "I'm one of the happiest people in North America tonight," Saxon wrote amid the festival in the *Times-Picayune* one year, "because New Orleans really had a good time on Mardi Gras."

For the Project's folklore division, Saxon delves even further into Mardi Gras flamboyance, finery, and human extravagance—a roller coaster of emotion:

Then there was an awed hush as a maid led the Queen out upon the platform, and sighs passed through the crowd that were a tribute to her beauty . . . She wore an expensive-looking white satin gown, lavishly trimmed in lace, a multi-colored train of metallic cloth, a rhinestone crown, and carried accessories to match. "The white lady I used to work for gave me all my accessories," Queen Zulu revealed later. "She said, 'Ceola, I want to fix you up right. I want you to be a damn good queen.'"

Mardi Gras encompassed everyone's dreams, no matter how fantastic or unconventional. Saxon documents this in *Gumbo Ya-Ya*, a book of folklore (the title is a Cajun term meaning "everyone talks at once"):

A group of Negro female impersonators headed by Corinne the Queen are perhaps the gayest of all. In evening gowns and wigs they try to outdo the real girls. Corinne always maintains her regal bearing, explaining, "I'm a real queen, and don't nobody never forget it!" She has genuine claims to majesty. In 1931 she was Queen of the Zulus! That year the king said he was disgusted with women, so he selected Corinne to reign as his mate over all of the Negro Mardi Gras!

The same New Orleanian character that exulted in that pageant could also deeply ponder death and the afterlife. Where else would a morgue-obsessed song like "St. James Infirmary" become a local standard? The dead in New Orleans lived in a style unlike that of any other city. As museums of folk and fine art and places for powerful encounters, cemeteries reveal societal values, and the way the dead are treated often can be a source of identity and strength for the living. Saxon personally had an ear tuned for these portals to the past (his novel *Children of Strangers* placed at least five scenes in cemeteries), and the *WPA Guide to New Orleans* paraphrased Mark Twain's comment that New Orleans had *no* architecture except in its cemeteries. It's the kind of arch remark that pleased Saxon.

Saxon, a lifelong Louisianan, stood more than six feet tall and was heavyset. He was born in Bellingham, Washington (though he never corrected the myth that his birthplace was Baton Rouge), and studied at Louisiana State University. A lively conversationalist, Saxon loved story-telling and befriended some of the best American writers of the 1920s: Sherwood Anderson, Thomas Wolfe, William Faulkner. He hoped to immortalize Louisiana life in a novel as Wolfe had done for North Carolina and Faulkner did for Mississippi. Saxon especially admired Anderson, the author of *Winesburg, Ohio*, who lived in the French Quarter for part of the 1920s. After Saxon's short story "Cane River" won the 1926 O. Henry Award, he started his novel with great ambition and a publisher's advance. With encouragement from Anderson, he went to New York to make his mark. But he came back when it didn't turn out as expected and began to work as a newspaperman. By the mid-1930s, his youthful ambition had withered.

"I'm getting ready to die through sheer lack of interest in life," he wrote in his diary in 1933. He still loved fiction, but it came out in compulsive book-buying sprees. "What insanity—the writing of the check leaves me nearly penniless," he wrote, after spending nearly $400 on books in three months. He moped around a plantation house he'd bought outside the city and expended a lot of effort avoiding writing. Saxon had many friends but few close relationships, and he often got drunk alone. He wasted time teaching his hens to perform a trick of flying up on his arm when he called them. The turning of a new year in January 1934 forced a bleak self-assessment. "For three years I have lain fallow, fattening, getting drunk, deteriorating," he wrote in his journal, "a repellent, fat middle-aged man. . . . Where is that man that I used to be? Have I lost him completely?"

He wanted a fascinating challenge to grab hold of him and make him forget himself and his long-overdue novel: "Lately I've been obsessed with the idea of closing doors, as one thing after another becomes impossible, or recedes into the past."

In late summer of 1935, Saxon received a letter from Washington, asking him to be the state director of the Louisiana Writers' Project.

A downtown New Orleans street, 1935.

He had known Harry Hopkins since 1919, when Hopkins, then the head of the Gulf division of the American Red Cross, had recruited Saxon to start a vocational education program. Saxon saw this new invitation as a deliverance from his listlessness. He accepted and moved from his country home into New Orleans. He set up an office in the Canal Bank Building on the main thoroughfare at the edge of the French Quarter and rented a room nearby in the St. Charles Hotel on St. Charles Avenue. Then he set to work recruiting indigent writers to report on the city. The unemployed on relief rolls were everywhere, from the city streets to houseboats on Lake Pontchartrain.

Saxon was careful to recruit from across the whole city. Since his first Mardi Gras, he had been sensitized to conditions faced by African Americans. His fiction dealt with the trials faced by interracial children and others whose place in society was uncertain, a sensitivity fueled perhaps by rumors of illegitimacy in his own background. Although his concern could be patronizing, he worked to dedicate a section of the Louisiana office to black studies. He also made sure that the publications of the Louisiana Writers' Project accounted for the divisions in New Orleans, both generally and specifically, in how they affected people's choices in housing, transportation, restaurants, and music.

In his first year as director, Saxon established the Project's "Negro unit" to examine black history, culture, and folklore, with Dillard University professor Lawrence Reddick as its director. Saxon helped get the black poet Marcus Bruce Christian appointed to the staff (Christian later became the unit's second director). Saxon also recommended him to the publisher Houghton Mifflin for a literary fellowship in 1936, writing, "Of all the writers that I have seen since I have taken this job, Marcus Christian is the one most likely to prove successful."

Saxon assigned the New Orleans guide's essay on race to Jeanne Arguedas, who wrote Creole poetry under the pen name Anne Labranche. She was born Jeanne Wogan and came from an old Creole family of New Orleans. Her husband, Gustave J. Arguedas, was Peru's consul general to Guatemala. Arguedas began her essay straightforwardly. "Like all cities of the South," she wrote, New Orleans drew clear lines between the races, with "still a great prejudice on the part of the white population against the negro. The Jim Crow law is in effect in the streetcars, busses, trains, railway stations, movies, and churches, but it has not yet affected the residential part of the city." Intermarriage, although prohibited, had happened anyway. (Editors muted the tone in the published version: "The melting pot has been simmering in New Orleans for over two centuries," it begins, in a way that would nonetheless unsettle white Southern readers. "Intermarriage has broken down distinctions and destroyed the boundaries of racial sections.") Arguedas explained how intermarriage had multiplied the number of racial categories: mulatto, terceron, quadroon, and quinteron. Quinterons were considered essentially white.

Arguedas's essay goes on to describe how the city was divided into racial districts in the 1800s, with Creoles in the Vieux Carré (the French Quarter), Anglo Americans in the Faubourg St. Marie and Lafayette, and Irish and German sections elsewhere. By the 1930s, these neighborhoods had been completely rearranged. The guide includes notes on an Italian neighborhood and a small Chinese enclave on Tulane Avenue near Rampart, Filipinos on Dumaine, and Orthodox Jews on Carondelet. Other sections of the guide describe the race barriers in churches and labor unions, from dockworkers to the construction trades.

The writer who was sent to cover the city's transportation, William de Brueys, laid out in detail the options in air, rail, and highway travel. His draft notes how streetcars on the city's main lines ran every two and a half to seventeen minutes. It describes the special transfers on the St. Charles line and tosses in the fact that there were roughly 127 miles of streetcar tracks in daily service and 94 miles of active bus service. De Brueys gives the Transportation Department's phone number (Main 4900) and details the Desire streetcar line's route from Canal and Royal, out Canal to Bourbon Street, out Pauger to Dauphine, down Dauphine to Desire, and out to Tonti, ending down on France Street. The editor scrawled his verdict in the margin: "Inadequate, should be rewritten."

Robert McKinney wrote the manuscript on black life and canvassed the restaurants, hotels, and taxi companies that were available to black residents and visitors. Readers learned about the black commercial district on South Rampart Street and the regional chain of "Negro restaurants" called the National Lunch Room, based in Memphis. Mr. C. A. Brown's Astoria Taxicab Company was the oldest black taxi company in the city, with fifty drivers, mechanics, car washers, and operators. Its fares were based on a zone system and ranged from 35 ¢ to $1.50 per hour.

Black orchestras could play for both white and black dances, and members of the Célestin Tuxedo Orchestra wore gray uniforms with black lines and toured in a customized bus. (Oscar Célestin lived on France Street in the Ninth Ward.) Leary's Society Syncopators had a roster of fifteen musicians on the WPA Music Project, and the fees they received for their gigs ($35 for five hours) supplemented the WPA budget.

The musical tradition for which New Orleans became famous was not at the top of the WPA writers' minds, but their account of the birthplace of jazz contains a lively description of the brash, spiky spasm bands that helped to midwife jazz in the 1890s and that still endured.

> You get to the corner of Royal and St. Peter Streets just in time to see a "spasm band" go into action. A "spasm band" is a miscellaneous collection of a soap box, tin cans, pan tops, nails, drumsticks, and little Negro boys. When mixed in the proper proportions this results in the wildest shuffle dancing, accompanied by a bumping rhythm. You flip them a coin, and they run after you offering to do tricks for "lagniappe"; and without your approval, one little boy begins to walk the length of the block on his hands, while another places the crown of his skull on a tin can and spins like a top. "Lagniappe" . . . is a little gift the tradesmen present to their customers with each purchase. By extension, it means something extra, something for nothing. . . . Playing in front of the theaters, saloons, and brothels of the city, these bands regaled the public with their informal "ear" music.

The Razzy Dazzy Spasm Band earned a gig in New York, where it changed its name to simply "Jazz Band." Jazz emerged as a musical gumbo of folk music, brass marches, and French dance forms. African American blues formed a strong tributary, and jazz classics with local titles like "Canal Street Blues," "Basin Street Blues," and "Milneburg Joys" reveal how that river flowed through New Orleans. The guide sounds decidedly archaic when it says that Louis Armstrong's "Negro jazz" "deserves mention," but it acknowledges him among the world's greatest trumpet players and describes unique aspects of his style. Jazz greats Sidney Bechet, Jelly Roll Morton, Joe "King" Oliver, and Kid Ory get shout-outs, along with Oscar "Papa" Célestin's previously mentioned Tuxedo Orchestra (which included Armstrong on second trumpet in 1921–1922), a leader among the fifty or more black bands active in the city. White musicians are mentioned, too, but apart from Louis Prima, few of them are remembered today.

Racial divisions existed in the houses of God, as elsewhere; most white Catholic churches in the city seated black parishioners in the rear pews. The WPA writers put together a list of parishes in twenty-eight denominations, from Adventists to Unitarians, including Jewish Reform, Rosicrucians, and Latter Day Saints, as well as various unaffiliated black ministers and sects.

"The cemeteries of New Orleans are truly cities of the dead," says the New Orleans guide, "closely built-up enclosures filled with house-like tombs, blinding white under the hot southern sun." One portal to the past that Lyle Saxon knew well was the door in the thick plaster wall around St. Louis I, which encloses a small part of what was once called the Basin Street burial ground. Only the cream of New Orleans's white and Creole societies could afford vaults in St. Louis I, and its grandiose archi-tecture of marble and wrought iron suggests that a person carried social status into the next world. Inspired by the Père-Lachaise Cemetery in Paris, the soaring monuments are packed tightly on a miniature city grid of narrow graveled paths, block after block, with hardly a swatch of typical cemetery green. The metal and stone mount in an impressive urban dis-play. Group tombs soar twenty feet high, with "drawers" and handles, like wardrobes for gods. Passengers on the road outside see the tombs' peaked white rooftops and crosses of whitened plaster above the walls.

WPA writer Frank Riley trawled records and old newspapers while researching the Cemeteries section of the guide. His draft lays out the hard-ships of burial in such a low-lying city and the practice of renting space in "oven vaults" in the graveyard wall. After a year or two in these vaults, one tenant makes room for another, with the remains being removed and buried elsewhere and the coffin destroyed. "This seemingly heartless procedure was the only possible way," Riley wrote, to comply with tomb burial laws in the space limitations of the old cemeteries. He also outlined the exceptions to tomb burial required by Jewish ritual and described the potters field located out Canal Street, segregated even in death.

"It must be admitted," Riley continued, "the appearance of these little cities of the dead is depressing. . . . It is as if the crowded, living city outside begrudged this little space to the dead." His editors deleted these reflections but let stand his observations on the city's headstones and voodoo graves and snatches from the more colorful epitaphs, including several for men felled in duels and one that Riley thought sounded like language in *Alice in Wonderland*: "Alas that one whose dornthly joy had often to trust in heaven should canty thus sudden to from all its hopes benivens and though thy love for off remore that dealt the dog pest thou left to prove thy sufferings while below."

St. Louis I Cemetery in New Orleans in the 1930s.

The guide's account of the departed reveals their interactions with the living. In the 1850s, St. Louis I Cemetery bustled as the result of a yellow fever epidemic, and mourners poured through the gates wearing splendid black silks, shawls, and gloves purchased from exclusive shops. The near-daily frequency of funerals and the fabulous stone surroundings made St. Louis I a site of regular outings and a centerpiece of social life. The wrought-iron benches in New Orleans graveyards set the mold for modern trends in lawn furniture.

The guide takes readers deep into the city's secrets, such as its link with voodoo, which most Americans had heard rumors about. Congo Square (now Louis Armstrong Park) was, during the pre–Civil War era, "given over to slaves on Sunday afternoons for dancing, singing, and the performance of Voodoo rites." Voodoo practices had continued in various forms. The folkways essay is typical of Saxon, coming as a dialogue with a local Creole host who keeps trying to change the subject. "Those Voodoo queens, they knew things no white man ever knew," the host says when pressed.

> "They could make people die, have them buried, and raise them again two weeks or a month later. I know, because my grandfather told me a story." Here your Creole's voice drops to a confidential whisper—he is going to take you into his confidence, let you hear one of the most jealously guarded of secrets. Obviously he likes you.

The discussion moves instead to zombies in Haiti, and the host never really divulges his secrets. He does take you to a disappointing voodoo woman on Claiborne Street and then by streetcar to a shop.

> You get off the street-car and right in front of you is the Voodoo drugstore. You go in, meet the proprietor. . . . He is very reticent, since he is in an illicit business, but by haggling you . . . leave carrying a vial of Love Oil and a list of all the charms to be purchased: Courting Powder, Anger Powder, Easy Life Powder, Mind Oil, Devil Oil, Mad Luck Water.

The local guide then shows the tomb of Marie Laveau, the famous voodoo queen, where people have left offerings to her. He climbs atop the tomb and grabs a handful of damp earth to give you as a powerful charm. Walking out, he explains how Laveau charmed policemen who were sent to arrest her, making them unable to move, and how she reputedly advised her disciples even after her death. Gris-gris, the African amulet, gets its own entry in the index, as well as in the glossary of Louisiana terms at the back.

Years earlier, the promise of learning voodoo secrets had drawn the folk-lorist Zora Neale Hurston to New Orleans. "I have landed here in the king-dom of Marie Laveau and expect to wear her crown someday," she wrote on her arrival in the summer of 1928. Hurston spent nearly half a year appren-ticing with several voodoo masters, learning their secrets of "the conjure" through patient initiation, chasing black cats through the streets for one mentor and bringing the skin of a copperhead to another. By the end, she was anointed "the Rain-Bringer," with a lightning bolt painted on her back. She came away convinced of her teachers' spiritual power and the belief that those at the deepest levels of society hold the greatest power. "That man in the gutter is the god-maker, the creator of everything that lasts," she wrote.

The WPA guide writers did not dwell on the gangs and corruption that New Orleanians had to navigate and that posed particular dangers for the poor. Huey Long, Louisiana's "virtual dictator," had reigned as governor for four years and as a U.S. senator for three more. He assembled his own independent police force before he was murdered in September 1935. Despite the fact that Long had forced through a law permitting the state to jail New Dealers for interfering with Louisiana affairs, the guide remembers him as the city's "most colorful citizen." While describing his assaults on democratic institutions, it nonetheless credits him with giving the city lakefront development, a hospital and a medical center, and free schoolbooks.

The guide devotes several pages to the tangy flavors of Cajun and Creole cuisines ("the difference between one clove of garlic and two cloves of garlic is enough to disorganize a happy home") and describes their roots in French, Spanish, and African ingredients. "The slaves of Louisiana had their share in refining the product," along with the "roots and pungent herbs" of local Native Americans. Tastes range from oranges and figs to cayenne pepper and pecans, black coffee and *pain perdu* in the morning, to crayfish bisque, jambalaya, red beans, and gumbo. The guide includes recipes laced with serious advice; it tells you how to add chicory to coffee in the New Orleans style and how to make drinks from absinthe to planter's punch (the trick is to use granulated sugar so fine that it's almost powdered). Food was a very public enjoyment in New Orleans, and the guide made that clear:

The vending of food in New Orleans streets is a custom as old as the city itself. Earlier counterparts of present-day hawkers were the Green Sass Men. . . . Each season had its special commodities. Early spring saw the arrival of strawberries, of Japanese plums. Later, watermelons, dewberries, blackberries and figs appeared. Wild ducks, rice birds and other game were sold on the streets during winter. At the French Market Choctaw Indian squaws sat stoically at the curbs, offering gumbo file—powdered sassafras, frequently used instead of okra to thicken gumbo—other herbs and roots, baskets and pottery.

The New Orleans writers also fanned out into the surrounding bayous and peninsulas and wrote up tour routes there. The Plaquemines tour notes the local color of muskrat and alligator trappers plying their trade on the finger of land that extended some eighty miles southeast of the city into the Gulf.

Saxon felt time escaping his grasp. In mid-1937, he wrote a friend, "I have been doing this Federal job for nearly two years now, editing four huge tomes on Louisiana. Some way I managed to get my own novel finished and published and now I hope to get along to something else for myself, although I am in a state of exhaustion at the moment."

The drama in his novel *Children of Strangers* focuses on a Creole town in western Louisiana and a mulatto girl's romance with a white soldier across the river. The book drew good reviews. *Time* magazine said that its strength lay in Saxon's character portraits and its "vivid local color," so much so that the real-life dramas of plantation life outshone the melodramatic storyline.

Buoyed by the novel's success, Saxon bought a house in the French Quarter at 536 Madison Street, a two-story Spanish-style home with sixteen rooms in the heart of the city, one short block from Jackson Square. From there, he could take a streetcar uptown or walk over to Bourbon Street.

Still, Saxon found managing the Louisiana Writers' Project exhausting and annoying. To relieve the tedium, he wrote limericks and he drank. From the correspondence with headquarters, one source of annoyance

People lounging in Jackson Square in New Orleans in 1935.

is clear. Letters from Alsberg complain that some of the tours are "very dull and dry" and ask, "When you do the polishing you said you were about to do, can you not give more visual description of the towns and routes?" In revising maps, Alsberg requested that Saxon add points of interest and then check the edited map. Then, Alsberg said, Saxon should make sure that the map sent to him by mistake be sent immediately to the printer in Boston. And he should send a progress report on the maps "by airmail and follow up with weekly reports thereafter on the form provided for this purpose."

Also burdensome was the demand for official trips around the state. On those occasions, Saxon was the face of the federal government and had to visit district offices and give speeches. Early in 1937, for example, he was scheduled to address the Rotary Club in Lafayette, the capital of Acadiana, where French was still the main language. Saxon confided to a friend his outrage at the idiocy that drove him to start drinking alone on a bus headed for Alexandria, in the middle of the state, one rainy afternoon. At another lunch in 1938, he told the gathered Rotarians that the Writers' Project was collecting so much cultural material that it wouldn't all fit into the Louisiana guide, but the rest would be placed in libraries across the state so that the public could use it. He also reassured them that most WPA writers in the state had returned to other jobs after a stint on relief.

Other tasks took him farther afield—for example, to Little Rock to get the Arkansas guide back on track. On the way, he wrote a bitter limerick:

> Although I have not traveled far
> I do not care for Arkansas
> Nor for my state of health.
> My multiplicity of woe
> Is caused by soreness of my toe
> And by my lack of wealth.
> Now, as my eyes grow dim and shifty
> And I approach the age of fifty
> This thought cuts like a knife:
> It makes me mad, it makes me furious
> To find that I'm no longer curious
> About the facts of life.

Travel involved its own baffling instructions. This from Alsberg: "It is also necessary that we know where you will be on the last day of the preceding month and the first day of the month for which we request travel before we put in the request. The information should reach us by the 20th of the preceding month."

In early 1938, when the New Orleans guide went to press, Alsberg estimated that WPA writers nationally had logged one million miles on the road. The New Orleans guide has a foreword in which Harry Hopkins asserts that Saxon and his staff "have . . . succeeded in conveying the quality of their romantic and powerful city; the sense of its strength and destiny, as well as its gaiety, ease and its art of living." He heralds the book as a leading example of the WPA guides in their effort to "portray honestly and completely the history, struggles, and triumphs of the American people." The *Washington Post* said that the guide "made the city and its environs live and breathe."

With that milestone, Saxon's attention shifted to the state guide and the folklore research.

A change of pace came in May 1939, when WPA folklorist Herbert Halpert showed up with a recording machine on loan from the Library of Congress to record Louisiana folk songs. He arrived in New Orleans driving an old ambulance outfitted with shelves for the latest traveling recording studio. He made a base at Saxon's office in the Canal Bank Building and prepared to record a range of songs, including French, Creole, and voodoo songs. In all, with the help of Jeanne Arguedas, they made fifteen disks. (Another WPA worker who occasionally came from Mississippi to New Orleans was a young publicity assistant and photographer for the Mississippi guide named Eudora Welty.)

Saxon wrote to a friend in October 1940, "We got the Louisiana Guide done at the right psychological moment. . . . I'm as pleased as a child about it. The book should be out around the Christmas holidays sometime. [Coeditor Edward] Dreyer and I are knee deep in folklore at the moment, editing like beavers building a dam, working with claw and tooth."

The Louisiana guide came out in March 1941. The folklore book would keep Saxon busy for another two years. In August 1942, he wrote to Marge Hunter again that he had the manuscript spread out on his desk. "I'm determined that I get it finished before I leave this job."

One who had already left the job was Rudolph Umland. Having completed the Nebraska guide, Umland had been drafted into the army and now found himself stationed with his young family in New Orleans. It was a new and strange climate and culture. He looked for grounding in a connection at the outpost of the Project office. "The Writers' Project is still operating down here," Umland wrote back to a Nebraska friend in 1942. "Saxon can drink like a fish."

That year, Umland wrote to his old professor Wimberly with a bit of news: "Lyle Saxon was called back to Washington for a couple weeks. He thinks June 30 will see the end for it in all States."

Saxon was not pleased with the prospect of heading to Washington for one last chore. "Why they picked on me to do this I have no idea," he wrote to a friend in January 1943, "but they did."

Lyle Saxon conducting folklore research
in a cemetery in the 1940s.

He had been the regional director, had traveled to see Jim Thompson in Oklahoma City when that state office was in turmoil, and now he was called on to mop up the mess at the national headquarters. Saxon was not in good spirits. "All I've got to show" for six years, he wrote in his diary, "is the sad fact that I'm much older, and my eyes are bad now, and I've published some guidebooks . . . what the hell?"

At age fifty-four, Saxon's health was failing as he finished the folklore collection *Gumbo Ya-Ya*. It expressed much about Louisiana life that he couldn't get across in fiction, with a combination of whimsy and skepticism that lured the reader on through its tempting multicultural stew. "Every night is like Saturday night in Perdido Street," the book begins, "wild and fast and hot with sin." Saxon's preface thanks the many anonymous authors of folklore, from chimney sweeps to Jean Lafitte, and the text relishes their outrageousness:

> Berthoud Cemetery, some twenty miles from New Orleans, is the source of the most fantastic legend in the entire state. Here, it is said, the remains of pirate Jean Lafitte, admiral John Paul Jones and Napoleon Bonaparte lie in three adjoining graves. Lafitte is supposed to have rescued Bonaparte from St. Helena, leaving a double in his place, and the Emperor died while being carried to Louisiana. John Paul Jones, according to the legend, joined the Lafitte band, was killed in action, and buried. . . . Then, when Lafitte died, his pirates buried him between the other two. The fact that Jones died when Lafitte was about twelve years old doesn't seem to bother anyone. On certain occasions the trio of ghosts appear.

The book came out a year before Saxon died of cancer and pneumonia. *Time* magazine called it a "somewhat violent, somewhat gamy anthropology of New Orleans below the belt . . . acrawl with underworld or otherworld manifestations."

The blend of life and death in New Orleans that kept Saxon engaged made a magical and haunting mix, as in the story that WPA interviewee Melinda Parker told about a visit she received from her long-gone brother:

> Just the other day I was sitting down here by my stove, praying to the Lord, when who walks in the door but my brother that's dead. He used to live in Detroit so I always called him a snowdigger. I says to him, "What you doin' down here now, you snowdigger?" And he says, "I just had some money an' I thought I'd come an' give it to you." And he puts five dollars in my lap. Just then it looked to me like my brother that's a minister comes in the door and he turns to my brother and says, "Jim, what you doin' here?" And Jim

says, "I come to give Melinda some money." So my brother that's a minister, he gives me five dollars.

I got so excited about havin' that money for Christmas that I went out the house and was goin' to tell my friend and was all the way to Saratoga Street and the money was gone. . . . I told my brother that's a minister about it on Christmas Day and he said that Jim knew that I'm lookin' for a job and that his spirit is goin' to help me find one soon.

In 1939, Saxon's staff in New Orleans may have also been hopeful, as they left the Writers' Project for other jobs, that the economy was picking up. But as Herbert Halpert rolled the recording machine toward Florida that summer, there remained a lot of work to be done.

9

CIGARS AND TURPENTINE
IN FLORIDA

Folklore is not as easy to collect as it sounds. The best source is where there are the least outside influences and these people, being usually under-privileged, are the shyest. They are most reluctant at times to reveal that which the soul lives by.

—ZORA NEALE HURSTON, *MULES AND MEN* (1935)

First time that any society has assigned some of its members to run around to interview people and take down their stories.... We were like kids on a treasure hunt.

—STETSON KENNEDY

FLORIDA IN THE 1930S WAS, IN ZORA NEALE Hurston's words, a frontier. "There is still an opportunity to observe the wombs of folk culture," she wrote in a 1939 WPA memo. Traveling through Florida was like backtracking through American history to Europe and Africa. Each continent had brought elements to Florida culture, Hurston noted: Africa by way of Cuba, the British West Indies, Haiti, Martinique, and Central and South America; Old England through black and white mediums; and Old Spain by way of many interpreters.

That was not how many white Floridians viewed their home. The state had already begun to recast its identity as a modern tourist paradise, a tropical resort for the Henry Fords, the Rockefellers, and the Thomas Edisons, and a getaway for the rest of the country. Real estate prices went through the roof in 1925 and seesawed after that.

Stetson Kennedy was born in Jacksonville in 1916 to a white middle-class family. He laughed to recall a tale that captured Florida's nature, which he said he heard from Zora Neale Hurston. "One day God was on his way to Palatka," Kennedy said. "Him and St. Peter was hoofing it, and they were so busy toting up in their heads the latest batch of angels at the pearly gates that they didn't notice the Devil lurking up ahead. But the Devil hid behind a stump and waited till they got up real close. Then the Devil jumped out and hollered, 'Christmas gift!' This was a Southern variation on yelling 'Trick or treat!' So God owed the Devil something. God thought about it for a minute and finally he looked up, said, 'Take the East Coast!' Meaning the east coast of Florida. And that's how come the Florida east coast got so many skeeters and hurricanes and big blows and scorpions and such like. It belongs to the Devil."

During Kennedy's childhood, Jacksonville was a city of about 125,000, the state's largest, spread on the banks of the Saint Johns River about sixteen miles inland from the Atlantic coast. During the booming 1920s, Jacksonville's riverfront sprouted towers and modern buildings; it was a transport hub and a thriving port with the largest timber market and turpentine yard on the Atlantic seaboard and the largest cigar factory in the world. But pine shacks stood not far from the port, and the city had more poor and homeless residents than Florida's tourist destinations farther south.

Power had a heavy tread in north Florida. Kennedy's mother came from an affluent family (the hat-making business for which Stetson was named), and his uncle Gordon was a big man in the politics of northeastern Florida. "The Jacksonville of my youth, especially, was very much a plantation psychology," he said. There and throughout the South, racial segregation was the rule.

On holidays, the family would watch the Klan parade up Main Street. Despite the anonymous hoods, Stetson could tell when his uncle Gordon marched past in the parade "because he wore high-topped leather boots. . . . Instead of holes for the laces, there were hooks. And I knew that was Uncle Gordon going by."

The thinly concealed threat of Jim Crow rules permeated life. "We got it with our mother's milk," said Kennedy, "and the air we breathed."

Kennedy's father came from a farm family and ran a Jacksonville furniture shop that catered to the "dollar down and dollar-a-week" trade, lending credit to poor whites and poor blacks. According to Kennedy, "In that business, the merchant owned the furniture until he got the last dollar." When a buyer couldn't make payments, a merchant didn't need a warrant to repossess an item. He just took it. "Sometimes a stove would be hot," the son recalled.

As a teenager in the early 1930s, Kennedy worked for his father's furniture business and sometimes made collections. When a family didn't have the weekly payment, the mother would say, "If I give you this dollar, my children will go to bed hungry."

"The entire system was flat on its face," he said. "Everybody was out of work, and no one had any money." Kennedy was struck by the ways that people talked and sayings such as "If you ain't got no education, you got to use your brain." He knew that he was "hearing a subculture, or two subcultures really, that had significance and flavor."

At one point later, he would tag along with an older white salesman (of "furniture, clothing, and burial insurance") identified only as Mister Homer, on his rounds in Jacksonville's black neighborhoods. Kennedy wrote down the conversational exchanges as a WPA life history. His account offers a glimpse of the way in which many whites in north Florida spoke and perceived race at that time:

The Negro shacks are dilapidated and unpainted; very few have plumbing, but are equipped with pump and sink on the back porch, and an outhouse. . . .

As we turn a corner Homer suddenly jams on the brakes [of his car]. A gray-haired Negro man is leaning on the fence.

"Well I'll be hanged!" Homer says to him. "I thought you was dead and in hell long ago! And here ya is lookin younger than ever. How many women ya keepin' now, Uncle Henry?"

The old Negro laughs. "Go on, Mister Homer." . . .

"How's Mary? And all them fine grandchildren? Near about growed, I guess?"

"Yes sir, they growed all right. But times is hard with them, like everybody else."

"Well Henry, here's my card. Better not lemme hear of you buyin from nobody but me."

Kennedy asks Mr. Homer about the issue of race directly, and the man gets caught in offensive, stock images even as he seems to acknowledge the hardships faced by African Americans:

"What beats me is why niggers ain't a heap sight worse than they is. They puts up with more than I believe any other race of people could stand. The nigger's cursed. The Bible says so. . . . He's cursed cause he's black—"

"What about the Chinese?" I interrupt. "Are they cursed because they're yellow?"

"Well, no. Yeller is the Chink's natural color. But niggers ain't like other peoples. They got no damn brain! Their heads is too thick. Ya can't hardly kill a nigger by beatin' him in the head. . . ."

[Kennedy asks] "Do you know that psychologists have tried to discover if there are any differences in the intelligences of whites and Negroes, and that they haven't found any that might not be attributable to a difference in cultural factors?"

"That might be true. All I'm a-sayin' is that there is differences— I ain't a-claiming to know what causes 'em."

We stop in front of a rickety and abandoned-looking frame house. Scrawled near the door with a piece of chalk I see: THIS OLD SCHOOL IS 43 YEARS OLD. There are no screens over the windows, and the glass panes are broken. Children of all ages are barely visible in the gloomy one-room interior.

"What are you going to do here?" I ask.

"Try and collect on a oil stove I sold the teacher. She owes for three weeks now. Generally when one of my customers misses two weeks I ties their tail in a knot. But these teachers don't get paid regular. Half the time they works for nothin. I don't never aim ta sell nothing ta no nigger teachers no more."

Kennedy studied natural science at the University of Florida in Gainesville for two years. He published stories in the university magazine and organized protests of the Spanish Civil War. But college life seemed irrelevant amid the seismic changes happening in society ("It looked like the world was going to explode, and the university seemed totally unaware of it"), so he dropped out and hitchhiked down the length of the state to Key West.

There he survived on gingersnaps, soup, and Cuban bread smeared with guava paste. It was his first exposure to Cuban culture, and he was fascinated. Cuban American families, including many skilled cigar workers, had come to Key West for the cigar industry decades earlier. When factories shut down and moved to Tampa to avoid dealing with unions, the Key West economy collapsed. By July 1934, the city treasury was empty. The city council asked the governor to declare a municipal state of emergency and take over local government duties. Most Key West families were on welfare. Yet they were not crushed. "They were really enjoying life in a way that I'd never seen anybody enjoying life," Kennedy later told folklore historian Peggy Bulger. The men played dominos and *bolita*, a gambling game. People valued song, dance, and food.

The homes in Key West shone with a velvetlike patina, Kennedy recalled, silver-gray from the salt air and sun. The sun hit the houses "and turned them all into pastel pinks and yellows and greens and purples. And it was quite a spectacle."

Kennedy took an emergency relief job raking seaweed on the beach. Every high tide, there was another batch of seaweed. "It was very much a job with a future," he said wryly. Other relief jobs on the island employed people to fix up rundown structures and build an aquarium for tourists to visit. In Key West, Kennedy met a young woman named Edith Ogden, whose mother was Cuban and whose father was an Anglo from the Bahamas, or Conch. Kennedy proposed.

"For the wedding Uncle Peter had smuggled in cases of Bacardi rum from Cuba," he said. The open windows were filled with little kids outside watching. They would hold up empty condensed milk cans, shouting, "Rum, rum, rum!" If the wedding party didn't give it to them, they would do a "tin-pan serenade outside the window," beating on cans, boxes, and garbage can lids.

Kennedy wrote down what he saw, just as he had written down the idioms people used along the furniture route in Jacksonville. In Key West, he listened to Anglo Bahamian Conch idioms, Cuban patter, and the Bahamian black speech. "I tried to make an exhaustive list of idioms." Kennedy interviewed Key West dancers, described the songs of marimba bands and street musicians known as *cantantes callejeros*, and documented local legends, beliefs, and rituals, including those of Afro-Cuban *ñañigo* religious groups and Bahamian *obeah*.

Newspapers reported on a government-sponsored project for writers. "The Palm beaches are soon to be combed by a staff of field and research workers," said the *Palm Beach Post*, "for an encyclopedic guide book of the United States." The paper quoted Henry Alsberg, who said that the work would be done mainly by local unemployed people. In the long term, the books would stimulate tourism.

Tourists having refreshments
near Tampa in 1939.

Stetson Kennedy joined the Writers' Project in Florida in December 1937, at age twenty-one. His title was junior editor, his assignment was writing natural history selections for the Florida guide, and his salary was $37.50 every two weeks. After he got the news that he'd been hired, he and his Edith "walked around window-shopping," thinking of all they could buy with that money. "Pork chops were eleven for a dollar," he recalled.

Zora Neale Hurston grew up in Eatonville, outside Orlando. That gave her childhood a rare atmosphere in the South: a predominantly black town with a black mayor, Hurston's father. John Hurston was also a successful carpenter and a preacher whose magnetism and command of language inspired people. Her mother was a lively dreamer who died when Zora was a teenager. Being the youngest, Zora was sent to live with her older brother's family. Soon, though, she left to join a traveling theatrical troupe. She stopped in Baltimore in 1917, staying with her sister Sara. Soon Zora was working and taking night classes, which led her to apply to Morgan College. "The Dean gave me a brief examination and credit for two years in high school," she wrote in her memoir *Dust Tracks on a Road.* "I was three years behind schedule." In fact, she was in her late twenties and ten years behind schedule, but she caught up partly by shaving at least seven years off her true age.

She was captivated by language and the power of stories. Her English teacher in Baltimore, Dwight Holmes, inspired her with his own enthusiasm for literature. His lecture on Coleridge's poem "Xanadu" mesmerized Hurston with a vision of a whole world of storytelling that she could make her own. She wrote one of her first stories on the blackboard of Morgan College, in which her teachers appeared as characters. To write it, she went in early one morning, "and when the bell rang for assembly, the big board was covered with the story."

Hurston went on to attend Howard University in Washington, D.C., supporting herself with jobs as a manicurist, a maid, and a waitress. She then studied in New York at Columbia University with Franz Boas, now considered the father of modern anthropology. As a student of Boas, Hurston returned to Florida and combed it for stories, working her way into communities as diverse as Miami's Bahamian Coconut Grove neighborhood and Tampa's Cuban quarter, Ybor City.

She found that she had the rare ability to connect with people almost instantly. In part, this came from her unique skill in communicating across a range of social frequencies. She could be clowning and joking one minute and the next be analyzing with clarity and precision a point for other academic folklorists, as the accomplished student of Franz Boas. Hurston had mastered many modes of communication because, as an African American woman who was independent of family and of male protection, she had to.

Through her folklore research during the 1920s, she came to know who had stories and where to find them. And to gather them, she ventured into sometimes dangerous jook joints, the nightspots in towns throughout Florida where men drank and women could get jealous. (*Jook* probably came from a West African word meaning "wicked" or "disorderly.") Most of the time, she traveled alone. "There's a picture of her with a gun belt around her waist and the gun in the belt," noted Ruthe Sheffey,

A jook joint in Belle Glade, Florida, in 1941.

a scholar and a professor at Morgan University, "because she felt if she had to use it, she would." Several times Hurston did find herself in danger. She was talking to men in drinking holes, after all, chatting them up to hear their stories, sometimes in front of their girlfriends.

In one instance, she barely escaped with her life. It was in a lumber camp in Loughman, southwest of Eatonville. Hurston was collecting stories and had befriended a powerful woman in the camp named Big Sweet, as well as a storyteller named Slim. Both aided her with the research, Big Sweet helping to open up reluctant informants and offering protection where needed. Slim's former girlfriend showed up at a jook joint after midnight looking for him, saw him talking with Hurston, and immediately made straight for Hurston with an open switchblade in her hand. Before she could use it, Big Sweet tackled the woman, giving Hurston time to flee as the place erupted in fighting. Zora jumped in her Chevy and didn't stop driving until she was miles away.

Hurston had the talent and the determination to plumb the deep reservoir of African American culture for its stories and use them to build magnificent new creations. She reimagined folktales as fiction and plays and became an important figure in the 1920s Harlem Renaissance, a flowering of black culture that was cut short by the Depression.

Hurston found a patron in New York who supported her work, although sporadically. By early 1932, she had returned to Florida, working with Rollins College in Winter Park to produce a concert program of African American performances. She wrote to her patron that she had "little food, no toothpaste, no stockings, . . . no soap." She was soon back in Eatonville, writing folklore essays, stories, and her first novel, *Jonah's Gourd Vine* (1934). It became a Book-of-the-Month Club selection and was followed by *Mules and Men* the next year. Both received strong reviews, but many black reviewers felt that her books omitted bitter truths of the black experience.

She traveled with her musical performances from Florida to Chicago and advised John Lomax when he launched a recording expedition through the South. In October 1935, Hurston joined the Federal Theatre Project's "Negro Unit" in Harlem, coaching productions at a wage less than half of what she'd received from her patron. For the federal theater, she helped Orson Welles and John Houseman prepare the Harlem unit's first production, *Walk Together Chillun!* But Hurston wanted to return to her own work, so by the spring of 1936 she immersed herself in field research in the Caribbean. It was a fruitful time for her. In Haiti, over a period of seven weeks, she wrote her landmark novel *Their Eyes Were Watching God*, which came out in 1937 to strong reviews. Another book, *Tell My Horse*, followed soon afterward. It was a great time for her artistic creation, but not for her finances because the publishing industry was reeling from the Depression. Still, Zora resisted returning to WPA work.

The Florida Project staff in Jacksonville was strictly segregated, with a separate office across town for the handful of workers in the so-called Negro Unit, housed at the Clara White Mission. They played a key role in the folklore division's effort to interview former slaves and conducted hundreds of interviews across the state. Many ex-slaves were interviewed in the Jacksonville area, but staff member Alfred Farrell also sought out many sources in Tallahassee, and Martin Richardson covered Pensacola. Their work turned up some of the most candid exchanges in the Ex-Slave Narratives program and would help yield a wide-ranging assembly of firsthand accounts of slavery. "They have the forthrightness, tang, and tone of people talking," Ben Botkin noted of the Ex-Slave Narratives, with "answers which only they can give, to questions we still ask: What does it mean to be a slave? What does it mean to be free?"

Still, the black Project workers were kept at arm's length; the only contact between the two Jacksonville offices was by courier. The prevailing racism outside the offices permeated the working atmosphere. For Kennedy, it felt like Jim Crow was the editor in chief, "looking over everyone's shoulders, white or black, with an eye as to what we were putting down."

Washington officials, white but suspect outsiders, experienced that same air of surveillance during their visits. During a trip to Jacksonville, Katharine Kellock wrote to Alsberg: "You better send all mail and telegrams to [me at] the Seminole Hotel, since all are opened in mail room and broadcast." Entering the Florida office, Kellock overheard a

A black neighborhood in Jacksonville in 1943.

secretary phoning the state director to say that Kellock had received a telegram from Washington, telling her to stay in Jacksonville until she received an airmail letter. Kellock hadn't yet seen the telegram herself. Everyone was watching her. "I am sure that the whole place will know what is in it before I do." Kellock added, "Tell Kel [her husband] I'm still alive."

So it startled Kennedy one day when the state director, Carita Doggett Corse, called an editorial meeting and announced that the black writer Zora Neale Hurston had signed on to the Writers' Project and would be paying a visit to their office.

"Zora has been feted by literary circles in New York and is given to putting on certain airs," said Corse, "such as smoking in the presence of white folks, so we're going to have to make allowance for Zora."

Zora Neale Hurston in 1935.

"And so Zora came, Zora smoked, and we made allowances," said Kennedy. For a black woman to smoke a cigarette in the presence of whites "bordered on impertinence or disrespect."

For her part, Hurston aimed to ignore the restrictions whenever she could. "Sometimes I feel discriminated against, but it does not make me angry," she wrote. "It merely astonishes me. How can any deny themselves the pleasure of my company? It is beyond me." She kept her focus on the individual. Hurston sums up her view in *Dust Tracks on a Road*:

Races have never done anything. . . . [A]chievement is the work of individuals. The white race did not go into a laboratory and invent incandescent light. That was Edison. The Jews did not work out Relativity. That was Einstein. The Negroes did not find out the inner secrets of peanuts and sweet potatoes. . . . That was Carver. . . . If you are under the impression that every white man is an Edison, just look around a bit.

This focus on the individual's freedom ironically put Hurston at odds with Richard Wright, whose articles lambasted Hurston and other Harlem Renaissance writers for not taking up the cause of social realism and justice in their writing. Hurston objected to a singular focus on injustice at the expense of other aspects of black life. She found Wright's book *Uncle Tom's Children* one-sided in its lack of sympathy and argued that black writers should feel free to write about the same wide range of topics and emotions as white writers.

In that debate, Stetson Kennedy sided with Wright. In August 1938, Kennedy wrote a letter to Wright congratulating him for his "leadership

in directing the writing of Federal Writers into socially conscious channels." Kennedy had read Wright's essay "Blueprint for Negro Writing" in
New Challenge and found it inspiring, having witnessed the oppression
that Wright described from the other side. Wright showed him that
the threat that hung over Jacksonville could be expressed, and that the
harder aspects of Florida life could have a place in the WPA guide.

"We were taking seriously the congressional mandate of holding up a
mirror to America, warts and all," recalled Kennedy, and this included
Jim Crow, lynchings, poverty, and illness. Others on staff argued that
the Florida guide should be a more conventional travel book, "to attract
tourists, and show what a beautiful place Florida was, meaning bathing
beauties and coconut palms and so forth . . . the moonlight and magno-
lia approach. . . . And so we had our work cut out for us."

The WPA writers combed the state, taking notes on everything about
Florida life, from the prison system's failings to horse racing. They
describe jai alai as an "exciting sport, brought from Cuba" ("faster than
tennis and more dangerous than football"), played on a paved court
known as a fronton, with the highest stakes in the Miami area. After
stating Florida's claim as the birthplace of softball and the home to major
league spring-training camps, the guide researchers note that blacks had
little share of the state's sporting industry, although they made up nearly
a third of the population.

Hurston joined the Florida Writers' Project in April 1938 with an
assignment to write for the state guide and revise the draft of *The Florida
Negro*, one in a series of books on black life. Although she had published
two books, more than any other staff member, she was given the title of
junior interviewer with a lower salary of $32.50 every two weeks. Com-
pounding that insult, she felt stifled by her supervisors. Folklore research
and interviews were her expertise, and she knew how to do them better
than the others did.

Hurston's visits to the state headquarters were rare, both because
Jacksonville was unwelcoming to blacks and because she didn't relish the
WPA atmosphere. Like Cheever, she was embarrassed by WPA relief.
Hurston would tell her niece in Eatonville that she was headed to see her
publisher in New York, when in fact she was going to the Project office

in Jacksonville. But the trips brought some personal changes. On June 27, 1939, Hurston married Albert Price, a WPA playground worker fifteen years her junior whom she'd met in Jacksonville. They were married in a small ceremony in the nearby fishing village of Fernandina. Theirs was a stormy relationship, and at several points she threatened Price with voodoo "spells" she had learned in New Orleans.

Kennedy, working in Jacksonville at the state office, always watched for the manila envelopes from Eatonville. "The mark of Zora," Kennedy called the Eatonville postmark; it signaled packages "stuffed with the most fabulous folk treasure imaginable."

Some material she sent for the Florida guide was straight reportage on her part of the state, verdant and harsh: "Around Lake Okeechobee, from December to April tomatoes, green beans, peppers and other winter vegetables are harvested, packed and shipped, for the most part by Negro labor. A municipal ordinance requires that all Negroes be off the streets by 10:30 pm." In Ocoee, west of Orlando, Hurston uncovered a history of murderous harassment:

> On election day 1920, a race riot broke out at Ocoee, following a disturbance at the polls. . . . The conflict arose when Mose Norman, prosperous grove owner and the town's most prominent Negro, ignored the threats of the local Ku Klux Klan and cast his ballot. . . . [When Norman took refuge at the home of a friend, July Perry,] Perry was . . . locked up in the Orlando jail. At sunrise the jail was stormed; Perry was . . . tied to the back of an automobile and finally hanged from a telephone pole. . . . Mobs surrounded the Negro section of town and fired it. . . . Some 35 Negroes perished. The conflict spread to Orlando, Apopka, and Winter Garden.

Hurston's base in Eatonville was a house known as Tuxedo Junction, which she chose for its solitude and beauty. As Pamela Bordelon noted in Hurston's *Go Gator and Muddy the Water!* the house overlooked a lakeshore with massive oaks and Spanish moss. There, Hurston sorted her field notes and typed up her manuscripts, often seated at a card table out under the trees. Many of her accounts made their way into the

Florida guide. In a gesture that was unusual for a Project publication, which typically followed a strict policy of anonymous authorship, the Florida guide names Hurston in the Eatonville entry and quotes from her work: "Eatonville is the birthplace and home of Zora Neale Hurston, and the locale of her novel *Their Eyes Were Watching God.*" Then it offers Eatonville "in her eyes":

> Maitland is Maitland until it gets to Hurst's corner, and then it is Eatonville. Right in front of Willie Sewell's yellow-painted house the hard road quits being the hard road for a generous mile and becomes the heart of Eatonville. Or from a stranger's point of view, you could say that the road just bursts through on its way from US 17 to US 441, scattering Eatonville right and left.
>
> On the right, after you leave the Sewell place, you don't meet a thing that people live in until you come to the Green Lantern on the main corner. That corner has always been the main corner, because that is where Joe Clarke, the founder and first mayor of Eatonville, built his store. . . . People have gotten used to gathering there and talking. Only Joe Clarke sold groceries and general merchandise, while Lee Glenn sells drinks of all kinds and whatever else goes with transient rooms. . . . After the shop you come to the Widow Dash's orange grove, her screened porch, "double hips," and her new husband. . . . West of it all, the sun makes his nest in some lonesome lake in the woods, and gets his night's rest.

In stark contrast with that idyll was the entry for another African American town nearby that had fared quite differently from Eatonville: West Sanford had been incorporated as Goldsborough, an African American town, in 1891. As the nearby white town of Sanford sought to expand westward, Goldsborough's legal status blocked the way, so an Orange County state senator got the state legislature to revoke both towns' charters long enough for Sanford to maneuver Goldsborough into its charter. "Thus ended the existence of the second incorporated Negro town in Florida," Hurston wrote for the guide.

Against that background of vanished towns and stolen sovereignty, Hurston's folkloric descriptions of towns such as West Hell and Diddy-Wah-Diddy are especially poignant. "Negroes have their mythical cities and countries which are discussed and referred to in everyday conversation," notes the guide. "Diddy-Wah-Diddy, the largest and best known, is a place of no work and no worry for man or beast. The road to it is so crooked that a mule pulling a load of fodder can eat off the back of the wagon as he plods along."

West Hell, another mythical town described on Tour 7, had a markedly different atmosphere, yet it shared a vital element of self-determination:

> West Hell, said to be the hottest and toughest part of that notorious resort, was once the home of Big John de Conqueror, who eloped with the Devil's daughter. The pair fled on her father's favorite steeds, Hallowed-Be-Thy-Name and Thy-Kingdom-Come. The Devil pursued them on his famous jumping bull, and when they met, Big John tore off one of the Devil's arms and almost beat him to death with it. Before Big John left Hell, he passed out ice water to everybody, and even turned down the dampers, remarking that he expected to return to visit his wife's folks pretty soon, and he didn't like the house kept so hot.

Besides her dispatches for the Florida guide, Hurston also worked extensively on the manuscript of *The Florida Negro*, including a chapter titled "The Sanctified Church," which is perhaps the best known of her writings for the Project. Ultimately, the WPA didn't publish *The Florida Negro*. It eventually appeared in 1993 without her contributions; her essays for it appear in the collection of her WPA work titled *Go Gator and Muddy the Water!*

In the summer of 1939, the Florida guide moved toward completion, and the air of suspicion and curiosity intensified. The pressures increased, not only within the Project but from communities across the state. The Tampa police department contacted Washington with concerns about material on the black section of their city. Within the office, editorial maneuvering came down to sleight of hand, according to

Kennedy, who said that after the final manuscript had been wrapped up for mailing to Washington, hidden forces on staff had untaped the package, removed incendiary material from the manuscript, and sent off the censored version. Whatever the case, the state guides often brought to a head local tensions about how communities saw themselves and how they wanted other Americans to see them.

With the guidebook finished, the Florida Writers' Project began to wind down. In late July, Kennedy, who had wanted to pursue the folklore interviews, sent a letter to Botkin, in which he noted it is "with deep regret that I learned that lack of sufficient travel funds was to prevent my cooperating with the Folklore Recording Expedition. . . . This letter to you is probably my final effort."

Kennedy evidently had a friendly spy among Corse's secretaries, for he received notice in the margin of a file copy that Herbert Halpert was leading a recording tour through the South and was then staying in the care of Lyle Saxon in New Orleans. The secretary informed Kennedy that the tour would spend twelve to fifteen days in Florida. The state director had nixed Kennedy's request to join the team in Ybor City, the secretary wrote, but there was a chance he could help record in Key West.

That summer Hurston received a rare acknowledgment of her folklore accomplishments from academia. Her alma mater in Baltimore, now called Morgan College, invited her to receive an honorary doctorate as part of its commencement activities. Her old professor Dwight Holmes, now the president of the college, had arranged the honor. Hurston was touched by his gesture, but as often happened when it came to someone else's schedule, she skipped the ceremony.

Hurston still hoped to pull something of her own design out of the Writers' Project. In a May 1939 memo to Ben Botkin, she had made the case for a recording tour and mapped a route through Florida's cultures, from the panhandle to the Gulf Coast and down to South Florida. It was an eloquent proposal, evoking Florida as a frontier still rich with cultural history that demanded to be tapped. But there was little reaction from Washington. That August, just as she was about to leave the Project, Herbert Halpert arrived in Florida with the recording machine on loan from the Library of Congress.

The machine represented the latest technology for capturing people's songs and stories. It resembled a heavy phonograph and used a sapphire needle to carve sounds into a spinning acetate disk. John Lomax had procured it a few years earlier for a recording tour with his son Alan, and they had carted it to where people lived and worked—in fields, homes, churches, and prisons. Such recording tours could raise suspicions among locals in the South. Once in Mississippi, Lomax was detained at police headquarters before they would let him record field hands. When he brought the recordings of prison songs sung by inmates to Washington, D.C., and replayed them in the marble halls of the Library of Congress, he told colleagues, the voices sounded liberated.

Hurston launched the Florida recording tour in Jacksonville at the Clara White Mission, a soup kitchen for African Americans that was named for the mother of the director, Eartha White. Hurston tapped a number of her folklore sources to sing: dockworkers calling out their work chants, a gospel choir, and Eartha White herself. Hurston acted as something of a conductor, Pamela Bordelon noted, directing the musicians and singing more than a dozen songs herself. The recordings of her exchanges with Halpert reveal his somewhat patronizing tone and her quicksilver mind, able to reply in depth to any question. The mission recordings also show how deeply Floridians held their culture. When Halpert asks one singer, Annie Whittaker, where the next song comes from, she replies, "It just come to me and I sung it out of my heart."

At the Clara White Mission, Hurston herself sang the bawdy song of Uncle Bud and his sexual escapades. For an artist with her ear, the song's flair and style were irresistible. Other stories and songs commemorate real, often tragic, events: hurricanes, shipwrecks, lost children, lynchings, and more. Songs memorialize two especially "big blows": the Miami Hurricane of 1926 and the "West Palm Beach Storm" of 1928. The first provides the backdrop for *Their Eyes Were Watching God*, and Hurston describes the storm in the guide: "Blowed so hard, blowed a well up out of the ground, blowed a crooked road straight, and scattered the days of the week so bad Sunday didn't get around 'til late Tuesday morning."

The WPA researchers played back a recording to the group at the mission, and it had a galvanizing effect. Eartha White asked for a moment of prayer. "Dear Lord, this is Eartha White talking to you again," Kennedy recalled her saying. "I just want to thank you for giving mankind the intelligence to make such a marvelous machine, and a President like Franklin D. Roosevelt, who cares about preserving the songs people sing."

From Jacksonville, the recording team set across the state toward the Gulf Coast, where Hurston had long mined working-camp communities for folktales and mythic characters, ranging from Daddy Mention and Uncle Monday to Big John de Conqueror and Kerosene Charlie. Segregation laws forbade whites and blacks to travel together, so Hurston went ahead as a location scout. The recording team, with Halpert and Kennedy, followed along to camp near Cross City. Hurston drove her Chevy down a dirt road and entered a pine plantation where turpentine was made.

Turpentine was a vestige of Florida's old economy, described in the WPA guide as "naval stores," which dated back to the 1500s when sailors used the "gummy substances" from scarring and chipping pine trees to caulk their ships' hulls. English admiral Sir John Hawkins had seen Florida as a great potential source of naval stores, and it had been one ever since. In 1938, the state was America's number-two producer of turpentine and supplied 20 percent of the world's production, most of it in the hands of large corporations. Observes the guide:

> Although the importance of rosin and turpentine in the maritime trade has greatly diminished, they are still known as naval stores. Actual field work is conducted by individual operators, each connected with an agent. The operator advances cash to his white and Negro workers throughout the season, deducting these loans at the end of the year. A representative turpentine camp comprises a fire still, spirit shed and glue pot, rosin yard, blacksmith and cooperage shed, cup-cleaning vat, barn and wagon shed, and living quarters for the manager and workers.

A turpentine worker, 1938.

Cross City was a rough patchwork of hardwood and pine trees, sometimes peaceful with cattle grazing knee-deep in shaded grassy ponds and herons feeding nearby.

"It was like entering a foreign country," said Kennedy. "You had to get almost a passport to get into a turpentine camp." Owners were reluctant for outsiders to see the old system of peonage, which referred to forced labor in payment of a debt. Families in the camps had no choice but to buy groceries and other supplies from their employers, usually on credit against future wages, which meant that their debt continued to mount and became nearly impossible to pay off.

Hurston arrived early to conduct advance interviews. She made notes of their work on turpentine, their entertainments, and their personal lives. One woman told Zora about a supervisor who beat the workers and said that some workers had been killed. Zora was shaken and wrote only a few pages of notes. When the recording team arrived at the

Aycock and Lindsay Turpentine plantation, she told one of the crew that the situation in the camp was terrible.

Simply recording American songs and stories put the WPA workers at risk of having confrontations with the white woodsrider, or company boss. Most Americans, then as now, didn't consider their country a place where forced labor existed. But it did. Kennedy recalled one turpentine worker named Cull Stacey, who, when asked why he didn't simply leave, replied, "If you tries to leave, they'll kill you." (The practice is unfortunately not a relic of the distant past. In July 2005, journalists confirmed that "modern-day slave farms" still existed in Florida, luring homeless recruits from soup kitchens and shelters, including the Clara White Mission, with promises of hot meals, good pay, and drugs.)

The WPA team set up the machine and recorded one worker, James Griffin, as he told the story behind his song "Worked All Summer Long." He had been jailed for ninety days at hard labor in the Dixie County Prison Camp to repay three months' rent to the lumber company, a total of $50. The song came to him while he was in jail. "I started singing it and thought it would be my theme song," Griffin said. He and the other inmates would take it up in the cool of the evening. "We'd be singing," he said. "It helps." Then he sang for the recording:

Oh my dear mother,
She prayed this prayer for me;
My dear mother,
She prayed this prayer for me.
She said, "Lord, have mercy on my son,
Wheresoever he may be."

On leaving the camp, Hurston informed the plantation's owner of the abuses, a move that itself carried risk. But she did not press further. She wrote up part of her visit, a ride through the woods with a black woodsrider, as a life history titled simply "Turpentine."

"Turpentine woods is kind of lonesome," the woodsrider told her.

Hurston left the Florida Project soon after the recording tour, and by September 1939, she was teaching at a college in North Carolina. But she would return again and again to the Florida stories from her WPA work, and the haunting tales from the turpentine camps seeped into her play *Polk County* and her novel *Seraph on the Suwanee*. She rarely wrote of her own response to the turpentiners' hardships but let them speak for themselves.

Kennedy continued to record farther south, interviewing Cuban relatives in Ybor City, the community where his wife, Edith, grew up. Ybor City was Tampa's Latin quarter, with clubs, restaurants, theaters, Spanish newspapers, and its own chamber of commerce. At that time, it was a self-contained enclave where stores posted signs to help outsiders: ENGLISH SPOKEN HERE. Rice and beans, steak catalana and garbanzo soups, and wines were the local cuisine. Clubs such as Centro Espanol and Circulo Cubano were landmarks. At the cigar factories, *tabaqueros* worked in double rows seated at long tables. Readers (*lectors*) entertained them by reciting from news and books, such as *Gallito el Torero*,

Robert Cook (left) and Stetson Kennedy record Edith Kennedy in Ybor City, 1939.

a novel about a bootblack who becomes a bullfighter. The *lector* role was terminated after a number of them began to read radical protest literature.

Kennedy had already interviewed several people in the cigar industry. "I'm surrounded by friends here," one cigar maker told him. "Even the paving stones in all Ybor City know me."

"I work in a cigar box factory," another man told Kennedy. "We make forty thousand boxes a day. I kinda hate to start work because I know I'll have to keep on working steady until this time next year. We work steady all the time." Then he gave Kennedy advice on his interview technique: "I tell you something: if you tell everybody you is a Federal Writer, that makes them think you is a police or something and they won't talk to you. If you just say you are a WPA relief writer, they will talk to you much better."

Returning later in August 1939 with the recording machine, Kennedy scheduled several musicians and also recorded his wife singing "Pipi Sigallo," a Cuban game song from her childhood. Farther on, they recorded in the small Conch fishing village of Riviera outside West Palm Beach, where WPA writer Veronica Huss had interviewed Izzelly Haines, a midwife of Bahamian and English background:

> I was born in the Bahamas and I'm still belonging to that country. We never got papers here, 'cause we never needed them. . . . I been a midwife ever since I was seventeen. . . . [M]y first case was sure pitiful. If I hadn't taken it the little mother woulda died. . . . This woman had given birth at about six o'clock in the morning and by four o'clock that afternoon the afterbirth hadn't come and she was dying from the poison that sets in. There warn't a soul around that could do nothing about it, so remembering what I could, I took two pounds of onions and pulverized them; then soaked it in a pint of gin. Then I took it all and put it in two cloth bags. One bag I put to the lower part of the woman's stomach and the other to her back. Inside of a half hour it had come and she was getting along fine. I learned a lot of things down there in the Bahamas and I tended a lot of cases.

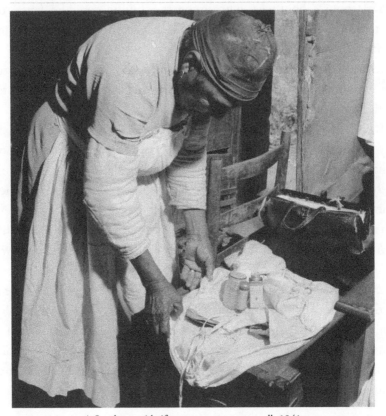

A Southern midwife prepares to go on a call, 1941.

Kennedy and coworker Robert Cook continued south past Florida City, where the highway ran straight across a yellow-green savannah, and the Card Sound Bridge crossed from the mainland to the first of the keys, Key Largo. Down at the end of the string of islands—past Plantation Key, Upper Matecumbe Key, Teatable Key, Indian Key, Lignum Vitae Key, Lower Matacumbe Key, Crawl Keys, Key Vaca, Bahia Honda Key, Big Pine Key, Little Torch Key, Sugarloaf Key, and Boca Chica Key—lay Key West.

One hundred miles off the mainland, Key West was crammed with docks where dories, launches, and "sturdy smacks" tied up alongside ocean liners and battle cruisers. Duval Street, the main thoroughfare, carved a line across the island. The town followed a tropical daily rhythm of closing during the hottest hours, with the iceman's bell announcing his delivery cart. As the guide notes, most restaurants were Cuban style, and coffee shops served small cups of "black, sweetened coffee and buttered, hard-crusted bread that comes from the oven in two-foot loaves."

In January 1940, the recording team spent three days capturing Bahamian and Cuban musicians singing traditional songs and their own songs, eighteen disks in all, from "Hoist Up the John B Sail" and "Bingo" to "Boil Them Cabbage Down" and "Bonefish."

Throughout Florida, the WPA recordings and interviews had continued to uncover vital and tragic sides of Kennedy's home state, as in a story his brother-in-law told of a Klan murder in Key West. Norberto Diaz, a Key Wester and Edith's half brother, told the tale of Isleño, a man from the Canary Islands whose name meant *islander*. He had become an American citizen and had fought in World War I. "Isleño was a good friend to everybody," Diaz said. Diaz thought of Isleño every time he passed the palm where the Klan had lynched him. When Isleño began to live with a mulatto woman, the Klan issued a threat: Stop or suffer the consequences. "But Isleño wasn't afraid of nobody," said Diaz. "He was strong as an ox." On Christmas Eve, about twenty Klan members marched down Duval Street in hoods, carrying guns and torches. They dragged Isleño down the steps from his second-story apartment, his head cracking on the metal stairs all the way down. "He put up an awful fight," Diaz said.

Duval Street, Key West, in 1938.

Kennedy considered the telling of such stories important, not maca-bre. "I think the human race has much blood on its hands," Kennedy said, and yet much of the violence could be prevented if it were exposed. "So therefore, keep writing about it."

In Key West, Kennedy had drafted notes about the Ernest Hemingway house for the WPA guide. Hemingway's 1937 novel *To Have and Have Not*, about rumrunners in the islands, drew on stories of Captain Antonio, whom Kennedy interviewed in 1938. "Hemingway's all right," Antonio said in the WPA life history. "Every now and then he comes around and drinks and cusses with us. But he put a lot of bunk in that book. All that stuff about monks, you know, Chinks. There were some Chinks smuggled, but they were handled out of Havana and landed up the Keys, never at Key West. Most of the people smuggled were Cubans, Spaniards, Mexicans, some Slovaks." The sailor went on to describe his scrapes with customs agents, pelicans, and a character named Cockeye Billy.

A Key West fisherman, 1938.

It's worth considering how Captain Antonio's tale intersects with that of Louis F., the Polish-born fishmonger whom Hilda Polacheck interviewed the same summer that Hurston and Kennedy hauled the recording machine across Florida. Louis spent a hellish night in a small boat that could well have been Antonio's. Louis had told Polacheck about his long journey from Poland to America by way of Cuba:

Now, in Cuba, the excitement started, I found a boarding house where I shared a room with two fellers. I wanted to get to Chicago, where I had three brothers and many uncles and aunts. The only way that I could go to Chicago was to be smuggled into America. After six weeks, I met a feller who said he would take me to America for $150.00. I had enough money to pay this, so I told him: all right.

One very hot night in March, this feller who said he could take me to America, came to the boarding house and told me to get ready. He said I could not take anything. Not even a drink of water. Well, I did not want to stay in Cuba, so I went with him. He told me to walk a few steps behind him, and not to talk. He said he must get some more fellers who wanted to go to America. If I saw him go into a house, I should follow. I do as he say. . . . And soon thirteen fellers was following him. We came to the yam [ocean]. It was a very dark night. But the feller who had the boat must have cat's eyes. He took our hands, one at a time, and put us in a small boat. Maybe there was place for four men, and he put thirteen in and he was fourteen. We lay in the boat like herring in a barrel. Because we had no water, we all got thirsty. It was very hot and the heat from our bodies made it hotter. We were not allowed to talk. We were not allowed to take off our clothes. There was no room to move even an inch. The only sound was the noise from the engine of the small boat. We travelled like this all night. The next day, we travelled all day. The sun made it hotter. The feller who was taking us went the longest way, so we did not meet any boats. That day was the worst day I ever spent in my life. . . . About nine o'clock in the evening, we got to Key West, Florida. The man pulled us out of the boat. We were more dead than alive. . . . Well, the next day we took a train for Jacksonville, Florida. We waited there six hours and then we took the train for Chicago.

Twelve of the state guides were published in 1939, and the folklore anthologies were coming together, following *These Are Our Lives,* a collection of oral histories that appeared early that year to warm reviews. But opposition to the WPA was gathering force, too. Even as Hurston was interviewing the turpentine workers in Cross City, Congressman Martin Dies planned a series of trips as part of his investigation on un-American activities. Federal funds for the arts projects had already been slashed, but their influence—and the potential infiltration of American institutions by foreign powers—remained a threat. That fall of 1939, Dies was more popular than ever and was taking his case to the American people.

10

AMERICAN AND UN-AMERICAN: BACK AROUND THE BOROUGHS

Millions of gullible Americans have been hoodwinked into joining
or working for the fifth columns of propaganda, ... [which] may
be more menacing to our national security than espionage. ...
Both constitute un-American and subversive activities.

—MARTIN DIES, *TROJAN HORSE IN AMERICA* (1940)

IN THE FALL OF 1939, ZORA NEALE HURSTON
visited New York for the publication of *Moses, Man
of the Mountain,* the novel she had finished while she
was in Eatonville working on the Florida Project.
She had gotten married just a few months earlier,
but what she wanted to discuss with her close friend,
the photographer Carl Van Vechten, was her concern over her book. Hurston took to heart several
criticisms in the otherwise positive reviews. The *New York Times* said
that "the stately Old Testament story comes handsomely to life again in
her pages," but that Hurston's "touch is not consistently sure" and "her
humor is not always the lightest."

"I fell far short of my ideal in the writing," she told Vechten. Later critics would be more generous, calling *Moses* one of Hurston's greatest accomplishments in fiction. A combination of fiction and folklore, the novel reinvented the Moses story with American blacks as the Israelites and Moses as a voodoo chief. It grew out of Hurston's work and life in the 1930s. Although she and Wright approached the black experience from very different viewpoints, they both saw it as an important lens for viewing the modern world. The force of their vision moved black culture from the margin, where blacks had always been portrayed, to a more central place.

Other WPA writers were helping to shift readers away from a single, conventional vantage point for viewing history. Vardis Fisher's novel *Children of God*, which came out the same month as *Moses*, put Mormon history on an epic footing as a saga of the West, warts and all.

John Cheever had returned to New York from the Project's Washington headquarters in the fall of 1938 to help finish the *WPA Guide to New York City*, but he mainly had come back out of a personal hunger to live in Manhattan and pursue his writing career. At twenty-six, Cheever viewed the Writers' Project as merely the latest in a series of odd jobs he'd held over the previous four years while submitting his short fiction to literary magazines. His friend and editor Malcolm Cowley got him started by placing his story "Brooklyn Rooming House" in the *New Yorker*, and a few other key publications followed. According to Cowley, Cheever was never politically opinionated; "by instinct he was a storyteller." Yet they both had belonged to the leftist John Reed Club for a while, and Cheever pursued his political education by reading Russian authors. He observed life on the streets from his cheap fourth-floor West Village apartment on Hudson Street, where his meals consisted of "stale bread, buttermilk, and raisins. Sometimes we got food from the government, usually free rice and canned fish."

Most of Cheever's neighbors were unemployed dockworkers, so his affected accent, gray flannel suit, and button-down shirts made him "a curiosity." His neighbors thought that he should be in the government. And in a way, he was.

John Cheever (center) at Yaddo artists' colony in 1934.

Cowley also got Cheever an assistant position at Yaddo, the artists' colony, and Cheever kept up a bantering exchange of letters with Elizabeth Ames, Yaddo's director. When she advised him to explore other jobs besides writing, he bristled. "I have thought about it continually," he responded. "The problem is not, I think, the evasion of occupation . . . but the inability to find occupation. . . . It is not a problem peculiar to writers but the problem of an entire generation of younger men. From the time when I took a job as a stock-boy in an abandoned subway tube when I was about fifteen, I have almost always worked. I have held the average run of jobs, driving a truck, working on a small newspaper, etc. But about two years ago the possibility of holding these jobs stopped. I have no trade, no degree, no special training."

This passage echoes a rabble-rousing speech by a Marxist organizer in an early Cheever story, "In Passing," who exhorts "the young men in your generation" who "had the good fortune to miss the boom period and all of that harmful, inflated ambition" and who had known only poverty and the fact that "[you] will never have money in this rotten world and that you will never have power." The rabble-rouser invokes "twenty million men of your age, cooling their heels right now." Cheever was tracking social movements like many writers in those times, but he also carefully steered his own course. When he could, he helped fellow writers, too. In time, he would put up Nebraskan Weldon Kees for a while in his cramped Village apartment and get Kees a spot at Yaddo for a summer.

Cheever closely watched the people around him and how they handled life's trials and irritations. When he stayed at Yaddo near Saratoga, Cheever hung out at the racetrack, watching the swells. Yet others he tracked were not the suburbanites of his later stories, but the waitresses, hoods, and hobos of his boardinghouse on the Lower West Side. An entry in his journal from one April day reads,

> The two tired waitresses in Childs at about half-past eight, one of them eating, mimicking an old, crotchety customer, the other telling her to go to hell. The two hoodlums in the park, running through the crowd shrieking: smell da refreshing air. Halcyon, halkyon, which is it. It means a day without any wind. A beautiful day. Like a day after a storm. No wind. At twilight. That's what Halcyon means. This from a bum on an abandoned pier near Bethune Street, explaining the name of a tug boat.

This range of humanity would inhabit the Manhattan essay that Cheever drafted for the *WPA Guide to New York City*. The opening scene on a ferry is cinematic, starting with an aerial approach over the water. "The liner steams through the Narrows," it begins. After describing the throng on the ferry, the perspective shifts to a train crossing the Meadowlands, bringing to New York "a sightseeing family (there are 115,000 of them daily—from Waco, Mobile, Los Angeles, Kansas City), the literary genius of Aurora High School, the prettiest actress in the Burlington dramatic club, a farm boy hoping to start for Wall Street, and a mechanic with an idea." Then, in the verbal equivalent of a low-angle camera shot, Cheever establishes downtown Manhattan, from the footsteps of night workers returning home and the wheels of a water wagon to the dawn light appearing in a midtown alley, the faint ringing of alarm clocks in the apartments of the morning workers, and a May Day parade "sixty thousand strong," both festive and ominous with its "tramp, tramp of regimented feet," slogans, and banners.

In the spring of 1939, Cheever logged many hours getting the New York guide into shape. (Vincent McHugh had left by then.) Cheever stayed late in the office evenings and worked weekends during the final stages of production, but he felt alienated by the radical politics of so much of the staff and the red-baiting in the newspapers. By the time the guide was published in late June, he had had enough.

The week the guide came out, English novelist Sylvia Townsend Warner gave an interview at the Project's Lower West Side headquarters, where she said that the Writers' Project was "the most exciting experiment that has ever been carried out." The *Times* called the WPA guide "a dictionary to the city," with an enjoyable range of history and contemporary stories, and said that it "should find a place in every New York household."

"It's not your ordinary guidebook," Michael Chabon has said of the WPA guide, although, he added, it can serve perfectly well as a walking guide. While he researched *The Amazing Adventures of Kavalier and Clay*, Chabon spent months wandering the streets and the subways with the WPA guide. He imagined the effect that the WPA work had on the younger writers: "It must have been a real apprenticeship for them, a kind of excuse to think about the city in ways that, certainly for Cheever and Ellison, obviously must have helped."

Reading the guide, Chabon got the sense that the gibes about lazy WPA workers may have produced a defensive counterreaction, the feeling that this was in fact a project of substance: "I have a sort of collective sense of these writers combing the city, every corner from Inwood to Staten Island, all the way out to New Lots—and that it's all being done, maybe partly as a *result* of the fact that in some weird way it was a make-work project.

"To maintain that spirit in the face of the things that they were facing in that period—granted, in 1939 things are beginning to look better, but still—to me, that's the mystery of the time, and the thing that speaks to me now the most."

For Chabon, the guide has "the democratic, all-encompassing impulse that people have been using to look at New York City at least since the time of Walt Whitman." Overall, the New York guide presents a tone of almost neutral judgment, like an observer who casts a wide look over the city at a time of extreme inequalities and doesn't make distinctions between high and low.

Cheever's fingerprints may also be found in the guide's section on Coney Island. "It just reads like him," said Chabon. The evocation of a day at Coney Island starts with the morning stillness and goes through the day, tracing people coming and going, and ending "on this sweet, kind of elegiac paragraph that is straight out of Cheever":

> Summer crowds are the essence of Coney Island. From early morning, when the first throngs pour from the Stillwell Avenue subway terminal, humanity flows over Coney Island seeking relief from the heat of the city. Italians, Jews, Greeks, Poles, Germans, Negroes, Irish, people of every nationality; boys and girls, feeble ancients, mothers with squirming children, fathers with bundles, push and collide as they rush, laughing, scolding, sweating, for a spot on the sand. . . . From the boardwalk the whole beach may be viewed: bathers splash and shout in the turgid waters close to shore; on the sand, children dig, young men engage in gymnastics and roughhouse each other, or toss balls over the backs of couples lying amorously intertwined. . . . The air is heavy with mixed odors of frying frankfurters, popcorn, ice cream, cotton candy, corn-on-the-cob, and *knishes*. . . . After sunset the Island becomes the playground of a mixed crowd of sightseers and strollers. . . . Riders are whirled, jolted, battered, tossed upside down by the Cyclone, the Thunderbolt, the Mile Sky Chaser. . . . In dance halls and honky-tonks, dancers romp and shuffle to the endless blare of jazz bands. About midnight, the weary crowds begin to depart, leaving a litter of cigarette butts, torn newspapers, orange and banana peel, old shoes and hats . . . and an occasional corset. A few couples remain behind, with here and there a solitary drunk, or a sleepless old man pacing the boardwalk. The last concessionaire counts his receipts and puts up his shutters, and only the amiable roar of the forgotten sea is heard.

A scene at Coney Island, 1941.

Cheever provides a comparable time-lapse view of the Lower West Side in an early short story, "Bayonne." It starts at a lunch cart in the market, the sidewalk outside crammed with produce, the aromas from the chicken market a block away, and the Ninth Avenue el roaring overhead.

In Queens, the 1939 World's Fair was taking shape. To present a beacon of modernity and a hopeful sign that the country was throwing off the Depression, the fair presented itself as the "City of the Future." The WPA guide describes the fair with a gimlet eye as something less than its ideal, based more on the "prospect of converting into a magnificent park a thousand acres of malodorous eyesore," and a chance to make money, the way Chicago had with the 1934 fair.

The red-baiting was intensifying. Earlier in the year, Congress had tarred the Project broadly with the brush of communism and managed to get FDR to slash the budgets of the arts projects under the WPA. By the fall of 1939, Congressman Martin Dies was stirring crowds at events in Madison Square Garden and the Brooklyn Academy of Music, claiming to possess a list of hundreds of Communists on the government payroll and pledging to expose people in high positions who had ties to the Communist Party.

Dies appeared at the Brooklyn Academy of Music in Fort Greene for a gathering of a veterans' association that filled the Italianate theater with three thousand people, to kick off a county-wide drive against Communism, fascism, Nazism, and other foreign influences. In his book, *Trojan Horse in America*, Dies rebuffed charges of extremism against his committee and defined his ideal of Americanism as "recognition of the fact that the inherent and fundamental rights of man are derived from God and not from governments, societies, dictators, kings, or majorities." In this way, Dies tried to align American values and equate class struggle with racism. He declared, "It is as un-American to hate one's neighbor because he has more of this world's goods as it is to hate him because he was born into another race or travels a different road to heaven."

Alongside Dies on the stage were the borough president of Queens and military officers and religious leaders, several of whom voiced support for a Dies presidential candidacy, according to the *New York Times*.

"This is one of the most critical periods in the world's history," Dies intoned, warning against saboteurs. "These groups are laying their groundwork now, making themselves solid, so that they will be in a position to strike and strike hard in case of war."

There were real perils overseas. Nazi Germany was marching into Czechoslovakia, and the Japanese invasion of China continued. Americans were on tenterhooks, to the point where Orson Welles's radio thriller *War of the Worlds* caused a public panic about aliens invading from outer space. Dies exploited this fear. Other congressmen objected to the lack of balance in the House Un-American Committee (HUAC) proceedings, including John Coffee from Washington. As reported in the *People's Herald*, he decried the committee's failure to pursue part of its mandate: the study of homegrown fascist and Nazi groups. "We have Silver Shirts, German-American Bunds, Ku Klux Klan, Christian Party, anti-Semitic organizations flourishing in this broad land," he said, "but the committee paid scant attention to their nefarious activities." Congressman Vito Marcantonio from New York complained that Dies had made no effort to go after the Klan.

Some members of the press challenged HUAC's leader as well. Columnist Walter Winchell charged that communists cherished America's democratic principles more than Dies did. In a defiant response to the congressman's fearmongering, Winchell declared in the *Daily Mirror*, "Communism is twentieth-century Americanism." The *Washington Star* deplored the hysterical atmosphere of the HUAC hearings, in which "members shout insults at each other or at witnesses" and where police had recently restrained one HUAC member "from assaulting a witness with his fists." The *Star* linked the rise of fascism in Europe to Dies's growing popularity:

> The Dies Committee came into being not long after Hitler's occupation of Austria. Its hearings were punctuated by the Anglo-French surrender at Munich, the annexation of Sudetenland and the overthrow of Czechoslovakia. Finally, there dropped into the committee's lap a godsend without parallel: the Nazi-Soviet pact. . . . If Hitler and Stalin could clasp hands, millions felt, then nothing in the world could be too fantastic for belief. So that it may be declared of Martin Dies . . . that Adolf Hitler made him what he is today.

Nonetheless, the Dies Committee had strong nationwide support. From the *Daily Republican* in Minnesota to the *West Virginia Farmer-Miner* and the *Binghamton Press* in New York, columnists affirmed the committee's work. "No greater general public service has been rendered the people of these United States since the world war than that of the Dies committee investigating un-American activities," proclaimed the *Chicago Herald American*. "It has lifted masks on foreign propaganda and has shown clearly the difference between American Americans and the alien-minded breed."

In the suspenseful air before FDR announced his bid for an unprecedented third term, Dies toured the country like a potential candidate testing the waters. That August, the *Christian Science Monitor* pointed out growing public discomfort with Roosevelt's "dominant and aggressive" role and applauded Republican gains in checking his powers. It signaled an opening for a "conservative or compromise" Democratic candidate in the next year's election.

September found Dies in Detroit conducting hearings on Communists in the autoworkers' union. The next month he was in Chicago, where he and several HUAC deputies made camp at the Palmer House hotel downtown, and where they heard testimony that, Dies said, confirmed that Chicago was a "nerve center" for foreign insurgents across the Midwest. He repeated his charge: "Communists have infiltrated the government, in high positions. . . . This is particularly true of the New Deal agencies, such as the WPA. . . . Their espionage systems could be turned into a sabotage ring overnight." His list of insurgents included 514 milkmen, 144 newspaper reporters, 112 lawyers, and 161 radio workers.

The crowds were growing. In a November rally at Madison Square Garden, the Texan drew an audience three to four times larger than he had in Brooklyn, and he pressed the administration to increase HUAC's funding for a more thorough investigation. (Still, newspapers noted that the crowd was *smaller* than that commanded by Communist Party leader Earl Browder not long before.) Dies entered the arena with a fanfare of drums and an escort guard. In his speech, he invoked George Washington's farewell address: "the jealousy of a free people ought to be constantly awake, since history and experience prove that foreign influence is one of the most baneful woes of republican government." Dies implied that foreign influences were shaping U.S. policy. Again, speakers mentioned the Texan as a possible candidate for higher office. "When the Revolution came along we had our Washington," said George Harvey, the Queens borough president, in the *New York Times.* "With the Civil War rose up a Lincoln, and now when our nation is threatened by foes within our borders, we have our Martin Dies of Texas."

One of Dies's targets in the HUAC hearings was an essay by Richard Wright. "The Ethics of Living Jim Crow" had appeared in *American Stuff,* an anthology of creative work written after hours by WPA writers. (The anthology also included Jim Thompson's story "The End of the Book"; a poem by Kenneth Rexroth; a story by Vardis Fisher; and seven "Negro convict songs," documented by John Lomax from prisons and chain gangs in Arkansas, Mississippi, South Carolina, and Texas.) HUAC committee member Joe Starnes read an excerpt from the essay, in which Wright recounts the reaction of white coworkers who, when he didn't perform a duty quickly, called him "a lazy black son-of-a-bitch," and who threaten him with a "f—kin' bar." At that point, Dies halted the reading and voiced his indignation over the language, saying, "That is the most filthy thing I have ever seen." He had no comment on the violence with which the white characters were threatening the narrator; it was the language that stirred Dies's wrath.

By 1939, Wright was living in Brooklyn, and his career was taking off. His book *Uncle Tom's Children* plumbed the alienation and violence of segregation, especially in the South. Its unvarnished dialogue and emotional intensity stirred publishers' interest in a novel, and by 1939, with research help from Margaret Walker's clippings on the murder trial in Chicago, he was ready to bring out *Native Son*.

His coworkers on the Project recognized that he was going places. Anzia Yezierska recounted in *Red Ribbon on a White Horse* how Wright had charmed her from the start, and how his rise stirred mixed feelings for her:

> I was in the noisy, smoke-filled cafeteria. Richard Wright was smiling down at me. . . .
>
> "There's a new shine in your eyes [I said]. Have you fallen in love?"
>
> "In love with the whole world. . . ."
>
> He handed me a copy of *Story* magazine. On the first page was his picture, with the announcement that the first prize of the WPA Writers' Contest was awarded to Richard Wright. . . . "It is a tribute to the entire Federal Writers' Project that its assistance . . . should have enabled a talent such as Wright's to emerge. . . ."
>
> "Five hundred bucks!" He held up the check for me to see. "And they're going to publish my book!"
>
> In his eyes I saw my own elation thirty years ago when my first story was published. . . . I thought of Hollywood, when I'd been

as intoxicated with the triumph . . . as Wright was now, wresting first prize from a white world. . . . He would know how to take success for what it was worth and not become rattled by it as I had been.

Yezierska recalled leaving the office with Wright then, watching him walk away, erect and purposeful. She empathized with Jeremiah, the old bohemian with writer's block, and felt the "despair of all aborted effort," the weight of all unrealized creative work. With the numbness of a sleepwalker, Yezierska felt compelled to throw out her own half-finished notes and manuscripts.

"For all the ghetto shrewdness," Yezierska was "sometimes frightened, uncertain, and easily defeated," wrote her daughter, Louise, in *Anzia Yezierska: A Writer's Life*. For both Wright and Yezierska, though, the WPA job provided intellectual and financial support.

The WPA's monthly checks contributed significantly to "the community life-blood," Wright noted in an essay on Harlem. Besides construction workers and tradesmen, the WPA supported the Harlem Community Art Center at Lenox Avenue and 125th Street, where painters Romare Bearden and Jacob Lawrence worked. Lawrence had considered becoming a writer first and took inspiration from WPA writer Claude McKay, as well as from gatherings with Wright and Ralph Ellison in those years. Lawrence "wanted to tell a story," he said, but he chose to tell it in paint. He created much of his *Migration Series* when he was twenty-three and living in a Harlem loft.

Wright felt a debt to his friends on the Project. In the flush of winning the *Story* prize in 1938, he had primed a radio audience for the WPA guide, promising that the guide would "go behind the scenes and show that phase of Harlem which the casual visitor or tourist does not see." Then, as a best-selling author who could buoy any book's sales with his name, he gave a bouquet to Algren with a glowing introduction to Algren's *Never Come Morning*. Wright hailed Algren as a "bold, vivid, and poetic" writer who revealed the Polish neighborhood of Chicago's North West Side in a way that "informs us all that there lies an ocean of life at our doorsteps":

Never Come Morning portrays what actually exists in the nerve, brain, and blood of our boys on the street, be they black, white, native, or foreign-born. . . . There will come a time in our country when the middle class will gasp (as they now gasp over the present world situation): "Why weren't we told this before?"

Wright's own writing about Harlem in the *WPA Guide to New York City* is not always inspired but does convey the intensity of nearly half a million people crammed into three square miles of city, distinguished by "its vivid population groups, with their national and racial cultures." The guide takes readers inside places that most outsiders would rarely glimpse, including the churches of the hugely popular preacher Father Divine:

At 152 West 126th Street is the most important Kingdom of Father Divine in Harlem. Father Divine, Negro religious leader of the "Righteous Government," has thousands of followers who call him "God" and who believe him to be God in the flesh. One of the chants holds: "He has the world in a jug and the stopper in his hand." His adherents are called angels. . . . Since Marcus Garvey's time no Negro has achieved a larger following among the masses of Harlem. Father Divine, a stocky bald-headed man with an intimate rhythmical style of Bible oratory, preaches a simple Christian theology emphasizing the principles of righteousness, truth, and justice. . . . Assistance from public relief agencies is prohibited. A kingdom serves as meeting hall, restaurant and rooming house.

The WPA life histories show the deep pools of mistrust in Harlem that came from experience. Lilly Lindo, a Harlem showgirl, dreamed of seeing her name in lights and in the newspapers, but it was a hope that ran up against past heartbreaks, like what had happened to the joyful Florence Mills, a dancer in the 1920s:

Her spirit was typical of the Negro, and did she have pride in her own people! . . . Lord, I can see and hear her now, singing: "I'm a little Blackbird lookin' for a Bluebird," in her small warbling voice, her fidgeting feet dancing as though she was walking on fine wires and had electric sparks going through her body. Jesus! She sure did her stuff with enjoyment. . . . Sometime I think God ain't as fair as He should be. Florence Mills died when she reached the top. . . . They had big plans for her and all of a sudden God came on the scene. She was one of His children. He stepped right in and clipped her wings. . . . People like Florence Mills make this world a better place to live in. She did a helluva lot to wipe out race prejudice. That was some year and month of disappointments in Harlem, November 1927. The Republicans swept Harlem, Marcus Garvey was being deported, and our Queen of Happiness died.

Speaking as a black man and a young writer, Wright addressed the need to nurture that hope in a radio appearance in 1939. He appeared with several others on "Can We Depend upon Youth to Follow the American Way?" which was on *America's Town Meeting of the Air*, soon after the budgets of the WPA arts projects had been slashed. Wright reminded the audience of how desperate the situation had been only a few years earlier, and of the New Deal's origins. "We created five cultural divisions of the WPA—five art projects—to keep alive the spirit of the tradition of the human race," he said, "to link the present with the past, and to link both the past and the present with the future." The arts projects were "trying to keep alive in the hearts of youth the dream of a free and equal mankind, a dream which, if allowed to die, will open the gates to a ruthless and brutal tide of fascism." Then he listed the harsh statistics of African American life: extreme poverty, virtually nonexistent professional and educational opportunities, and a hundred lawyers for nine million blacks in the South. "The test of the American Way, in a sense, is embodied in the fate of the Negro in America."

In his short speech, Wright recognized the WPA for preserving hope, highlighted the risk if young people lost the opportunities he had had, and issued a challenge for reform. If the American Way can't work for African Americans, then it doesn't work, period. This dramatically changed the "race question." Wright's experience on the Writers' Project and with the Communist Party had given him a new historical context for the black experience. (He would get a chance to explore it further in a photo essay, *12 Million Black Voices*, about the African American experience and migration. Later, when Ralph Ellison received a copy of the newly published book, he was deeply moved by the historic sweep of an experience that was finally gaining recognition.) At the Project office, Wright discussed this growing awareness with Ellison, and the two shared their ideas on fiction.

Ellison, meanwhile, was gaining his own sense of that history as he interviewed Harlem residents for Botkin's folklore division. He talked with Pullman porters, unemployed truck drivers, musicians, and children. One day at the corner of 135th Street and Lenox, Ellison met a gifted storyteller who had come to New York from South Carolina. That afternoon in June 1939, Leo Gurley told Ellison a story that was both incredible and mythic:

> I hope to God to kill me if this ain't the truth. All you got to do is go down to Florence, South Carolina and ask most anybody you meet and they'll tell you its the truth.
>
> Florence is . . . hard . . . on colored folks. You have to stay out of the white folks' way; all but Sweet. That the fellow I'm fixing to tell you about. His name was Sweet-the-monkey. I done forgot his real name, I can't remember it. But that was what everybody called him. . . . My mother and grandmother used to say he was wicked. He was bad all right. He was one sucker who didn't give a damn bout the crackers. . . . I can't ever remember hear tell of any them crackers bothering that guy. . . .
>
> It was this way: Sweet could make hisself invisible. . . . Sweet-the-monkey cut open a black cat and took out its heart. Climbed up a tree backwards and cursed God. After that he could do anything. The white folks would wake up in the morning and find their stuff gone. He cleaned out the stores. He cleaned up the houses. Hell, he even cleaned out the damn bank! He was the boldest black sonofabitch

ever been down that way. Hell, he had everybody in that lil old town scaird as hell, black folks and white folks.

The white folks started trying to catch Sweet. . . . The police would come up and say: "Come on Sweet" . . . and they'd put the handcuffs on him and start leading him away. He'd go with 'em a little piece. . . . Then all of a sudden he would turn hisself invisible and disappear. The police wouldn't have nothing but the handcuffs. . . .

That was about five years ago. My brother was down there last year and they said they think Sweet done come back. But they can't be sure because he won't let hisself be seen.

Gurley's tale about Sweet summed up life in many parts of the South, where only a black man with supernatural powers could act freely and without fear. At the end of each day, Ellison typed up his notes and turned them in, but the stories stayed in his head.

May Swenson grew up in the town of Logan, Utah, the eldest of ten children in a home where English was a second language. Her Swedish parents had come to the United States as converts to Mormonism. After finishing college in Utah, Swenson headed east to take part in New York's literary scene. In 1938, she joined the Federal Writers' Project, where she met and befriended Anzia Yezierska, another independent-minded daughter of immigrants. Swenson, like Ellison, worked in the folklore unit. She compiled more than twenty life stories, ranging from an old-timer's recollections of a vanished Bronx landscape to "Folklore of Drug Store Employees" and "Lore of Department Store Workers."

Ralph Ellison in 1937.

In the Bronx on East 242nd Street, Swenson met Mrs. J. Elterich at a large frame home. Elterich had lived in the Bronx for fifty-eight years and recalled as a girl going for picnics and strawberry festivals on the ball field at 136th Street. She told Swenson a girlhood story about the Frog Hollow Gang, a group of petty thieves who holed up in shacks that were much like Hoovervilles. They never seemed to rob anybody, but everyone in the neighborhood was "scared to death of the Frog Hollow Gang." Supposedly, its members "could see in the dark like cats or owls but couldn't see in daylight" and "if you kept a light burning they would be blinded and would go away." Mothers invoked the gang to get children to behave. Eventually, Elterich said, the police cleared out the squatters and made Frog Hollow into a sort of park, which, although it was a "pretty little place," she said, always felt strange afterward. "And at night especially, with the sound of the frogs and all, nobody would go near it."

Swenson interviewed a man from Tennessee living on West 93rd Street and talked with a bachelor on East 79th Street about his arrival from southern Italy and his trips back there to see his family. She paid close attention to the ways that people expressed themselves, observing of this gentleman: "While talking, he moves his plump little hands with agility, and when trying to think of a word that is slow in coming off the tip of his tongue, the thumb and forefinger of his left hand go to his brow; sporadic wrinkles appear in a sharp V over the bridge of his nose."

"I reckon you've come to pester me for a story," John Rivers said with a smile when Swenson approached him in Washington Heights one brisk October day. He was seventy-two years old and wore a threadbare overcoat. "Well, come on in."

Swenson wasn't put off when he joked about how his wife would be jealous if she found him with a young lady. "Will you think me too personal," she said, "if I ask how you lost your finger?"

Swenson also wrote up Hungarian stories and Czech tales, as well as the lives of marine radio operators, union organizers, a tramp poet in Washington Square, and workers at the National Biscuit Company, whose sufferings on the job blended with a sensual exuberance that Swenson captured:

The heat is terrible. The foreman was every five minutes hollering at us today, because we couldn't work fast. Our fingers were bleeding from the hot crackers that stick to the pans, and nearly everyone of us had to go for plaster to the nurse. One girl fainted in Building A. Spanish Mary got fired in spite of the busy season, because she danced the Tango during lunch hour—lifted up her skirts above her knees—the girls clapped and the men workers hollered. But the foreman, that old joy-killer, came in, and later we heard she got the air. We were so sad, this made us more sad than any sad story told by Shirley.

Swenson, Ellison, and the other interviewers were saving people's accounts of the past but also their sense of the present, their memories and expressions. The Depression was fading, but new forces pulled the WPA writers and the people they interviewed in strange ways.

The *WPA Guide to New York City* includes a special twenty-page section featuring the 1939 World's Fair, so that the guide itself—that dictionary to the city—also contains a bulletin of the year's big happening with a map of the fairgrounds. The fair's theme, "Building the World of Tomorrow," was intended as a bold statement of the future, but among all the families who wandered through the fairgrounds and left exhausted, the uncertainty of tomorrow caused many hearts to fill with dread. The fair reflected events in Europe as the pavilions for Poland and Czechoslovakia closed after Germany invaded those countries. Months later, two New York policemen were killed by an explosive placed at the British pavilion.

11

CONVERGING ON
WASHINGTON

We went up in that monument in Washington. But I don't
like to go up high any more. And I like to froze to death, too.
Coldest place I was ever in.

—G. O. DUNNELL, YANKEE MERCHANT, IN A WPA
INTERVIEW WITH ROBERT WILDER

MANY WPA WRITERS AND EDITORS
entering the nation's capital were met by
the daunting marble shrine of Washington's
Union Station. Arriving by train, they passed
through the city's gritty neighborhoods, yet
when they disembarked, they were sud-
denly surrounded by the gleaming monuments and museums. The first
of the giant-scale, marble public buildings that line the Mall, Union
Station was designed by Daniel Burnham, the architect who conjured
up the dramatic White City for Chicago's 1894 World's Fair. His super-
sized classicism set the tone for the public Washington of the twentieth
century. "Make no little plans. They have no magic to stir men's blood,"

Burnham urged (as quoted in the Washington, D.C., guide). "Make big plans, aim high in hope and work."

The station made that sentiment real with its white marble façade and soaring vaulted roof, which was "calculated to dwarf the individual into insignificance," the WPA guide notes, "while inflating his breast with civic pride." Burnham modeled the vast waiting area on the Baths of Diocletian, with rows of stone guardians peering down on travelers from a great height and a barrel-vaulted ceiling soaring ninety feet overhead. The concourse in Union Station—nearly as big as the concourses of New York's Penn and Grand Central stations combined—was designed to handle crowds for presidential inaugurals. By the 1930s, roughly forty thousand passengers filed through it each day.

Hundreds of Project workers came through the great hall, their footsteps sounding on the stone floor on the way to the taxi stand. Many reported to headquarters with a mixture of awe and anxiety. "The floor where you stand has been trod by presidents and kings," wrote Cheever, conveying a sense of that arrival through the eyes of a young character in *The Wapshot Chronicle*:

> You come . . . at nine in the evening to Washington, a strange city. You wait your turn to leave the coach, carrying a suitcase, and walk up the platform to the waiting room. Here you put down your suitcase and crane your neck, wondering what the architect had up his sleeve. . . . You follow the crowds and the sounds of a fountain out of this twilight into the night. You put down your suitcase again and gape. On your left is the Capitol building, flooded with light.

Burnham's edifice and the humanity passing through it embodied the challenge to the WPA writers: How do you present the mammoth scale of American history and yet capture the human scale of the people who made it? "Think of it, to tell the story of America!" exclaims a character in *Lamps at High Noon*, WPA writer Jack Balch's novel about the Project. "What a huge job this was!"

When the *WPA Guide to Washington, D.C.*, came out in 1937, many people felt that Alsberg had taken the giant scale too far. The five-pound

Boys playing in the fountain outside Union Station, 1938.

guide, one reviewer noted, was so big "not even Samson could have carried it from the depot to his hotel." Apart from its ungainly size, however, that review in the *Christian Science Monitor* went on to say that the guide "makes a living, understandable and likable city out of what sometimes seems to be a vague conglomeration of scarcely related worlds." It depicted Washington as "both small-town America and the political capital" of the Western world.

The *WPA Guide to Washington, D.C.*, may be the first travel guide that was ever praised on the floor of Congress, where a representative hailed it as "more than a guide, as a splendid job of writing as well as an invaluable source of information." Reviewers noticed that it wasn't simply promotional froth but a social critique. The *New York World-Telegram* called it a cross section of the city, showing "the marbles of the Capitol and the disease-infested alley tenements." The guide even stirred a sex scandal of a sort in Congress by noting that George Washington's stepson had fathered a child with a slave, Maria Syphax.

Cheever spent the summer of 1938 near Dupont Circle in Mrs. Gray's boardinghouse at 2308 Twentieth Street, Northwest. Despite the sense of importance he felt at being in the nation's capital, he was at the mercy of strangers at the boardinghouse dinner table. There, an elderly lodger mocked WPA workers while Cheever ate in silence, ashamed. The bitter taste gave him fodder for "Washington Boardinghouse," a story that appeared in the *New Yorker* in March 1940.

Every day he walked to his job as junior editor in the Project's headquarters, housed in an old theater that had once been home to prizefights and dog shows. Cheever hated Washington bureaucrats and the smugness he found, and he longed to be back in New York. His letters to friends included biting asides about the city's Southern accents and conformity. The aura of social climbing informs a portrait in *The Wapshot Chronicle.*

The Writers' Project staff in its Washington, D.C., office.

Members of the Project staff at the D.C. headquarters.

The man who had the room next to Moses in the boardinghouse . . . had been in Washington for two years and he invited Moses into his room one night and showed him a chart or graph on which he had recorded his social progress. He had been to dinner in Georgetown eighteen times. His hosts were all listed and graded according to their importance in the government. He had been to the Pan-American Union four times: to the X Embassy three times: to the B Embassy one time (a garden party) and to the White House one time (a press reception).

"This town has a way of making a man feel like he's living in a fool's *paradise*," says a character in Ralph Ellison's story "Cadillac Flambé." Washington's mix of officialdom and local residents, including many middle-class blacks, affected Ellison. What's more, it was the hometown of Ellison's hero, Duke Ellington, who had defined vitality, elegance, and style for a generation.

The neighborhood around U Street, Northwest, where Ellington had grown up, was a pocket of relatively prosperous African American families in a deeply segregated city. That district was shaped by the black migration from the South, the image of Washington as a safe haven for blacks, and the growth of Howard University as the first in the country dedicated to educating African Americans. Zora Neale Hurston studied at Howard in the early 1920s, and in 1921 published her first literary story and poem in Howard's literary journal.

Sterling Brown, the Howard professor who headed the "Negro Affairs" division on the Writers' Project, grew up in Washington, too. His father, born a slave in Tennessee, became a university professor at Howard in 1892. Sterling grew up surrounded by books and education. Besides managing the states' black studies programs, he drafted the section of the Washington guide on black life. Pulling no punches, his essay indicted the system that kept blacks segregated in ghettos within sight of the Capitol.

Alley residents in Washington, D.C., 1941.

Education, economic opportunity, and entertainment converged on U Street. The *WPA Guide to Washington, D.C.*, described U Street as the city's "thoroughfare of Negro businesses," bustling with poolrooms, cabarets, beer gardens, "and eating places from fried-fish 'joints,' barbecue, and hamburger stands to better-class restaurants." The grand Lincoln Theatre stood next to a small movie house built in 1910 for black audiences. A person could stand on the sidewalk on U Street in the evening and watch "crowds go by, togged out in finery, with jests upon their lips—this one rushing to the poolroom, this one seeking escape with Hoot Gibson, another to lose herself in Hollywood glamour, another in one of the many dance halls" or in the Howard Theatre, with its mix of Broadway, vaudeville, and jazz.

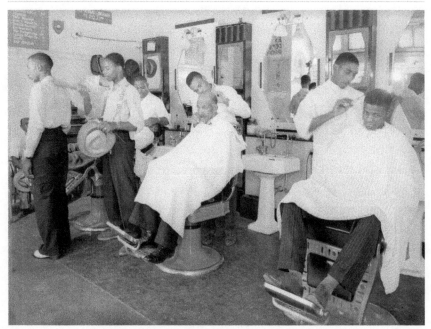

A barbershop in Washington's U Street neighborhood, 1942.

A focus of neighborhood life, the Howard stood near the corner of Seventh and T streets. Like the Apollo in Harlem, the Howard was a community pillar and a platform for new jazz talents, as well as for more famous performers who passed through: Louis Armstrong, Fats Waller, Jimmie Lunceford, Andy Kirk and the Clouds of Joy, and Ellington himself.

A vibrant music scene percolated, unseen by most of official Washington, yet it gave testimony to the city's local culture. Ellington described locales from his youth in his memoir *Music Is My Mistress.* "There was a demonstration of how all levels could and should mix at Frank Holliday's poolroom," next to the Howard Theatre, he wrote. "Guys from all walks of life seemed to converge there. You do a lot of listening in a poolroom," where stories ranged from hospital interns' discussions to forgery experts listing their skills. Everything got discussed: sports, racing, medicine, law, and politics. "At heart, they were all great artists."

At Eleventh and U streets, the Crystal Caverns was another beacon for great jazz. Ahmet Ertegun, who came to Washington in 1935 as the twelve-year-old son of the Turkish ambassador, heard bands at the Caverns when it was managed by Cab Calloway's sister. "The house band at the Crystal Caverns was terrific. They had a great, flashy drummer—one of the best drummers I ever heard, named Streamline Burrell," Ertegun said in an interview. He also heard Jelly Roll Morton, who lived in the city briefly in the late 1930s and appeared occasionally in a small second-floor nightspot on U Street. Morton also recorded songs for Alan Lomax at the Library of Congress. Although Ertegun lived in a diplomatic enclave, he and his brother, Nesuhi, were drawn to U Street because music stores downtown didn't carry any of the jazz or blues records they sought. The boys would enlist the embassy's chauffeur for a ride to U Street and leave the car waiting at the curb while they hunted the racks for jazz rarities at Max Silverman's Quality Music Shop. The Ertegun brothers also went door-to-door for blocks, asking people whether they had any old records to sell, like young urban Lomaxes. Ertegun later said that Washington gave him the background for going into the music business and founding Atlantic Records.

Ben Botkin collected jazz records, but most of all he loved live music. He also relished hearing people's stories and often fell into the role of informal interviewer, even with friends. In his work, he relied on his wife, Gertrude, who did all of his typing and proofreading, usually at night after she finished with the housework and child-raising. They lived in a house in the Southeast section of the city, out Pennsylvania Avenue from Capitol Hill. During their time in Washington, their daughter, Dorothy, recalled a morning ritual they developed, in which she would stand at the top of the stairs and watch Botkin through the bathroom door as he shaved. "And while he shaved, he'd tell me stories or make up nonsense poems."

Botkin had a rich sense of humor that came out in puns and off-the-cuff wit. He marked every birthday or holiday by penning a nonsense rhyme. Although his hopes for a public recognition of folk culture were grand, his own ambitions were modest. "I swing a mop occasionally," he told a reporter once. "I am a pretty good housekeeper."

He was slow to accept the gathering wrath of the Dies Committee, perhaps believing, like Alsberg, that the threat would pass when the public became aware of the facts. "One can forgive 'folksiness' almost everything—its nostalgia, its quaintness," he wrote of those who simplified the past, "but not its clannishness" or its talk about "racial heritage." As the Project came under more intense fire, the Botkins realized that the consequences could be dire for his career. "That was a terrible time in my father's life," Dorothy recalled in an interview. "And my mother was even more concerned." One of the things that worried them in 1939 was that Botkin wouldn't be able to return to a professorship because of the red-baiting fallout from the HUAC hearings.

Still, he continued his work with the Project well into 1939. At the start of the year, he estimated that they had more than a quarter of a million words of folklore interviews from New York alone, from street vendors and lawyers to circus workers, who struggled with the bizarre views that millions held of their work in popular culture. "Circus people are just like other human beings," Maude Cromwell told a WPA interviewer in New York. Cromwell and her husband were Ringling Brothers veterans, wire walkers who had survived many falls. Sometimes during the act she would scream and fake a fall, terrifying the audience.

Heading up Pennsylvania Avenue from the Botkinses' home in the Southeast toward the Capitol, one encountered a stark transition through poor neighborhoods. The WPA guide writers showcased the monuments of the Mall, but they also fathomed the city's layers of humanity. At the National Archives, for example, on the ground beneath its windowless marble cube on Seventh Street, Northwest, once stood the old Center Market where slave auctions took place regularly until 1850.

From the wide steps of the Capitol, a visitor could look out over the Mall and see the Washington and Lincoln monuments. Here at the Capitol came the hearings that drew the curtain on the Project's final act.

Increasingly, Congressman Dies led HUAC with an eye for publicity. He allowed vague accusations about Communist ties and questionable testimony to stand unchallenged, in a process that President Roosevelt called "sordid." With few resources, the investigation would have been a monumental task if it were approached systematically. Instead, the HUAC staff relied on innuendo and file cabinets full of thousands of index cards, typed with names and addresses of suspected Un-Americans.

Congressman Martin Dies of Texas in 1938.

These were gleaned from petitions, magazine mastheads, and leaflets. It was a haphazard method that turned up an assortment of people, including Ash Can artist George Bellows, the owner of a Georgetown bookshop, and several members of the Writers' Project, including Jack Conroy.

Dies and his fellow committee members led witnesses through barrages of leading questions, as they pressed for stories of communists and radicalism.

Alsberg was feeling the heat. When he came to give testimony to the Dies Committee, he arrived pushing a cart full of the Project's publications and attempted to win over the congressmen by acting ingratiating.

"The history of this project is a little different from the other three projects," he had told Congress in early 1938, perhaps to create some distance between his staff and the more radical Federal Theatre. Alsberg pointed out how writers had helped with government administration and emergency relief—for example, after a 1937 flood in Pennsylvania. They didn't merely report on the 1937 flood but "actually got on the phone and informed the officials where help was needed." Alsberg quoted Lewis Mumford on the value of the national self-portrait coming out of the Project, "the finest contribution to American patriotism that has been made in our generation." He described how work on the Project could equip a young writer for later creative work. "[W]e all have a novel in us," he said.

So Alsberg felt confident appearing before Dies in December 1938, despite the warning signs. Several former staff members had painted the Project as a haven for Communists. Ellen Woodward, a WPA administrator, had stood up for the Project, saying that it employed "thousands of people who are pretty well licked by this Depression," and calling the committee itself "un-American" in its tactics. Hallie Flanagan defended the Federal Theatre with even more poise and verve, talking Dies to a draw. She did not get a chance to make the closing statement she requested, however, or to have her written statement entered into the public record.

Alsberg came next and portrayed himself as a staunch anti-Communist and a manager who had struggled with the unions and strikes. When asked about Katharine Kellock, the tours director, he described her as someone who would easily be admitted to the Daughters of the American Revolution. The session ended with surprising equanimity. "The Chair wants to commend you for your frankness," Dies said in closing.

Alsberg's cooperative testimony before the Dies Committee did not save him. With war looming, Roosevelt had already decided to sacrifice the arts projects to congressional politics. Alsberg resisted heavy pressure to leave immediately, saying that he wouldn't go until the principal remaining guides were published. He lost that battle, too. He was forced to resign that spring.

Hallie Flanagan, already deposed from the Theatre Project, wrote him a note of consolation. "Dear Henry," it read, "In the years to come when miles of asphalt will be broken up and my clippings about the Theater Project will crumble, your books will survive."

Alsberg's replacement, a stern and crisply dressed retired colonel, F. C. Harrington, aimed to bring the last state guides to press with the efficiency of a train conductor and steer the Project to a close. It had lost its federal budget; its remaining work devolved to state offices for its final three years, just as most of the guides were published and were receiving warm reviews. In describing the WPA guides for the April 26, 1939, issue of *New Republic*, Robert Cantwell wrote,

> The America that's emerging from the Writers' Project books is like nothing we've ever seen. Nothing in our academic histories prepares you for it. The guides are a vast catalogue of secret rooms. It is a grand, melancholy, formless, democratic anthology, a majestic roll call of national failure, terrible and yet engaging. The American Guides make some of the horrors of the present less difficult to endure. Even Martin Dies seems all right in this company.

Critic Alfred Kazin wrote in *On Native Grounds* that the Project, which "began by reporting the ravages of the Depression," ended with triumphant "reporting on the national inheritance." It changed American literature forever.

In the fall of 1941, the last guides came out with the fanfare of American Guide Week, a publicity campaign to cap the series. It signaled a reevaluation of the guides. FDR announced, "At this time of crisis, when every student needs to know what America is and what it stands for, educators everywhere should be aware of the invaluable contribution made by the American Guide series." Privately, his assessment of the WPA arts projects was more qualified: "Some of it good, some of it not so good, but all of it native, human, eager and alive."

The recasting of the guides as patriotic occurred just weeks before Pearl Harbor was bombed and America entered World War II. Every G.I. who shipped out received a copy of the WPA guide to his home state, a reminder of what he was fighting to protect.

Lyle Saxon had shepherded the Louisiana Project to its completion and then served as Southern regional director, where he had given what he called the "last rites on the Oklahoma guide" and managed other disagreeable tasks. Now he was called upon once more. He arrived in Washington to oversee the final accounting of the Writers' Project as the last of the WPA guides rolled off the presses.

Zora Neale Hurston at a Writers' Project publicity event in 1937.

Saxon was in a foul mood. He felt that the previous five years had been wasted and wrote to a friend in early 1943, "I'm . . . doing a final, overall report on the defunct WPA. Why they picked on me to do this I have no idea, but they did; and it seems fairly important that someone should do it, so that if and when it is necessary to have a work-relief program again—the same mistakes will not be made. For some of it worked and some of it didn't."

He loathed the task. He was staying at a "dump" with a shared bathroom and working at the corner of Eighteenth and E Streets, two blocks from the White House. Washington's gray winter desolation was palpable, and letters poured in from the states, pleading that the Project last until spring because older people on staff had no other job prospects. "I've been in this hellhole for ten days," he wrote, "and it seems a century." Everyone he had known had scattered to different branches of the

AMERICAN
GUIDE
★ WEEK ★

TAKE PRIDE   IN YOUR COUNTRY

NOV. 10-16

STATE BY STATE
THE WPA WRITERS PROJECTS DESCRIBE
AMERICA TO AMERICANS

"Through these guides to the forty-eight states, Alaska,
Puerto Rico, the District of Columbia, and the principal Cities
and major regions of the United States, citizens and visitors to our
country now have at their finger-tips, for the first time in our
history, a series of volumes that ably illustrate our national way
of life, yet at the same time portray variants in local patterns
of living and regional development." *President Roosevelt.*

A poster for the 1941 publicity campaign for
the WPA guides.

service as the war ramped up. He longed for the fine lodging options that were open to him in Louisiana, but instead, "here I stay in a 9 × 12 room with linoleum on the floor and listen to Miss Feurst wash her clothes all night," he fumed. "There's no sense to it."

In April the last day came, almost in silence. There was no last-minute scramble by the writers to retrieve work they had done before it was hauled away to warehouse files, the way that Jackson Pollock and a few other WPA artists had rushed to pay a few dollars each for their own paintings. (Later, Willem de Kooning and Franz Kline tried to find the paintings *they* had done for the WPA, and ended up in a plumbing warehouse on Staten Island, sorting through hundreds of stacked canvases, according to *American-Made.* They left empty-handed.) "We dribbled out without anyone even saying goodbye," wrote Katharine Kellock.

As the country turned to the war effort, there was no time for assessments of the Writers' Project except for a perfunctory financial tally: the total federal cost of the Writers' Project during its span from 1935 through 1943 amounted to about $26 million, less than 1 percent of the WPA total. *Time*'s epitaph for the Project noted, "Credit for planning the State Guide series goes to the Project's first national director, slow-moving, slow-speaking Henry Alsberg."

People who had been on the Project moved on to other employment. Some, like Rudolph Umland, went on to careers in government. Henry Alsberg became an editor for a commercial publisher. Ben Botkin followed Lomax's path to the Library of Congress, where he plowed much effort into anthologies of folklore that the Project had gathered. Some of the staff members became literary and art critics; others, screenwriters.

Gauging the Project's longer-term effects on its members and the country is a tricky matter. For one thing, what measure does one use? Impact on the U.S. economy through the promotion of tourism, the rationale deployed by Henry Alsberg and Harry Hopkins? Alsberg's hope of influencing "real American writing," based on inspiring writers with the evidence from their research for the guides? Or a greater democratic understanding, as Botkin hoped? These gauges pose obvious challenges. Tracing influence to creative output is always risky, due to the variety of factors that go into producing any work of art or literature. What's more, many people associated with the Project later washed their hands of it. It was a relic of the bad old Depression, and when anticommunist fever resumed with even greater intensity after World War II, there seemed to be little point in revisiting old arguments.

Nonetheless, by the mid-1950s, Alsberg could claim a Project link to remarkable contributions to American fiction. Zora Neale Hurston published her most ambitious novel, *Moses, Man of the Mountain*, within months after leaving the Project. Richard Wright's *Native Son*, written while he was on the Project, showed a man caught in a violent downward spiral and marked a new era in social realist fiction. A dozen years later, Ralph Ellison's novel *Invisible Man* would challenge stereotypes that Wright's novel raised. Vardis Fisher's best-selling novel *Children of God*, written while he edited the Idaho guide, pushed the historical novel in new directions. Many consider it his finest work. (Fisher's better-known legacy is that his 1965 novel *Mountain Man* provided a basis for the Hollywood film *Jeremiah Johnson*.) In 1950, Anzia Yezierska's memoir of her life and the Project, *Red Ribbon on a White Horse*, became a best seller and revived her reputation. In that book's preface, W. H. Auden called the Writers' Project "the most noble and absurd undertaking ever attempted by any state. No other [government] has ever cared whether its artists as a group lived or died."

Project workers racked up a string of nominations and National Book Awards. The first award in fiction was given to Nelson Algren in 1950 for *The Man with the Golden Arm*, about a war veteran addicted to heroin. Algren was followed by Ralph Ellison, Saul Bellow, John Cheever, and Eudora Welty in fiction; and Conrad Aiken, May Swenson, and Kenneth Rexroth in poetry. While they may well have made their marks with or without government support, the fact is that they rose from the ranks of WPA emergency relief.

Yet having the Project on your résumé did not open doors; it was more likely to slam them shut. With the advent of Joseph McCarthy's round of HUAC hearings, some Project alumni were blacklisted and others left the country. Richard Wright and his family emigrated to Paris in 1947 and would never live in the United States again. He and Ralph Ellison remained friends for years but eventually drifted apart. In Paris, Wright also fell out with his old friend Nelson Algren. Stetson Kennedy visited Wright in Europe in the 1950s. Frank Yerby, Wright's colleague in Chicago, became one of the most prolific African American writers, publishing twenty-eight novels. He lived with his wife in France and Spain from the 1950s until his death in 1991.

Studs Terkel, Jim Thompson, and Meridel Le Sueur were blacklisted from writing jobs for years during the 1950s. Le Sueur reported being hounded from working at correspondence courses and even waitress jobs. Terkel became a radio deejay and an interviewer, grounded in the WPA principle of democratic history as he took oral history to a popular audience. He wrote many best-selling and prize-winning books, such as *Working* and *The Good War: An Oral History of World War II*. "The Writers' Project changed everything for me," he said. "I think it changed everything."

Loren Eiseley, who wrote about nature and history for the Nebraska WPA guide, would win many awards for his books on science and natural history. And the poetry of Weldon Kees has gained new admirers in recent years.

Jim Thompson never again lived in Oklahoma. He spent many years in Los Angeles, unsuccessfully as a scriptwriter. In the late 1950s, he worked with Hollywood director Stanley Kubrick on *The Killers* and *Paths of Glory* and inspired later filmmakers from Sam Peckinpah to Quentin Tarantino. Most of his novels, however, were out of print when he died in 1977. He told his wife, Alberta, "Just you wait, I'll become famous after I'm dead about ten years." In the mid-1980s, all of his crime novels were republished and esteemed as classics of the genre.

Margaret Walker published novels and poetry and won a large following as a mentor for many young female writers, including Alice Walker, Nikki Giovanni, and Sonia Sanchez. "The WPA accomplished what nobody believed was possible at that time," Margaret Walker wrote in *Richard Wright: Daemonic Genius,* "a renaissance of the arts and American culture. It afforded some of the most valued friendships in the literary history of the period."

Zora Neale Hurston died in 1960, poor and largely forgotten by the public. It was Alice Walker who rediscovered her and helped to bring her work renewed public attention. Since then, Hurston's novel *Their Eyes Were Watching God* has gained the stature of a classic. In the early years of this century, her unpublished play *Polk County,* featuring people's songs and stories—many of them collected while she was on the Project—came alive onstage before packed theaters in Washington, D.C., and won a Helen Hayes Award for best musical.

For Saul Bellow, the Project's lone Nobel prizewinner, the WPA marked a crucial period in his development as a writer, according to his biographer James Atlas. As Bellow wrestled with the question of how to become a writer in his city of Chicago, which didn't seem to prize literature highly, he found models for his vocation in fiction on the Project.

The life histories never appeared in the full glory that Ben Botkin had envisioned for them. He published a collection of the narratives of former slaves as *Lay My Burden Down,* and folklore from the Project made its way into *Treasury of American Folktales.* Most of the interviews reached the public only decades afterward.

Many lesser-known authors from the Project penned books later, including Hilda Polacheck (*I Came a Stranger: The Story of a Hull House Girl*), Ruby Wilson (*Frank J. North: Pawnee Scout Commander and Pioneer*), and Julia Conway Welch (*The Magruder Murders: Coping with*

Violence on the Idaho Frontier). Polacheck spent months living with her daughter in New Jersey in the 1950s while she devoted time to documenting her life story as a woman, an immigrant, and a writer.

In Utah, Juanita Brooks wrote penetratingly about the land and the Mormons who lived there, including in her 1950 book *The Mountain Meadows Massacre*, which Jon Krakauer has called "groundbreaking" and "an extraordinary work of history." In *Under the Banner of Heaven*, Krakauer said that "every book about the Mormon experience in nineteenth-century Utah published after 1950 is a response to Brooks's book."

Even reluctant recruits John Cheever and Vardis Fisher, while keeping the Project at arm's length, maintained ties with some Project colleagues. Fisher became more fervently anticommunist as a columnist for Idaho newspapers. He eventually found a kind word for the Project that he had branded a boondoggle, telling an interviewer, "The cost of the arts projects was ridiculous, but I think it was a magnanimous gesture on the part of the government toward a better understanding of the nation . . . which is necessary at any time."

Cheever made lasting friendships with several of his WPA coworkers, including Ellison, and in private moments admitted that the Writers' Project offered the elements of a novel. "The social life of the project, the diversity of the cast—drunken stringers and first-rate men—the bucking for power, the machinations of the Dies Committee and the sexual and political scandals all make an extremely interesting story," Cheever conceded. "But it doesn't seem to be my kind of thing." In the 1970s, Cheever taught writing to inmates at Sing Sing Prison, an experience that helped to inspire *Falconer*, the novel that revived his career. In an essay for *Newsweek* in 1978, "Why I Write Short Stories," he expresses a hope for fiction that resembled Ben Botkin's speech in 1937: "narrative fiction can contribute to our understanding of one another and to the sometimes bewildering world around us." Ellison regarded Cheever's fiction as remarkable for its careful reporting of "the folkways, the conflicts of values, the joys and sorrows, the defeats and triumphs" of people.

Ellison, while on the New York Writers' Project, had chosen writing over music and learned to hear the music in speech that inspired his masterpiece. In the thirtieth-anniversary edition of *Invisible Man*, he explained how that had happened. He had returned from a stint in the merchant marine during World War II and was staying on a farm in Vermont, trying to write a war novel. His previous stories had always grown from concrete images and familiar characters, but that time, he wrote,

> I was confronted by nothing more substantial than a taunting, disembodied voice. I was most annoyed to have my efforts interrupted by an ironic, down-home voice that struck me as being as irreverent as a honky-tonk trumpet blasting through a performance, say, of Britten's *War Requiem*. . . . The voice was so persuasive with echoes of blues-toned laughter that . . . current events, memories and artifacts began combining to form a vague but intriguing new perspective. . . . Details of old photographs and rhymes and riddles and children's games, church services and college ceremonies, practical jokes and political activities observed during my prewar days in Harlem—all fell into place.

Ellison listened and realized that the voice belonged to "one who had been forged in the underground of American experience" and "a blues-tinged laugher-at-wounds who included himself in his indictment of the human condition." Ellison came to believe that even when the real world posed insurmountable hurdles to equality, fiction offered a place where he could blend the richness of the folktale and the culture of the novel, high and low, black and white, "the northerner and the southerner, the native-born and the immigrant are combined to tell us of transcendent truths and possibilities such as those discovered when Mark Twain set Huck and Jim afloat on the raft."

At a panel discussion about the Writers' Project, held in 1983 at the New York Public Library, Ellison was roused to a heated defense of the WPA regional and ethnic histories. "Let's face it," he said, "there is something called official history. Perhaps it's only academic, but you couldn't find the truth about *my* background in that history. You could not find the truth about other ethnic groups." He continued:

> We are a country which improvises. . . . The greatest, of course, is the Constitution. We are constantly moving toward it and moving away. . . . One of the things that the WPA did . . . was to allow that intermixture between the formal and the folk. The real experience

of people as they feel it, perceive it, act it out and try to embody it in art and narrative, in jokes and so on. . . . But we are *creating* American history, we are not reliving European or African history. We must still improvise our culture and we do that best when we make use of all that is at hand.

"Writing is an act of salvation," Ellison had written to Wright back in November 1941. After recounting hardships and pain they had shared coming from similar backgrounds, Ellison burst out, "God! It makes you want to write and write and write, or murder."

"The amazing resilience of people!" marvels Anzia Yezierska in *Red Ribbon on a White Horse*. "How they cling to life, even on the edge of an abyss!"

12

TRAVELING BEYOND

I see Roosevelt is tryin' to get a billion and a half more for WPA and if Congress won't give him that, they may lay off all the white-collar workers. That means fellows like you, I suppose.

—HENRY MITCHELL, PENOBSCOT CANOE MAKER,
IN A WPA INTERVIEW WITH ROBERT GRADY

DAY-TRIPPERS AND ARMCHAIR TRAVELERS HAVE used the WPA guides for sixty years now and have found them to be, in Robert Cantwell's phrase, "a vast catalogue of secret rooms." Soon after the guides appeared, the British journalist Alistair Cooke pledged in a letter to Henry Alsberg to "buy, beg, steal, annex, or 'protect' a complete library of the guides before I die." He did gather a substantial collection and used them to map a cross-country reporting trip, which was published only recently as *The American Home Front, 1941–1942*.

At the start of the 1960s, John Steinbeck set out across the country with many of the WPA guides in his trunk. He wrote in *Travels with Charley*:

The complete set comprises the most comprehensive account of the United States ever got together, and nothing since has even approached it. It was compiled during the Depression by the best writers in America, who were, if that is possible, more depressed than any other group while maintaining their inalienable instinct for eating. . . . They were reservoirs of organized, documented, and well-written information, geological, historical, and economic.

The Project's view of America influenced later writers as well. William Least Heat-Moon has said that without the WPA guide to Nebraska, he might never have written his epic-scale *PrairyErth*. The late *New York Times* reporter and author R. W. Apple Jr. used the WPA guides often in his wide-ranging travels. "I have long been a fan of the WPA guides," he wrote, "ever since I came across the excellent Virginia volume while serving there in the Army in the late 1950s." Apple used the WPA guide to Virginia to find the burned ruin of a plantation house, Rosewell, hidden off a rural road and overgrown with vines.

"They were living in a dark and troubled time," said Michael Chabon of the WPA writers in an interview, "yet they kept a positive attitude not only toward their enterprise, but toward art and life and culture."

The late Grace Paley understood how the WPA connected its writers to the city. The Writers' Project, she said, was "marvelous at helping people to find their own ears" as artists, and for getting people "talking about what their lives were really like." The Project pushed writers out into their neighborhoods, she believed, showing them "how to be literary and yet at the same time how to write about ordinary people in their own language."

"I had no idea how much these writers influenced me as a reader," said novelist Dagoberto Gilb. "The books that I fell for tended to be from writers from that period," such as *Native Son* and Studs Terkel's *Working*. "Once I read *Working* I knew that this was . . . like a literary parent." Gilb has also found rich material in the WPA life histories of the Southwest, including those collected by Lorin Brown in New Mexico.

One of the appeals of the WPA guides, noted novelist David Bradley, is seeing what they say about your hometown. Even if the entry is only two paragraphs in a seven-hundred-page guide, that representation of your home in a national publication "has a profound effect on people's beliefs and the way they see themselves in the world."

"You pick up the guide and you hear somebody saying, '2.2 miles beyond some little geezy town that doesn't even have a highway exit, there is something,'" Bradley said with a laugh. "Sometimes the guides get way off the beaten track, and it's amazing."

Besides the previously suggested methods, travelers can find other creative ways to use the 1930s guides and narratives. Start as an armchair traveler through the WPA guide of your choice. That may lead you to take the book on the road. Historian William Leuchtenburg and his wife take a copy of the relevant WPA guide on most of their U.S. trips. One of them will read aloud from the passenger seat, narrating the tour of sites they pass.

Commuters who pass daily through a place such as Grand Central, for example, might look at that very scene in the guidebook: "While a crowd of commuters just arrived from the suburbs over New York Central and New Haven trains is storming the turnstiles on its way to downtown offices, a greater crowd from the city is pushing the stiles in the other direction." The hordes on the platforms and in the narrow stairwells gradually subside. "Nickles jingle, signal bells clang, turnstiles bang until the faint thunder of footsteps on the wooden passageway connecting the Lexington Avenue lines with the Times Square-Grand Central shuttle sounds human and restful." Today's commuter might then search the Library of Congress's WPA Life Histories Web site for "Grand Central" and find a Manhattan cabbie from December 1938 talking about taking an "apple pusher" (out-of-towner) the long way to Grand Central by way of the Queensborough Bridge, Long Island, and Brooklyn.

Even without much advance reading, if you simply walk along an unexpected path it can bring surprises. Trenton can feel like several eras squished together under the manufacturing chutzpah of the lighted bridge sign over the Delaware River, visible to riders on Amtrak's Northeast line: TRENTON MAKES, THE WORLD TAKES. The New Jersey WPA guide explains that the span stands on piers from the original span across the river that was built in 1806; the bridge got its big-talking electric sign in 1935. In a fifteen-minute walk across from the Pennsylvania side at rush hour, the steel-blue river shines beneath the golden dome of the Trenton state house in the day's last sunlight. Follow Bridge Street down the old brick-paved blocks and you pass from a cobblestone sense of preindustrial Jersey to scruffy, postindustrial decay and twentieth century, inner-city grit. It's not the grand vista of the Sierras, but in the words of Black Elk, the Oglala Sioux leader, "Anywhere is the center of the world."

Sometimes, though, clues can help us get past the surface noise. You can find further resources in the appendix and the sources.

APPENDIX

RESOURCES FOR READERS AND TRAVELERS

WPA Guide Reprints and Related Books

Two very good anthologies that distill highlights from the WPA guides are *The WPA Guide to America: The Best of 1930s America as Seen by the Federal Writers' Project*, edited by Bernard A. Weisberger (Pantheon, 1985), and *Remembering America: A Sampler of the WPA American Guide Series*, edited by Archie Hobson (Columbia University Press, 1985). Each has a different take on what makes the guides valuable, and together they make fine starting points for an exploration of the American Guide series.

Many of the original WPA guides were republished by Pantheon in the 1980s, most of them with new introductions that provide context for modern readers. Other reprints of selected WPA guides have appeared in the last few years, including the Iowa, Kentucky, Minnesota, Nebraska, South Dakota, and Wisconsin guides. Publications such as *Maryland: A New Guide to the Old Line State* (Johns Hopkins University Press, 1999) use the original WPA guide as a starting point. *State by State: A Panoramic Portrait of America*, an anthology edited by Matt Weiland and Sean Wilsey (Ecco, 2008), is a collection of essays, one for each state, inspired by the WPA guides.

Some Books in the Tradition of the WPA Guides

Six Heritage Tours of the Lower East Side: A Walking Guide, by Ruth Limmer, New York University Press, 1997.

Hard Times: An Oral History of the Great Depression, by Studs Terkel, W. W. Norton, 2000.

Washington Schlepped Here: Walking in the Nation's Capital, by Christopher Buckley, Crown Journeys, 2003.

Apple's America: The Discriminating Traveler's Guide to 40 Great Cities in the United States and Canada, by R. W. Apple Jr., North Point Press, 2005.

Two for the Road: Our Love Affair with American Food, by Jane and Michael Stern, Houghton Mifflin, 2006.

America Eats: On the Road with the WPA, by Pat Willard, Bloomsbury, 2008.

Oral History Resources for Travelers

The Library of Congress has most but not all of the WPA life histories. In addition to the Web site given below, some life histories remain archived in state libraries and historical societies. For example, the Library of Virginia has more than a thousand WPA life histories (www.lva.lib.va.us/whatwehave/gov/wpalhabout.htm). Here are a few resources that may be of interest:

Crossing the Blvd.: Strangers, Neighbors, Aliens in a New America, by Warren Lehrer and Judith Sloan, W. W. Norton, 2003. This oral history project features people living in the many communities within Queens, New York: www.crossingtheblvd.org.

America's Highway: Oral Histories of Route 66, by Jay Crim and Shekar Davarya, published online in 2007, consists of a dozen interviews gathered from people living along the old Route 66, providing a glimpse of life on the highway: route66map.googlepages.com.

Listening Is an Act of Love: A Celebration of American Life from the StoryCorps Project, by Dave Isay, Penguin, 2007. This effort, inspired by the WPA life histories, brings oral history into the twenty-first century with digital recording. See also www.storycorps.net.

Cell phone walking tours: Talking Street has pioneered this approach with tours of New York's Lower East Side; Boston; Chicago; Philadelphia; Seattle; Washington, D.C.; and other cities: www .talkingstreet.com.

Online Resources

Some WPA guides are available as pdf files that you can call up on a laptop or a handheld device. A number are available at the Internet Archive, www.archive.org. The Washington Trust for Historic Preservation has adapted *Washington, a Guide to the Evergreen State* as an interactive program, which is downloadable at http://revisitingwashington.org.

WPA Life Histories at the Library of Congress

Nearly three thousand personal life histories from the 1930s are available on the Library of Congress Web site, at "American Life Histories: Manuscripts from the Federal Writers' Project, 1936–1940." For more information, visit http://memory.loc.gov/ammem/wpaintro/wpahome.html.

More resources at the Library of Congress Web site include the following:

Images of Depression-Era America: Photographs from the 1930s and 1940s taken by the Farm Security Administration are available at http://memory.loc.gov/ammem/fsowhome.html.

Voices from the Days of Slavery: Transcripts and recordings of more than twenty-three hundred interviews with former slaves can be found at http://memory.loc.gov/ammem/snhtml/snhome.html.

Posters from the WPA: Check out WPA posters at: http://memory .loc.gov/ammem/wpaposters/wpahome.html.

Florida Folklife from the WPA Collections: For a multiformat ethnographic field collection, visit http://memory.loc.gov/ammem/ collections/florida.

Zora Neale Hurston Plays: The scripts for nine Hurston plays and musicals can be found at: http://memory.loc.gov/ammem/znhhtml/znhhome.html.

Additional Resources

The American Library Association's (ALA) Public Programs Office developed *Soul of a People* programs in thirty libraries with a grant from the National Endowment for the Humanities. Visit the ALA Web site at www.ala.org/soulofapeople for an array of information and materials.

The National Park Service has online travel itineraries of historic places at www.nps.gov/history/nr/travel/.

The National Endowment for the Arts has posted a state-by-state list of books of interest to teachers and travelers of all ages at www.nea.org/readacross/resources/statebooks.html.

A searchable list of murals that the WPA created for schools, post offices, and libraries is at www.wpamurals.com.

The Online Archive of California brings together material from many of the state's museums and historical societies, including images, documents, and oral histories: www.oac.cdlib.org.

The Chicago Historical Society has created a Chicago encyclopedia: http://encyclopedia.chicagohistory.org.

The Literary Map of Manhattan on the *New York Times* Web site links specific addresses in New York City history to the works of authors of all eras, including Richard Wright, John Cheever, Ralph Ellison, and Saul Bellow: www.nytimes.com.

An online Almanac of Massachusetts history from the Massachusetts Foundation for the Humanities offers daily doses of the state's history, along with lesson plans and podcasts: www.massmoments.org.

The Texas Historical Society has made available the Handbook of Texas Online: www.tshaonline.org/handbook/online.

Roadside America is an online guide to odd tourist attractions across the country: www.roadsideamerica.com.

SOURCES

Most of the WPA life histories cited are on the Library of Congress Web site: http://lcweb2.loc.gov/ammem/wpaintro/wpahome.html.

Prologue

Bordelon, Pamela, ed. *Go Gator and Muddy the Water!: Writings by Zora Neale Hurston from the Federal Writers' Project.* New York: W. W. Norton, 1999.

Internet Archive. *Investigation of Un-American Propaganda Activities in the United States.* Hearings before a Special Committee on Un-American Activities, House of Representatives, Seventy-Fifth Congress, Third Session, Seventy-Eighth Congress, Second Session, archive.org/details/investigationofu193906unit, accessed August 19, 2008.

Mangione, Jerre. *The Dream and the Deal: The Federal Writers' Project, 1935–1943.* Boston: Little, Brown, 1972.

McDaniel, Dennis. Personal communication, and "Martin Dies of Un-American Activities: His Life and Times." PhD dissertation, University of Houston, 1988.

New York Times. "Further Dies Committee Inquiry Is Favored by Most Voters in U.S., Gallup Survey Finds." November 1, 1939.

Introduction

Boland, E. P. "Letter to Rep. Joshua L. Johns." In Herb Lewis, ed., *Oneida Lives: Long-Lost Voices of the Wisconsin Oneidas*. Lincoln: University of Nebraska Press, 2005.

Chabon, Michael. Phone interview with the author, tape recording, September 8, 2004.

Denning, Michael. *Cultural Front: The Laboring of American Culture in the Twentieth Century*. New York: Verso, 1998.

Schleuning, Neala. *America: Song We Sang without Knowing: The Life and Ideas of Meridel Le Sueur*. Mankato, MN: Little Red Hen Press, 1983.

1. The Writers' Project

Banks, Ann. *First-Person America*. New York: W. W. Norton, 1991.

Bold, Christine. *The WPA Guides: Mapping America*. Jackson: University Press of Mississippi, 1999.

Botkin, B. A. Introduction to *A Treasury of American Folklore*. New York: Crown, 1944.

———. "WPA and Folklore Research: Bread and Song." *Southern Folklore Quarterly 3*, no. 1 (1939): 7–14.

Brinkley, Douglas. "Unmasking the Writers of the WPA." *New York Times*, August 2, 2003.

Bulger, Peggy. "New Deal and Folk Culture." In Jan Brunvand, ed., *American Folklore: An Encyclopedia*. New York: Routledge, 1998.

Cornelius, Carol. Phone interview with the author, September 30, 2004.

Cronyn, George. Office memorandum to Henry Alsberg dated December 26, 1935. National Archives, Washington, DC.

Ellison, Ralph. "American Music: A Personal Glance after 200 Years," speech given at New York University, the Society for the Libraries, April 28, 1976. Ralph Ellison Collection, Manuscripts Division, Library of Congress.

Hayden, Dolores. *The Power of Place: Urban Landscapes as Public History*. Cambridge: MIT Press, 1995.

Hirsch, Jerrold. *Portrait of America: A Cultural History of the Federal Writers' Project*. Chapel Hill: University of North Carolina Press, 2003.

Hurston, Zora Neale. *Dust Tracks on a Road: An Autobiography*. Urbana: University of Illinois Press, 1984 ed.

Kaplan, Carla. *Zora Neale Hurston: A Life in Letters.* New York: Doubleday, 2002.

Kellock, Katharine. Letter to Henry Alsberg dated January 20, 1936. National Archives, Washington, DC.

Kuckhorn, Frank. "Uncle Sam Expands as an Arts Patron." *New York Times,* October 6, 1935.

Leuchtenburg, William. *The FDR Years.* New York: Columbia University Press, 1997.

Lewis, Herb, ed. *Oneida Lives: Long-Lost Voices of the Wisconsin Oneidas.* Lincoln: University of Nebraska Press, 2005.

Mangione, Jerre. *The Dream and the Deal: The Federal Writers' Project, 1935–1943.* Boston: Little, Brown, 1972.

McLester, Gordon. Author interview, May 2, 2006, Oneida, Wisconsin.

New York Times. "Relief Top Issue, Survey Indicates," June 4, 1939.

Stott, Bill. Introduction to *Remembering America: A Sampler of the WPA American Guide Series.* New York: Collier Books, 1987.

Taylor, Nick. *American-Made: The Enduring Legacy of the WPA: When FDR Put the Nation to Work.* New York: Bantam, 2008.

Twain, Mark. *Essays on Paul Bourget.* Project Gutenberg EBook #3173, 2004, www.gutenberg.org/etext/3173, accessed. August 11, 2008.

Watkins, T. H. *The Hungry Years: A Narrative History of the Great Depression in America.* New York: Henry Holt, 1999.

Weisberger, Bernard, ed. *The WPA Guide to America: The Best of 1930s America as Seen by the Federal Writers' Project.* New York: Pantheon, 1985.

2. Point of Departure: New York

Adamic, Louis. "New England's Tragic Towns." In Don Congdon, ed., *The '30s: A Time to Remember.* New York: Simon & Schuster, 1962.

Cheever, John. Early journal dated 1934–1935 (Folder 2, p. 36). Houghton Library, Harvard University.

Donaldson, Scott. *John Cheever: A Biography.* New York: Random House, 1987.

Federal Writers' Project. *WPA Guide to New York City.* New York: Pantheon, 1982 reprint.

Henriksen, Louise L. *Anzia Yezierska: A Writer's Life.* New Brunswick, NJ: Rutgers University Press, 1988.

Paley, Grace. Phone interview with the author, tape recording, September 10, 2004.

Quinn, Susan. *Furious Improvisation: How the WPA and a Cast of Thousands Made High Art Out of Desperate Times.* New York: Walker & Co., 2008.

Roskolenko, Harry. *When I Was Last on Cherry Street.* New York: Stein & Day, 1965.

Seltzer, Leo. Film interview with the author and Andrea Kalin, New York City, June 7, 2005.

Universal Newsreel. "Congressman Dies Comments on Immigration." June 25, 1935.

Yezierska, Anzia. Letter to Celia Ager dated May 6, 1935. Anzia Yezierska Collection, Howard Gotlieb Archival Research Center of Boston University.

————. *Red Ribbon on a White Horse: My Story*, with an introduction by Louise Levitas Henriksen. London: Virago, 1987.

3. Chicago and the Midwest

Except where otherwise indicated, Studs Terkel's quotations in this chapter come from two interviews with the author: tape recording, April 6, 1999, and film recording, Chicago, Illinois, February 18, 2004.

Algren, Nelson. Letters and postcards to Richard Wright between April 1938 and November 1941, in the Richard Wright collection of the Beinecke Rare Book and Manuscript Library at Yale University.

Atlas, James. *Bellow: A Biography.* New York: Random House, 2000.

Banks, Ann. *First-Person America.* New York: W. W. Norton, 1991.

Barnouw, Erik. *A Tower in Babel: A History of Broadcasting in the United States*, volume 1. New York: Oxford University Press, 1966.

Burrough, Bryan. *Public Enemies: America's Greatest Crime Wave and the Birth of the FBI, 1933–1934.* New York: Penguin, 2004.

Conroy, Jack. "Literary Underworld of the Thirties." A lecture at the Newberry Library, Chicago, April 17, 1969.

Denning, Michael. *The Cultural Front: The Laboring of American Culture in the Twentieth Century.* New York: Verso, 1998.

Donohue, H. E. F. *Conversations with Nelson Algren.* New York: Hill and Wang, 1963.

Drew, Bettina. *Nelson Algren: A Life on the Wild Side.* New York: Putnam, 1989.

Epstein, Dena Polacheck. Film interview by Andrea Kalin, Chicago, Illinois, February 21, 2004.

Federal Writers' Project. *The WPA Guide to Illinois.* New York: Pantheon, 1983 reprint.

Hauptman, Laurence. *The Iroquois and the New Deal.* Ithaca, NY: Syracuse University Press, 1988 reprint.

Jaffey, Bessie. "Staff Conference in Industrial Folklore." Notes of a staff meeting. Library of Congress, *American Life Histories from the Writers' Project,* http://lcweb2.loc.gov/ammem/wpaintro/wpahome.html, accessed August 12, 2008.

Le Sueur, Meridel. *The Girl,* 2nd rev. ed. Albuquerque: West End Press, 2006.

———. Film interview with Al Stein, Chicago, Illinois, September 23, 1989.

Lewis, Herb, ed. *Oneida Lives: Long-Lost Voices of the Wisconsin Oneidas.* Lincoln: University of Nebraska Press, 2005.

McCray, Judith. "*For My People: The Life of Margaret Walker,*" a video documentary. Chicago: Juneteenth Productions, 1998.

Morgan, Mindy. "Constructions and Contestations of the Authoritative Voice: Native American Communities and the Federal Writers' Project, 1935–1941." *American Indian Quarterly 29,* no. 1–2 (Winter/Spring 2005): 56–83.

Parker, Tony. *Studs Terkel: A Life in Words.* New York: Henry Holt, 1996.

Partnow, Hyde. "I'm a-Might-Have-Been." *Direction* (May/July 1939).

Polacheck, Hilda. *I Came a Stranger: The Story of a Hull-House Girl.* Urbana: University of Illinois Press, 1991.

Ross, Sam. Interview with Al Stein, Library of Congress Center for the Book, Washington, D.C., December 8, 1994.

———. *Windy City: A Novel.* New York: G. P. Putnam's Sons, 1979.

Rowley, Hazel. *Richard Wright: The Life and Times.* New York: Henry Holt, 2001.

Schlesinger, Arthur M., Jr. "The Rise of Federal Relief." In Don Congdon, ed., *The '30s: A Time to Remember.* New York: Simon & Schuster, 1962.

Terkel, Studs. *Hard Times: An Oral History of the Great Depression.* New York: Pantheon, 1970.

Ulrich, Mabel. "Salvaging Culture for the WPA." *Harper's,* May 1939, 653–664.

Walker, Margaret. "For My People." In *This Is My Century: New and Collected Poems.* Athens: University of Georgia Press, 1989.

———. "Richard Wright." In Ray, David, and Robert M. Farnsworth, eds., *Richard Wright: Impressions and Perspectives.* Ann Arbor: University of Michigan Press, 1973.

———. *Richard Wright, Daemonic Genius: A Portrait of the Man, a Critical Look at His Work.* New York: Warner Books, 1988.

———, with Maryemma Graham. *Conversations with Margaret Walker.* Jackson: University Press of Mississippi, 2002.

Wright, Richard. *Black Boy: A Record of Childhood and Youth.* New York: HarperPerennial, 1993.

———. "Ethnographical Aspects of Chicago's Black Belt," and "Amusements in Districts 38 and 40." WPA manuscripts in the Vivian G. Harsh Research Collection of Afro-American History and Literature, Chicago Public Library, n.d.

———. Letters to Nelson Algren dated May 21, 1940, and September 7, 1940. Richard Wright Collection, Beinecke Rare Book and Manuscript Library, Yale University.

———. *12 Million Black Voices.* Reprinted with an introduction by David Bradley. New York: Thunder's Mouth Press, 1988.

———. *Works.* New York: Library of America, 1991.

4. Gathering Folklore, from Oklahoma to Harlem

Botkin, B. A. "Regionalism and Culture." In Harry Hart, ed., *The Writer in a Changing World: American Writers' Congress.* New York: Equinox Cooperative Press, 1937.

———. "WPA and Folklore Research: Bread and Song." *Southern Folklore Quarterly* 3, no. 1 (1939): 7–14.

Ellison, Ralph. "February." In John F. Callahan, ed., *The Collected Essays of Ralph Ellison.* New York: Modern Library, 1995.

Federal Writers' Project. *Oklahoma: A Guide to the Sooner State.* 2nd ed., 1945.

Garrison, D. M. "Rigbuilders Marry Women." Unpublished WPA manuscript in the Southern Historical Collection, Manuscripts Department, Wilson Library, University of North Carolina–Chapel Hill.

Jackson, Lawrence. *Ralph Ellison: Emergence of Genius.* Hoboken, NJ: John Wiley & Sons, 2002.

L'Amour, Louis. *Education of a Wandering Man.* New York: Bantam, 1989.

McCauley, Michael J. *Jim Thompson: Sleep with the Devil.* New York: Mysterious Press, 1991.

New York Times. "Defends Writings of WPA Authors: Henry G. Alsberg Replies to Charges of Incompetence and Unproductivity." July 22, 1937.

Polito, Robert. *Savage Art: A Biography of Jim Thompson.* New York: Knopf, 1995.

Rampersad, Arnold. *Ralph Ellison: A Biography.* New York: Knopf, 2007.

Thompson, Jim. "The Drilling Contractor." Unpublished WPA manuscript in the Southern Historical Collection, Manuscripts Department, Wilson Library, University of North Carolina–Chapel Hill.

———. *The Killer inside Me.* In *Crime Novels: American Noir of the 1950s.* New York: Modern Library, 1997.

———. Letters to B. A. Botkin, March–December 1939. Benjamin A. Botkin Collection of Applied American Folklore, Archives and Special Collections, University of Nebraska-Lincoln Libraries.

———. "Solving Okahoma's Twin Slayings." *Master Detective,* 26–31ff, March 1938.

———. "The Strange Death of Eugene Kling." *True Detective,* 56–59ff, November 1935.

———. "Time Without End." In *Economy of Scarcity: Some Human Footnotes.* Norman, OK: Cooperative Books, 1939.

5. Rising Up in the West: Idaho

Bold, Christine. *The WPA Guides: Mapping America.* Jackson: University Press of Mississippi, 1999.

Brooks, Juanita. *Quicksand and Cactus: A Memoir of the Southern Mormon Frontier.* Salt Lake City: Howe Brothers, 1982.

———. *The Mountain Meadows Massacre.* Norman: University of Oklahoma Press, 1991 reprint.

Brown, Lorin W., with Charles L. Briggs and Marta Weigle. *Hispano Folklife of New Mexico: The Lorin W. Brown Federal Writers' Project Manuscripts.* Albuquerque: University of New Mexico Press, 1978.

Conway Welch, Julia. Letter to James Mirabello, October 9, 2005.

Federal Writers' Project. *Idaho: A Guide in Word & Picture.* Caldwell, ID: Caxton Press, 1937.

Fisher, Vardis. Film interview with John Milton, March 20, 1967, South Dakota Public Television.

———. Letters to H. G. Merriam and Elizabeth Nowell, December 1931 through November 1935, in the Vardis Fisher collection at the Beinecke Rare Book and Manuscript Library at Yale University.

———. *Orphans in Gethsemane.* Denver: Allan Swallow, 1960.

———. "Writers on Relief." *Idaho Statesman,* June 22, 1941.

Greenwood, Annie Pike. *We Sagebrush Folks.* Moscow: University of Idaho Press, 1988.

Mangione, Jerre. *The Dream and the Deal: The Federal Writers' Project, 1935–1943.* Boston: Little, Brown, 1972.

Swetnam, Susan Hendricks. *Lives of the Saints in Southeast Idaho: An Introduction to Mormon Pioneer Life Story Writing.* Boise: Idaho State Historical Society, 1991.

Watkins, T. H. *The Hungry Years: A Narrative History of the Great Depression in America.* New York: Henry Holt, 1999.

Woodward, Tim. *Tiger on the Road.* Caldwell, ID: Caxton Press, 1989.

6. Nailing a Freight on the Fly: Nebraska

Cloyd, Stephen. *The Nebraska Federal Writers' Project: Remembering Writers of the 1930s.* Web exhibit of the Lincoln City Libraries, www.lincolnlibraries.org/depts/hr/wpa/, accessed August 18, 2008.

Federal Writers' Project. *Nebraska: A Guide to the Cornhusker State.* New York: Viking, 1939.

Kees, Weldon. *The Ceremony and Other Stories,* selected and with an editorial introduction by Dana Gioia. Lincoln: University of Nebraska Press, 1983.

———. *The Collected Poems of Weldon Kees.* Lincoln: University of Nebraska Press, 1967.

Reidel, James. *Vanished Act: The Life and Art of Weldon Kees.* Lincoln: University of Nebraska Press, 2003.

Umland, Rudolph. "The Federal Writers' Project: A Nebraska Editor Remembers." *Nebraska History 78*, no. 3 (Fall 1997): 110–115.

———. "Lowry Wimberly and Others: Recollections of a Beerdrinker." *Prairie Schooner* 51 (Spring 1977): 17–50.

Witt, Richard C. "The WPA Federal Writers' Project in Nebraska." Master's thesis, University of Nebraska, 1980.

7. Poetic Land, Pugnacious People: California

Chesworth, Darren. *The Outsider: The Story of Harry Partch.* Documentary for BBC4, 2002.

Federal Writers' Project. *The WPA Guide to California.* New York: Hastings, 1939.

Gibson, Morgan. *Revolutionary Rexroth, Poet of East-West Wisdom.* North Haven, CT: Archon Books, 1986.

Gilmore, Bob. *Harry Partch: A Biography.* New Haven, CT: Yale University Press, 1998.

Hamalian, Linda. *A Life of Kenneth Rexroth.* New York: W. W. Norton, 1991.

McDaniel, Eluard Luchell. "Bumming in California." In Federal Writers' Project, ed., *American Stuff.* New York: Viking, 1937.

Partch, Harry. *U.S. Highball.* Recorded by the Kronos Quartet on Nonesuch Records, 2003.

Rexroth, Kenneth. *Autobiographical Novel,* rev. and expanded, edited by Linda Hamalian. New York: New Directions, 1991.

———. Unpublished WPA drafts for "Mt. Shasta," "State Line to Sacramento," "Tour 1," "Mineral King," and "Sequoia." Kenneth Rexroth papers, Department of Special Collections, Charles E. Young Research Library, University of California–Los Angeles.

Wald, Alan M. *Exiles from a Future Time: The Forging of the Mid-Twentieth-Century Literary Left.* Chapel Hill: University of North Carolina Press, 2001.

8. Raising the Dead in New Orleans

Boyd, Valerie. *Wrapped in Rainbows: The Life of Zora Neale Hurston.* New York: Scribner, 2003.

Federal Writers' Project. *The WPA Guide to Louisiana.* New York: Hastings, 1941.

———. *The WPA Guide to New Orleans.* New York: Pantheon, 1983 reprint.

Harvey, Chance. *The Life and Selected Letters of Lyle Saxon.* Gretna, LA: Pelican, 2003.

Klein, Sybil, ed. *Creole: The History and Legacy of Louisiana's Free People of Color.* Baton Rouge: LSU Press, 2000.

New York Times. "WPA Writers Travel Much." February 9, 1938.

Saxon, Lyle. *Children of Strangers.* Gretna, LA: Pelican, 1989.

———. *The Friends of Joe Gilmore. And Some Friends of Lyle Saxon,* edited by Edward Dreyer. Gretna, LA: Pelican, 1998.

———, et al., eds. *Gumbo Ya-Ya: A Collection of Louisiana Folk Tales.* Gretna, LA: Pelican, 1987 reprint.

———. Letter to Paul Brooks, Houghton Mifflin, February 18, 1936, in Letters from the Archives of Marcus Bruce Christian, www.nathanielturner.com/selectedletters.htm, accessed August 16, 2008.

9. Cigars and Turpentine in Florida

Except where otherwise indicated, Stetson Kennedy's quotations in this chapter come from two interviews with the author and Andrea Kalin: tape recording, September 7, 2000: and film recording, July 13–15, 2004, Jacksonville, Florida.

Bordelon, Pamela. Biographical essay. In *Go Gator and Muddy the Water!: Writings by Zora Neale Hurston from the Federal Writers' Project.* New York: W. W. Norton, 1999.

Boyd, Valerie. *Wrapped in Rainbows: The Life of Zora Neale Hurston.* New York: Scribner, 2003.

Bucuvalas, Tina, Peggy A. Bulger, and Stetson Kennedy. *South Florida Folklife.* Jackson: University Press of Mississippi, 1994.

Egerton, John. *Speak Now against the Day: The Generation before the Civil Rights Movement in the South.* Chapel Hill: University of North Carolina Press, 1994.

Federal Writers' Project. *Florida: A Guide to the Sunshine State*. New York: Oxford, 1939.

Griffin, James. Song and interview recorded by the Federal Writers' Project. Library of Congress Web site, *Florida Folklore from the WPA Collections*, http://memory.loc.gov/ammem/collections/florida/, accessed June 19, 2008.

Hemenway, Robert E. *Zora Neale Hurston: A Literary Biography*. Urbana: University of Illinois Press, 1980.

Hurston, Zora Neale, *Dust Tracks on a Road: An Autobiography*. Urbana: University of Illinois Press, 1984 ed.

———. *Folklore, Memoirs, and Other Writings*. New York: Library of America, 1995.

———. *Go Gator and Muddy the Water!: Writings by Zora Neale Hurston from the Federal Writers' Project*, edited and with a biographical essay by Pamela Bordelon. New York: W. W. Norton, 1999.

———. "How It Feels to Be Colored Me." *The World Tomorrow*, 215–216, May 1928.

———. "Mules and Men." In *Folklore, Memoirs, and Other Writings*. New York: Library of America, 1995.

———. *Their Eyes Were Watching God*. New York: HarperPerennial Modern Classics, 2006 ed.

Kahn, Carrie. "Modern-Day Slave Farms in Florida." National Public Radio, *Morning Edition*, July 14, 2005. Transcript at www.npr.org.

Kaplan, Carla. *Zora Neale Hurston: A Life in Letters*. New York: Doubleday, 2001.

Kennedy, Stetson. "Florida Folklife and the WPA, an Introduction." In *Reference Guide to Florida Folklore from the Federal WPA*. Deposited in the Florida Folklife Archives. Tallahassee: Florida Department of State, n.d.

———. Letter to Richard Wright dated August 18, 1938. Stetson Kennedy collection.

———. "Working with Zora." In Proceedings of the Academic Conference of the First Annual Zora Neale Hurston Festival of the Arts, January 26–27, 1990, Eatonville, Florida.

Library of Congress. "Florida Folklife from the WPA Collections, 1937–1942." *American Memory* Web site, http://memory.loc.gov/ammem/flwpahtml/flwpahome.html, accessed June 19, 2008.

Library of Congress, *Center for the Book.* "Jean Trebbi Interviews Stetson Kennedy." Transcript of taped interview, December 8, 1994.

McDonough, Gary W., ed. *The Florida Negro: A Federal Writers' Project Legacy.* Jackson: University Press of Mississippi, 1993.

Sheffey, Ruthe. Film interview with the author, Baltimore, Maryland, November 16, 2006.

10. American and Un-American: Back around the Boroughs

Canham, Erwin D. "Roosevelt as an Issue." *Christian Science Monitor,* August 5, 1939.

Chabon, Michael. Phone interview with the author, tape recording, September 8, 2004.

Cheever, John. Early journal dated 1934–1935 (Folder 2, p. 53). Houghton Library, Harvard University.

———. Letter to Elizabeth Ames dated May 4, 1935. Houghton Library, Harvard University.

———. *Thirteen Uncollected Stories,* edited by Franklin H. Dennis. Chicago: Academy Chicago Publishers, 1994.

Chicago Daily Tribune. "Dies Calls City Powerhouse of Subversive Acts." October 4, 1989.

Crumbley, Paul, and Patricia M. Gantt, eds. *Body My House: May Swenson's Work and Life.* Logan: Utah State University Press, 2006.

Dies, Martin. *Trojan Horse in America.* New York: Dodd, Mead, 1940.

Donaldson, Scott. *John Cheever: A Biography.* New York: Random House, 1987.

———, ed. *Conversations with John Cheever.* Jackson: University Press of Mississippi, 1987.

Ellison, Ralph. *Interviews on the American Life Histories* Web site: "Harlem," "City Street," "Colonial Park." http://lcweb2.loc.gov/ammem/wpaintro/wpamap.html, accessed June 20, 2008.

———. Letter to Richard Wright dated November 3, 1941. Ralph Ellison Collection, Manuscripts Division, Library of Congress.

Fisher, Vardis. Film interview with John Milton, March 20, 1967, South Dakota Public Television.

Hurston, Zora Neale. *Moses, Man of the Mountain,* with a foreword by Deborah McDowell. New York: HarperPerennial, 1991.

Internet Archive. Investigation of Un-American Propaganda Activities in the United States. Hearings before a Special Committee on Un-American Activities, House of Representatives, Seventy-Fifth Congress, Third Session, Seventy-Eighth Congress, Second Session, www.archive.org/details/ investigationofu193906unit, accessed August 18, 2008.

Kaplan, Carla. *Zora Neale Hurston: A Life in Letters.* New York: Doubleday, 2001.

Lawrence, Jacob, in a public conversation with Henry Louis Gates Jr. at the Portland Art Gallery, Portland, Oregon, April 23, 1994.

New York Times. "Dies at Rally Here Warns U.S. to Stop Its 'Aping' of Europe." November 30, 1939.

People's Herald. "Congressional Colleagues Rake Dies over the Coals." November 15, 1939.

Swenson, May. Interviews on the American Life Histories Web site: Mrs. J. Elterich, "Southern Customs," "National Biscuit Company Workers," "Lumberjack Region." http://lcweb2.loc.gov/ammem/wpaintro/wpamap .html, accessed August 19, 2008.

Taylor, Nick. *American-Made: The Enduring Legacy of the WPA: When FDR Put the Nation to Work.* New York: Bantam, 2008.

Washington Sunday Star. "Un-American Probe Epochal: Turn of Events Makes Dies International Figure." October 29, 1939.

Wright, Richard. Comments in "An Editorial Conference." Radio broadcast concerning Federal Writers' Project, New York City, April 13, 1938.

———. Comments in "Can We Depend upon Youth to Follow the American Way?" NBC's *America's Town Meeting of the Air*, April 24, 1939.

Yezierska, Anzia. *Red Ribbon on a White Horse: My Story*, with an introduction by Louise Levitas Henriksen. London: Virago, 1987.

11. Converging on Washington

Balch, Jack S. *Lamps at High Noon.* Urbana: University of Illinois Press, 2000 reprint.

Botkin, B. A. "Introduction." In *A Treasury of American Folklore.* New York: Crown, 1944.

Cheever, John. *The Wapshot Chronicle.* New York: Harper and Bros., 1957.

Christian Science Monitor. "The Bookshelf: Guide to the Capital," September 4, 1942.

Dies, Martin. *Martin Dies' Story*. New York: Bookmailer, 1963.

———. *Trojan Horse in America*. New York: Dodd, Mead, 1940.

Donaldson, Scott. *John Cheever: A Biography*. New York: Random House, 1987.

Ellington, Duke. *Music Is My Mistress*. New York: Doubleday, 1973.

Ellison, Ralph. "Cadillac Flambé." In *Living with Music: Ralph Ellison's Jazz Writings*, edited by Robert O'Meally. New York: Modern Library, 2002.

———. Panel comments at "FDR and the Arts: The WPA Arts Projects," seminar held at the New York Public Library, March 1, 1983.

Ertegun, Ahmet. Phone interview with the author, April 18, 2001.

Internet Archive. Investigation of Un-American Propaganda Activities in the United States. Hearings before a Special Committee on Un-American Activities, House of Representatives, Seventy-Fifth Congress, Third Session, Seventy-Eighth Congress, Second Session, www.archive.org/details/investigationofu193906unit, accessed August 18, 2008.

Mangione, Jerre. *The Dream and the Deal: The Federal Writers' Project, 1935–1943*. Boston: Little, Brown, 1972.

Morgan, Ted. *Reds: McCarthyism in Twentieth-Century America*. New York: Random House, 2003.

Rosenthal, Dorothy. Phone interview with the author, September 1, 2004.

Saxon, Lyle. *The Life and Selected Letters of Lyle Saxon*, edited by Chance Harvey. Gretna, LA: Pelican, 2003.

Taylor, Nick. *American-Made: The Enduring Legacy of the WPA: When FDR Put the Nation to Work*. New York: Bantam, 2008.

Terkel, Studs. Film interview with the author, February 18, 2004, Chicago, Illinois.

U.S. Government Printing Office. Henry Alsberg testimony before the Department of Science, Art and Literature. Hearings before the Committee on Patents, Seventy-Fifth Congress, February 7–11, 1938.

12. Traveling Beyond

Apple, R. W., Jr., e-mail message to the author dated August 1, 2005.

Bradley, David. Film interview with Andrea Kalin and the author, August 18, 2007.

Brown, Lorin W., with Charles L. Briggs and Marta Weigle. *Hispano Folklife of New Mexico: The Lorin W. Brown Federal Writers' Project Manuscripts.* Albuquerque: University of New Mexico Press, 1978.

Callahan, John, ed. *The Collected Essays of Ralph Ellison*, with an introduction by Saul Bellow. New York: Modern Library, 1995.

Chabon, Michael. *The Amazing Adventures of Kavalier and Clay.* New York: Random House, 2000.

———. Phone interview with the author, tape recording, September 8, 2004.

Cheever, John. "Why I Write Short Stories." *Newsweek*, October 30, 1978, 24–25.

Cooke, Alistair. *The American Home Front, 1941–1942.* New York: Atlantic Monthly Press, 2006.

Ellison, Ralph. Author's introduction to *Invisible Man.* New York: Vintage International ed., 1983.

———. Howells Medal Speech, on John Cheever, given at the American Academy and Institute of Arts and Letters, New York, May 1965.

———. Letter to Richard Wright dated November 3, 1941. Ralph Ellison Papers, Manuscripts Division, U.S. Library of Congress, Washington, D.C.

Federal Writers' Project. *New Jersey: A Guide to the State.* New York: Viking, 1939.

Gilb, Dagoberto. Film interview with Andrea Kalin and the author, November 5, 2007.

Hurston, Zora Neale, and Dorothy Waring. *Polk County: A Comedy of Negro Life on a Sawmill Camp with Authentic Negro Music in Three Acts.* Library of Congress, Zora Neale Hurston Plays, http://memory.loc.gov/ammem/znhhtml/znhhome.html, accessed August 10, 2008.

Konzett, Della Caparoso. *Ethnic Modernisms: Anzia Yezierska, Zora Neale Hurston, Jean Rhys, and the Aesthetics of Dislocation.* New York: Palgrave Macmillan, 2002.

Least Heat Moon, William. *PrairyErth (a deep map).* Boston: Houghton Mifflin, 1991.

Mangione, Jerre. *The Dream and the Deal: The Federal Writers' Project, 1935–1943.* Boston: Little, Brown, 1972.

Paley, Grace. Phone interview with the author, tape recording, September 10, 2004.

Steinbeck, John. *Travels with Charley.* New York: Bantam, 1963.

Walker, Margaret. "For My People." In *This Is My Century: New and Collected Poems.* Athens: University of Georgia Press, 1989.

———. *Jubilee.* Boston: Houghton Mifflin, 1966.

———, with Maryemma Graham. *Conversations with Margaret Walker.* Jackson: University Press of Mississippi, 2002.

Wright, Richard. *12 Million Black Voices.* Reprinted with an introduction by David Bradley. New York: Thunder's Mouth Press, 1988.

———. *Works.* New York: Library of America, 1991.

Yezierska, Anzia. *Red Ribbon on a White Horse: My Story*, with an introduction by Louise Levitas Henriksen. London: Virago, 1987.

CREDITS

Text

Chapter 2: Excerpts from John Cheever's journal (1934–1946) and letter to Elizabeth Ames, copyright © 1946 by the John Cheever Estate, are reprinted with permission of the Wylie Agency, Inc.

Chapter 3: Richard Wright's letters to Nelson Algren are quoted with permission of Julia Wright. Nelson Algren's correspondence to Richard Wright is quoted with permission of Robert Joffe. Margaret Walker's "For My People" is quoted with permission of the University of Georgia Press.

Chapter 4: Jim Thompson's letters to B. A. Botkin and passages from "The Strange Death of Eugene Kling" are quoted with permission of the Thompson Estate.

Chapter 5: Vardis Fisher's letters are quoted with permission of Grant Fisher.

Chapter 6: Rudolph Umland's writings are quoted with permission of Yvonne Umland Jameson.

Chapter 7: Passages from Kenneth Rexroth's unpublished WPA manuscript on Mount Shasta and *Autobiographical Novel* are reprinted with permission of the Kenneth Rexroth Trust. All rights reserved. The libretto from *U.S. Highball,* by Harry Partch, is quoted with permission of Danlee Mitchell, executive director of the Harry Partch Foundation.

Chapter 8: Lyle Saxon's poetry, letters, and journal are quoted by permission of Pelican Publishing.

Chapter 12: Ralph Ellison's introduction to the Vintage international edition of *Invisible Man* (1983) and his correspondence to Richard Wright are quoted with permission of his literary executor, Professor John Callahan.

Illustrations

AP Images: 15

Philip Blackburn, from "Enclosure Three: Harry Partch": 136

Family of B. A. Botkin and the University of Nebraska, Love Library: 18

Henry Bowden/Hulton Archive/Getty Images: 125, 130

Chicago History Museum, Photographer: Stephen Deutch: 39, 66

Courtesy of Scott Gipson, Caxton Press, Caldwell, Idaho: 99

Idaho State Historical Society: 97, 101

Courtesy of Robert Joffe: 61

James Weldon Johnson Memorial collection, Yale's Beinecke Library: 189, 204

Russell Lee collection, Center for American History, University of Texas at Austin: 13

Library of Congress: 9, 14, 25, 50, 83, 104, 127, 132, 138, 141, 150, 172, 182, 219, 220

Library of Congress; Marjory Collins: 213

Library of Congress; Jack Delano: 40, 184

Library of Congress; Walker Evans: 145

Library of Congress; Dorothea Lange: 102, 129, 139, 140, 180

Library of Congress; Russell Lee: 42, 45, 79, 84, 91

Library of Congress; Alfred T. Palmer: 195

Library of Congress; Gordon Parks: 171

Library of Congress; Edwin Rosskam: 212

Library of Congress; Arthur Rothstein: 185, 186

Library of Congress; Ben Shahn: 154

Library of Congress; John Vachon: 41, 73, 115, 117

Library of Congress; Marion Post Wolcott: 142, 161, 166, 168, 209

Courtesy of Lincoln City Libraries, Lincoln, NE: 111, 113, 120

Milwaukee Public Museum: 70

Minnesota Historical Society: 72

National Archives and Records Administration: 16, 17, 23, 24, 207, 210, 211

Pelican Publishing: 157

Courtesy of the Thompson Family: 75, 88

Carl Van Vechten: 48

Photography Collection, Miriam and Ira D. Wallach Division of Art, Prints and Photographs, New York Public Library, Astor, Lenox and Tilden Foundations: 31, 36

Washington Star Collection, Washington, D.C. Public Library; © *Washington Post*: 216

Richard Wright Papers, Yale Collection of American Literature, Beinecke Rare Book and Manuscript Library, with permission from John Hawkins & Associates, Inc. on behalf of the Estate of Richard Wright: 37

Yaddo Records, Manuscripts and Archives Division, New York Public Library, Astor, Lenox and Tilden Foundations: 191

INDEX

Page numbers in *italics* refer to illustrations

Aaron, Abe, 59

Aiken, Conrad, 222

Algren, Nelson, 9, 21, 44, 48–50, *50,* 51, 53, 58–67, 200, 222
postcard to Richard Wright, *61*

Alsberg, Henry, 14–16, *16,* 17, 33, 44, 62, 69, 77–78, 100, 108, 128, 154–55, 166, 170, 208–9, 214, 216–17, 220–21, 227

Amazing Adventures of Kavalier and Clay, The (Chabon), 7, 193

American Folklore: An Encyclopedia (Bulger), 20

American Guides. *See* WPA Guides

American Guide Week, 218, *220, 227*

American Home Front, The, 1941–1942 (Cooke), 227

American Stuff (anthology), 60, 137, 198

American Town Meeting of the Air (radio program), 202

American Writers' Congress, 75, 77

Ames, Elizabeth, 191

Anderson, Sherwood, 49, 122, 144

Anvil (periodical), 71

Anzia Yezierska: A Writer's Life (Henriksen), 25, 200

Apple, R. W., Jr., 228

Archiquette, Oscar, 10, 69–70, *70*

Arguedas, Jeanne, 146–47, 156

Armstrong, Louis, 46, 149, 213

Assiniboine (Native American tribe), 69

Atlantic Monthly (periodical), 123

Atlas, James, 223

Auden, W. H., 21, 221–22

Author's Playhouse (radio program), 66

Autobiographical Novel (Rexroth), 126–27, 134

Baedeker (travel guide series), 16

Balch, Jack, 208

Banks, Ann, 55

Barber, Jim, 94

"Basin Street Blues" (song), 149

"Bayonne" (Cheever), 195

Bearden, Romare, 200

Bechet, Sidney, 149

Beiderbecke, Bix, 54

Bellow, Saul, 20–21, 44, 49, 222–23

Bellows, George, 53, 216

Best Short Stories 1941 (book), 124

Binghamton Press (newspaper), 197

"Bingo" (song), 185

Black Boy (Wright), 43

Blackhawk, Ida, 68

Black Legion (film), 20

"Blueprint for Negro Writing" (Wright), 173

Boas, Franz, 37, 69, 167

"Boil Them Cabbage Down" (song), 185

Boise (Idaho), 100, 107–8
landscape in the 1930s, *97, 101*

Bolero (film), 52

"Bonefish" (song), 185

Bontemps, Arna, 44

Bordelon, Pamela, 174, 178
Botkin, Benjamin, 18, *18*, 20, 50, 54, 76–78, 81, 87, 89–90, 94, 118, 170, 177, 203, 214–15, 221, 223–24
Bradley, David, 228–29
Brice, Mrs. Mary Anna, 106
Brimhall, Noah, 105
"Brooklyn Rooming House" (Cheever), 190
Brooks, Juanita, 20, 103, 224
Browder, Earl, 198
Brown, Lorin, 109, 228
Brown, Sterling, 212
Bulger, Peggy, 20, 165
"Bumming in California" (McDaniel), 137
Burks, Albert, 122
Burnham, Daniel, 207–8
Burrell, Streamline, 214

"Cadillac Flambé" (Ellison), 211
Calloway, Cab, 214
"Canal Street Blues" (song), 149
"Cane River" (Saxon), 144
Cantwell, Robert, 218, 227
"Can We Depend upon Youth to Follow the American Way?" (radio forum), 202
Capital City (Sandoz), 123
Caxton Press, 108
Célestin, Oscar "Papa," 148–49
Célestin Tuxedo Orchestra, 148–49
Chabon, Michael, 7, 193–94, 228
Chaucer, Geoffrey, 19
Cheever, John, 20, 36–38, 173, 190–91, *191*, 192–95, 208–10, 222, 224
Chicago, 12, 39–48, 126
    downtown, *41*
    musicians, *45*, 54–55
    Near West Side neighborhood, *42*
    skyline, *40*
    South Side neighborhood, 42–46, 53–54
Chicago Herald American (newspaper), 197
Chicago Tribune (newspaper), 12, 41
Children of God (Fisher), 99, 190, 221
Children of Strangers (Saxon), 144, 153
Christian, Marcus Bruce, 146
Christian Science Monitor (newspaper), 197, 209
Civilian Conservation Corps (CCC), 107
Coffee, John, 196–97
communism, the Communist Party and communists, 3, 23, 27, 44, 49, 51, 71, 93, 114, 128, 194–95, 198, 203, 215–17
Conflict: Love or Money, The? (Martin), 115

Conroy, Jack, 44, 50–51, 58, 65, 216
Conversations with Margaret Walker (Walker), 49
Conway, Julia, 107
Cooke, Alistair, 227
Cook, Robert, *182*, 184
Cornelius, Carol, 9–10
Corse, Carita Doggett, 171, 177
Coughlin, Father, 41–42
Cowley, Malcolm, 190
Crazy Horse (Native American leader), 123
Cromwell, Maude, 215
Cronyn, George, 17, *17*, 137
Cultural Front, The (Denning), 44

Daily Mirror (newspaper), 197
Daily Oklahoma (newspaper), 77
Daily Republican (newspaper), 197
Daily Worker (newspaper), 93
Daring Detective (periodical), 81
Daumier, Honoré, 53
de Brueys, William, 147
de Kooning, Willem, 220
Delano, Jack, 12
Denning, Michael, 7, 44, 51
Diaz, Norberto, 185
Dictionary of Oklahomaisms (book manuscript), 89–90
Dies, Martin, 3, 28–29, 187, 188, 195–99, 214–16, *216*, 217–18, 224
Dillinger, John, 68
Direction (periodical), 58
Disinherited, The (Conroy), 50
Dream and the Deal, The (Mangione), 11, 113
Dreyer, Edward, 156
"The Drilling Contractor" (Thompson), 87
Dunham, Kenneth, 44
Dunnell, G. O., 207
Dust Bowl, 97, 112, 114–15
Dust Tracks on a Road (Hurston), 12, 167

Eakins, George, 53
Earth Day, 68
Economics of Scarcity: Some Human Footnotes, The (pamphlet), 89
Eiseley, Loren, 118, 222
Eliot, T. S., 93, 128
Ellington, Duke, 91, 93, 211–13
Ellison, Ralph, 19–20, 36, 64, 75, 78, 90, 92–95, *189*, 193, 200, 203–4, *204*, 206, 211, 221–22, 224–26

Elm, Guy, 10
Elterich, Mrs. J., 205
Emergency Relief Act, 12
"The End of the Book" (Thompson), 198
Engstrand, Stuart, 58–59
Epstein, Dena Polacheck, 56–57
Ertegun, Ahmet, 213–14
Ertegun, Nesuhi, 214
"Ethics of Living Jim Crow, The" (Wright), 198
"Ethnographical Aspects of Chicago's Black Belt"
    (Wright), 46
"Exposing Soviet Plot to Overthrow U.S.A."
    (article), 82

Falconer (Cheever), 20, 224
farm for sale in Boundary County (Idaho), 102
Farm Security Administration, 12, 123
Farrell, Alfred, 170
Federal Emergency Relief Administration
    (FERA), 52
Federal Theatre Project, 169, 216
Federal Writers' Project, 1–3, 5–6, 8, 10–14,
    16–17, 20–21, 28–30, 51–54, 71, 73, 77,
    93, 193, 199, 203, 207–8, 219, 223–24, 228
  Arizona Project, 136
  California Project, 17, 126–28, 130–37, 139
  end of, 217–21
  evaluation of, 20–21, 221–22, 225–26
  Ex-Slave Narratives Project, 170
  Florida Project, 167, 170–71, 173, 177,
    181, 189
  Folklore Division, 17–20, 50, 55, 58–59, 77,
    79, 89, 109, 203, 205, 215, 221, 223
  Idaho Project, 99–109
  Illinois Project, 43–49, 53–54, 56–57, 59–61,
    64–67
  Life Histories Division and Project, 123, 163,
    201, 223, 228
  Louisiana Project, 145–46, 156, 218
  Minnesota Project, 71
  Nebraska Project, 111–20, 120, 121–24
  Negro Affairs Division, 212
  New Mexico Project, 104, 109
  New York Project, 31–38, 52, 58, 60, 94,
    190, 224
  Oklahoma Project, 83–87, 89–90
  opposition to, 3, 28, 98, 195, 198–99, 214–17
  public conception of writers on project,
    98, 114
  Radio Division, 53, 55
  Recording Project, 177–81, 182, 183, 185
  startup and planning for, 14–17

Utah Project, 103
Wisconsin Project, 68
Federal Writers' Project staff at (Washington) DC
    headquarters, 207, 210, 211
"Fire and Cloud" (Wright), 60
Fisher, Vardis, 97–99, 99, 100–104, 106–9, 137,
    190, 198, 221, 224
Flanagan, Hallie, 217
Florida Negro, The (book), 173, 176
Foley, Samantha Brimhall, 104–6
"Folklore of Drug Store Employees" (Swenson),
    204
Ford, Henry, 95, 162
"For My Daughter" (Kees), 124
"For My People" (Walker), 61–62
Frank J. North: Pawnee Scout Commander and
    Pioneer (Wilson), 223
Freeman, Bud, 54
Freisen, Gordon, 88

Gallup (poll), 3, 10
Garrison, Dan, 89
Garvey, Marcus, 36, 202
Gellhorn, Martha, 75
German American Bund, 28, 196
Getty, Norris, 121, 124
Gilb, Dagoberto, 228
Gilmore, Bob, 137
Girl, The (Le Sueur), 72
"Git Along Little Dogies" (song), 18
Glass, Phillip, 138
Go Gator and Muddy the Water! (Hurston), 174, 176
Gooden, A. L., 116
Good War: An Oral History of World War II, The
    (Terkel), 222
Gould, Joe, 32, 34
Grady, Robert, 227
Grantham, Ed, 119–20
Great Depression, 2, 7, 12, 23, 23, 26, 28, 41,
    81, 97, 112, 169–70, 195, 206, 217–18,
    221, 228
Greenwood, Annie Pike, 103
Grey, Zane, 108
Griffin, James, 181
Grifters, The (Thompson), 21, 78
Gros Ventre (Native American tribe), 69
Gumbo Ya-Ya (Saxon), 143–44, 157
Gurley, Leo, 75, 203–4
Gutheim, Frederick, 11

Haines, Izzelly, 183
Halpert, Herbert, 156, 159, 177–79

Hard Times (Terkel), 41
Harlem (New York City) Community Art
    Center, 200
Harper's (periodical), 71
Harrington, F. C., 217
Harry Partch: A Biography (Gilmore), 137
Hartman, George, 116
Harvey, George, 198
Haskins, Joe, 89
Hawkins, Coleman, 54
Heat-Moon, William Least, 228
Helen Hayes Award, 223
Hemingway, Ernest, 75, 93, 186
Hickock, Wild Bill, 119–20
Hitler, Adolf, 20, 28, 94, 197
"Hoist Up the John B. Sail" (song), 185
Holmes, Opal, 109
"Home on the Range" (song), 18
Hopkins, Harry, 14, *15,* 146, 155, 221
Horowitz, Morris, 56
Houseman, John, 170
House Un-American Committee (HUAC), 3,
    196–99, 214–17, 222
"How Bigger Was Born" (Wright), 65
Hughes, Langston, 93
Hungry Hearts (Yezierska), 25
Hurston, Zora Neale, 1–2, 7, 12, 19, 21, 37,
    152, 161–62, 166–70, 171–72, *172,*
    173–81, 187, 189–90, 212, *219,* 221, 223
Huss, Veronica, 183

I Am Thinking of My Darling (McHugh), 34
I Came a Stranger (Polacheck), 56–57, 223
Idaho Statesman (newspaper), 107
"I'm a Little Blackbird lookin' for a Bluebird"
    (song), 202
"I'm a-Might-Have-Been" (article), 58
"In Passing" (Cheever), 191
Invisible Man (Ellison), 20, 78, 221, 225

Jacksonville, 162–63, 166, 170, 174
    black neighborhood, *171*
Jacobson, Bud, 39, 54–55
Jaffey, Bessie, 58
James, Henry, 93
Jane Addams's Hull House, 55
Jeremiah Johnson (film), 221
Jim Crow laws, 43, 147, 163, 170, 173
Joe Gould's Secret (Mitchell), 32
John Reed Clubs, 7, 44, 48, 51, 190
Johns, Orrick, 32–33
Jonah's Gourd Vine (Hurston), 169

jook joint in Belle Glade (Florida), *161, 168*
Journal of a Floater (Umland), 112
Joyce, James, 103
Juneteenth (Ellison), 79

Kansas City Star (newspaper), 123
Kass, Marie, 128–29, 134
Kazin, Alfred, 218
Kees, Weldon, 120–24, 128–29, 192, 222
Kellock, Katharine, 16, *17,* 71, 170–71, 217, 220
Kennedy, Edith, 182, *182,* 185
Kennedy, Stetson, 161–66, 170–74, 176–80,
    181–82, *182,* 183, 185–86, 222
Kenny, Anna, 66
Key West, 165–66, 184–86
    Duval Street, *185*
    fisherman, *186*
Killer inside Me, The (Thompson), 21, 78
Kline, Franz, 220
Kling, Eugene, 81–82
Krakauer, Jon, 224
Ku Klux Klan, 2, 162, 174, 185, 196

La Guardia, Fiorello, 33
Lake, Samantha, 104–5
L'Amour, Louis, *75,* 87–88, *88*
Lamps at High Noon (Balch), 208
Lange, Dorothea, 12
Laveau, Marie, 151–52
Lawrence, Jacob, 200
Lay My Burden Down (Botkin), 223
Lazell, Louise, 3
Ledbetter, Huddie ("Lead Belly"), 18
Leopold, Aldo, 67–68
Le Sueur, Meridel, 6–7, 70–72, *72,* 73, 222
Leuchtenburg, William, 229
Levinsky, King, 46
Library of Congress, 18, 214, 221
    American Memory Web site, 11, 119
    WPA Life Histories Web site, 229
Lincoln (Nebraska), 12, 80–81, 111, 113–14,
    120, 122
Lindo, Lilly, 201
Lindsey, Mrs. Robert, 80
Li Po, 136
Locke, Alain, 93
Lomax, Alan, 17, 178, 214
Lomax, John, 17–18, 77, 169, 178, 199, 221
Long, Huey P., 141, 152
"Lore of Department Store Workers"
    (Swenson), 204
Los Angeles Times (newspaper), 137

Louis, Joe, 46
Lounsbury, Floyd, 69–70

*Magruder Murders: Coping with Violence on the
    Idaho Frontier, The* (Welch), 223–24
Mallon, Mary ("Typhoid Mary"), 37
Mangione, Jerre, 11, 113
Man with the Golden Arm, The (Algren), 222
Marcantonio, Vito, 197
Mardi Gras (New Orleans), 141–44, 146
    costumes advertising, *142*
Marsh, Reginald, 37
Martin, Father, 115
Master Detective (periodical), 81–82
Matisse, Henri, 53
McCarthy, Joseph, 222
McCray, Judith, 48
McDaniel, Eluard Luchell, 125, 137
McHugh, Vincent, 33–34, 193
McKay, Claude, 200
McKinney, Robert, 147
McLester, Gordon, 10
Mencken, H. L., 43
Merriam, H. G., 99–100
Migration Series paintings (Lawrence), 200
Miller, Joaquin, 133
Mills, Florence, 201–2
"Milneburg Joys" (song), 149
Milton, John, 100
Mitchell, Henry, 227
Mitchell, Joseph, 32
Morton, Jelly Roll, 149, 214
Moses, Man of the Mountain (Hurston),
    189–90, 221
Mountain Man (Fisher), 221
Mountain Meadows Massacre, The (Brooks),
    20, 224
Mount Shasta (California), *132*
Muir, John, 132–33
Mules and Men (Hurston), 169
Music Is My Mistress (Ellington), 213

National Book Award, 20, 222
Native Son (Wright), 62–64, 199, 221, 228
Nebraska History (periodical), 113
Negro Folk Songs as Sung by Lead Belly
    (songbook), 18
Nelson, Gaylord, 68
Never Come Morning (Algren), 64–65, 200–201
New Challenge (periodical), 173
New Deal, 3, 42, 100, 198, 202
New Deal "Brain Trust," 37

New Masses (newspaper), 93
New Orleans, 141–144, 146–153, 156,
    158–59, 174
    downtown street, *145*
    Jackson Square, *154*
New Orleans Time-Picayune (newspaper),
    137, 143
New Republic (periodical), 218
Newsweek (periodical), 224
New York City, 13, 19, 23–28, 30–38, 75,
    93–94, 98, 144, 167, 189–90, 192–96,
    199–201, 204–6
    Coney Island, *195*
    Greenwich Village store, *31*
    Harlem scene, *36*
    Lower East Side scene, *24*
New Yorker (periodical), 32–33, 190, 210
New York Post (newspaper), 19
New York Times (newspaper), 15, 75–76, 139,
    189, 193, 196, 198, 228
New York Underground (proposed book), 34
New York World-Telegram (newspaper), 209
Nobel Prize, 223
Norwood, Robert, 76

O'Connor, Ellen, 50–51
O. Henry Award (book award), 144
"Oil Field Vignettes" (Thompson), 80
oil rigger, *79*
Okies in California, *140*
Oklahoma City, 77–78, 80, *83,* 84, 88, 90–91
    segregation, *91*
    "Stringtown," *84*
Old Jules (Sandoz), 123
Oliver, Joe "King," 55, 149
Omaha, 115–118
    Armistice Day parade, *117*
    unemployed man, *115*
Oneida (Native American tribe), 9–10, 68–70
Oneida Language and Culture Project, 10, 69
On Native Grounds (Kazin), 218
Ornitz, Samuel, 30
Orphans in Gethsemane (Fisher), 108
Ory, Kid, 149

Pacific Coast Musician (periodical), 138
Paley, Grace, 25, 228
Palm Beach Post (newspaper), 166
Parker, Melinda, 158–59
Parks, Gordon, 12
Partch, Harry, 136, *136,* 137–40
Partnow, Clyde, 58

People's Herald (newspaper), 196–97
"Pipi Sigallo" (song), 183
Polacheck, Hilda Satt, 55–60, 186, 223–24
Polk County (Hurston), 182, 223
Pollock, Jackson, 220
Prairie Schooner (periodical), 81, 111–12, 121
PrairyErth, a deep map (Heat-Moon), 228
Price, Albert, 174
Prima, Louis, 149

Reddick, Lawrence, 146
Red Ribbon on a White Horse (Yezierska), 24,
   26–29, 32–33, 35, 37, 199–200, 221, 226
"Regionalism and Culture" speech (Botkin), 76
Reidel, James, 121, 124, 128
Rexroth, Kenneth, 21, 125, *125*, 126–30, *130*,
   131–36, 198, 222
Richardson, Martin, 170
Richard Wright: Daemonic Genius (Walker), 223
Riley, Frank, 149–50
Rivers, John, 205
Roberson, Calvin, 86
Rockefeller, John D., 11, 95, 162
rooming house women (St. Paul, MN), *73*
Roosevelt, Eleanor, *16*, 20
Roosevelt, Franklin D., 2–3, 10, 12, *15*, 20, 42,
   71, 100, 179, 195, 197–98, 215, 217–18
Roskolenko, Harry, 36
Ross, Sam, 39, 53–55, 58, 60

Sand County Almanac (Leopold), 68
Sandoz, Mari, 123–24
San Francisco, 126–129, *127*, 137
   Potrero Hill, *129*
   WPA workers protest, *139*
Santa Fe, 109
Santee, Ross, 136–37
Saturday Review of Literature (periodical), 11
Saxon, Lyle, 141–46, 149, 153–55, *157*, 177,
   218–19
Seltzer, Leo, 27
Sentinel (periodical), 55
Seraph on the Suwanee (Hurston), 182
Sheffey, Ruthe, 168–69
Silent City of Rocks (Idaho), 103–4, *104*
Smart, Fredda, 117–18
Smith, I. B., 122
Social Security Administration, 123
"So Cold Outside" (Kees), 121
Southern midwife, *184*
South Side Writers' Group, 46, 51
Southwest Writers Conference, 77, 87

Spanier, Mugsy, 54–55
Spanish Civil War, 75, 137, 165
Starnes, Joe, 199
Stegner, Wallace, 99
Stein, Al, 53
Steinbeck, John, 122–23, 227–28
"St. James Infirmary" (song), 144
St. Louis I Cemetery (New Orleans), *141*, 150, *150*
Story (periodical), 60, 137, 199–200
Story of a Hull House Girl, The (Polacheck), 223
"Strange Death of Eugene King, The"
   (Thompson), 76, 81
Sul Ross State Teachers College, 48
Swenson, May, 21, 204–6, 222
Swetnam, Susan, 103

Tell My Horse (Hurston), 170
Terkel, Louis "Studs," 12, 21, 39–42, 44, 52, 56,
   60, 66, *66*, 222, 228
Texas Monthly (periodical), 80
Their Eyes Were Watching God (Hurston), 170,
   175, 178, 223
These Are Our Lives (collection), 58, 187
"Thieves of the Field" (Thompson), 80
Thompson, Big Jim, 80–81, 88–89
Thompson, Jim, 7, 21, *75*, 76–88, *88*, 89–90,
   157, 198, 222–23
Time (periodical), 158, 220
"Time Without End" (Thompson), 89
To Have and Have Not (Hemingway), 186
tourists with refreshments near Tampa
   (Florida), *166*
Travels with Charley (Steinbeck), 227–28
Treasury of American Folktales (Botkin), 223
Trojan Horse in America (Dies), 196
True Detective (periodical), 76, 81, 83
turpentine worker (Florida), *180*
Twain, Mark, 5, 19, 21, 144, 225
12 Million Black Voices (Wright), 203

Ulrich, Mabel, 8, 71–72
Umland, Rudolph, 111, *111*, 112–13, *113*, 114,
   120–24, 156, 221
Umland, Yvonne, 123–24
Uncle Tom's Children (Wright), 50, 60, 172, 199
Under the Banner of Heaven (Krakauer), 224
Unemployed Writers' Association, 13
Union Station (Washington, DC), 207–9, *209*
U.S. Highball (Partch), 139–40

Valdez, John, 119
Van Gogh, Vincent, 53

Vanished Act (Reidel), 128
Van Vechten, Carl, 189–90
Von Baum, Theresa, 98
Voynow, Richard, 54

Wada, Misao, 111, 119
Walker, Margaret, 21, 44, 48, *48,* 49, 51–52,
    58–59, 61–62, 64, 199, 223
Walk Together Chillun! (play), 170
Wapshot Chronicle, The (Cheever), 208, 210–11
Warner, Sylvia Townsend, 193
"Washington Boardinghouse" (Cheever), 210
Washington, Booker T., 91
Washington, D.C., 38, 207–14, 218–19
    alley residents, *212*
    barbershop in U Street neighborhood, *213*
    boys in fountain outside Union Station, *209*
Washington, George, 67, 198, 209
Washington Post (newspaper), 155
Washington Star (newspaper), 197
"Waste Land, The" (Eliot), 93
Weisberger, Bernard, 14
Welch, Julia Conway, 223
Welles, Orson, 170, 196
Welty, Eudora, 156, 222
We Sagebrush Folks (Greenwood), 103
West Virginia Farmer-Miner (newspaper), 197
White, Eartha, 179
Whitman, Walt, 194
Whittaker, Annie, 178
"Why I Write Short Stories" (Cheever), 224
Wilderness Society, 68
Wilder, Robert, 207
Wilson, Ruby, 111, 119–20, 223
Wimberly, Lowry, 81, 112, 118, 120–21,
    123, 156
Winchell, Walter, 197
Windy City (Ross), 53–54
Winesburg, Ohio (Anderson), 144
Woodward, Ellen, 217
"Worked All Summer Long" (song), 181
Workers Alliance, 71–72
Working (Terkel), 222, 228
Works Progress Administration (WPA), 9, *13,*
    14, 18–19, 36, 39, 56, 60, 62, 66–67, 69,
    75, 77–78, 80, 83, 85, 98, 107, 119, 121,
    161, 173, 200, 206, 217–20, 222–26, 228

budget restrictions, 202
criticism of, 94, 100, 114, 210
opposition to, 10, 12–13, 28–29, 31–33, 187,
    195, 198
posters, *9, 14*
prerequisite for job position in, 29, 52
startup, 2
A World to Win (Conroy), 50
WPA folk anthologies, 187
WPA guides, 6–7, 11, 20, 30, 57, 77, 108, 187,
    218, 227–28
    and Native American voices, 68–69
    publicity poster, *220, 227*
    style restrictions, 102
WPA Guide to Arkansas, 155
WPA Guide to California, 126, 130–35, 139
WPA Guide to Florida, 166–67, 173–77, 179
WPA Guide to Idaho, 77, 100–104, 108, 221
WPA Guide to Illinois, 44–47, 66–67
WPA Guide to Lincoln, Nebraska, 77, 114
WPA Guide to Nebraska, 111, 113–19, 121–24,
    156, 222, 228
WPA Guide to New Jersey, 229–30
WPA Guide to New Mexico, 109, 228
WPA Guide to New Orleans, 6, 141–44, 146–53,
    155–58
WPA Guide to New York City, 7, 30, 33–37, 94,
    190, 192–95, 200–201, 206, 229
WPA Guide to Oklahoma, 84–87, 218
WPA Guide to Virginia, 228
WPA Guide to Washington, D.C., 6, 77, 108, 208,
    212, 215
WPA Guide to Wisconsin, 67–68
WPA Music Project, 148
WPA workers protesting (San Francisco), *139*
WPA Writers' Contest, 199
Wright, Richard, 35–37, *37,* 42–52, 60–66, 93,
    172–73, 190, 198–203, 221–22, 226
Writers Union, 13

Yaddo artist colony (New York), 37, 191, *191,* 192
Yerby, Frank, 222
Yezierska, Anzia, 24–25, *25,* 26–35, 37,
    199–200, 204, 221, 226
Yezierska Levitas Henriksen, Louise, 25–26

Zakheim, Bernard, 128

ABOUT THE AUTHOR

DAVID A. TAYLOR wrote the article for *Smithsonian* that is the basis for this book and the Smithsonian/Channel HD special of the same title. He writes for the *Washington Post*, the *Village Voice*, and other publications, as well as scripts for television documentaries. His work has aired on the Discovery Channel, The Learning Channel, and elsewhere. He is the author of the award-winning book *Ginseng: The Divine Root* and a book of fiction, *Success: Stories*. Visit www.davidataylor.com.